BIKER GANGS AND ORGANIZED CRIME

THOMAS BARKER
EASTERN KENTUCKY UNIVERSITY

Biker Gangs and Organized Crime

Copyright © 2007

Matthew Bender & Company, Inc., a member of the LexisNexis Group
Newark, NJ

ISBN-10: 1-59345-406-6
ISBN-13: 978-1-59345-406-7

Phone   877-374-2919
Web Site www.lexisnexis.com/anderson/criminaljustice

Library of Congress Cataloging-in-Publication Data

Barker, Thomas
    Biker gangs and organized crime / Thomas Barker
        p. cm.
    Includes bibliographical references and index.
    ISBN 1-59345-406-6 (softbound)
    1. Motorcycle gangs--United States. 2. Organized crime--United States. 3. gang members--United States. 4. Criminal Justice, Administration of. I. Title.
HV6439.U5B38 2007
364.1'060973--dc22   2007036325

Cover design by Tin Box Studio, Inc./Cincinnati, Ohio   EDITOR Ellen S. Boyne
                                          ACQUISITIONS EDITOR Michael C. Braswell

Table of Contents

Chapter 1: Introduction 1
Overview 1
One-percent Bikers: American Popular Culture 2
Previous Works on Biker Clubs 3
    Popular Literature 3
        Journalistic Accounts 3
        Photodocumentaries 4
        Autobiographies 5
    Scholarly Literature 6
Criminal Activity and Violence 8
Biker Wars 9
Organized Crime 12
    Network Approach to Organized Crime 14
Methodology 18
Summary 19
References 20

Chapter 2: Conventional and Deviant Clubs 23
Introduction 23
Outlaw Motorcycle Clubs 25
    The Original Wild One: "Wino Willie" Forkner 26
    The Boozefighters Motorcycle Club (1946) 27

Hollister Motorcycle Incident/Riot (1947): Birthplace of
   the American Biker   28
Moral Panics and Folk Devils   30
Bikers as Folk Devils.   31
Riverside Motorcycle Riot (1948)   32
Cyclist's Raid.   32
The Wild One: First of the Biker Movies   33
Hells Angels Motorcycle Club and the One-Percenters   34
Ralph "Sonny" Barger   35
Oakland HAMC Chapter: The Early Years.   36
One-Percent Bikers   37
HAMC in the Mid-1960s   37
Altamont Speedway: One-Percent Bikers on Display   38
Summary   42
References   43

Chapter 3: One-Percent Clubs—The Outsiders   45
Introduction.   45
One-percent Clubs: Characteristics   46
Clubs for White Males   46
Females in the Biker Subculture.   47
Blacks in the One-percent Biker Subculture.   52
Clubs for the Lower/Working Class   55
The Motorcycle: American Iron   56
Summary   57
References   58

**Chapter 4: Becoming a Member: Righteous Biker to
            Patchholder**   61
Introduction.   61
The Club Bar   63
Four Stages in Becoming a Member   65
First Stage—Righteous Biker   65
Second Stage—Friend of the Club/Hang-around   67
Third Stage—Striker/Prospect/Probate.   68
Love of Biking.   69
Love of Brothers and Love of Club   69
Fourth Stage—Initiation-Patchholder   71
Patch/Colors.   72
Summary   73
References   73

Chapter 5: The Deviant Clubs: Big Five, Major Independents, and Others   75
Introduction   75
The Big Five One-percent Biker Clubs   76
   Hells Angels Motorcycle Club (HAMC)   76
   Bandidos Motorcycle Club   78
   Outlaws Motorcycle Club   79
   Pagans Motorcycle Club   80
   Sons of Silence Motorcycle Club   82
Major Independents   84
   The Warlocks Motorcycle Club   84
      Pennsylvania Warlocks MC   84
      Florida-Based Warlocks MC   85
   The Mongols MC   86
   The Iron Horsemen   87
Puppet Clubs   88
Black or Interracial One-percent Biker Clubs   89
Organizational Structure   90
   HAMC Structure   91
Summary   92
References   93

Chapter 6: Evolution from Clubs to Gangs: Outlaw Motorcycle Gangs   95
Introduction   96
Biker Literature   97
   Angel Autobiographies   97
Early Law Enforcement Efforts 100
Outlaw Motorcycle Clubs as Gangs 103
   Members' Criminal History 104
Summary 108
References 110

Chapter 7: Biker Gangs as Organized Crime 115
Introduction 115
Gang and Member Criminal Activity 116
   Focus: Gang/Club Criminal Activity 116
   Focus: Member Criminal Activity 121
Group Criminal Activity and Evolution into Criminal
   Organizations 124
Criminal Organization Continuum 125
Conclusion 126
References 127

**Chapter 8: Criminals Without Borders: Exporting American
            Organized Crime** 129
Introduction 129
International Expansion 130
OMG Criminal Activities in Selected Countries 133
  Australia 133
  Canada 138
  Denmark 138
  The Netherlands 139
  New Zealand 140
  Other Countries 141
Summary 142
References 142

**Chapter 9: The Hells Are No Angels:
            Organized Crime, Death, and Mayhem
            in Canada** 145
Introduction 145
Canadian Law Enforcement Activities 146
  Criminal Intelligence Service Canada (CISC) 146
    CISC Annual Report—1997 146
    CISC Annual Report—1998 147
    CISC Annual Report—1999 148
    CISC Annual Report—2000 149
    CISC Annual Report—2001 151
    CISC Annual Report—2002 152
    CISC Annual Report—2003 154
    CISC Annual Report—2004 155
    CISC Annual Report—2005 156
  The End of the Canadian Biker War 156
  The Bandidos Massacre 157
Summary 158
References 159

Chapter 10: Biker Gangs Now and in the Future 161
Introduction 161
Clubs-to-Gangs Evolution 162
Now and in the Future 162
The Criminal Activity of Other American
  One-Percent Clubs 163
The Criminal Activity of Other One-Percent Clubs Outside
  the United States 164
OMG Violence 165
Clubs-vs.-Gangs Controversy 166

Law Enforcement Intelligence 168
References 169

Appendix A: By-Laws—Bandidos Motorcycle Club, 1999 171

Index 175

1

Introduction

OVERVIEW

Four million Americans ride motorcycles. These motorcycle riders are a diverse group of all ages, races, gender, and income levels. They come from all walks of life, from blue-collar mechanics to billionaires like the late Malcolm Forbes. Actors Peter Fonda and Larry Hagman along with ex U.S. Senator Benjamin "Nighthorse" Campbell (R-Colorado) ride and belong to the Ugly Motorcycle Club. Motorcyclists ride foreign and domestic bikes from Harleys to so-called "crotch rockets." They join together in groups, clubs, and interest associations, riding for pleasure, companionship, and support for charitable causes. They go on national annual runs. Since 1947, motorcyclists roar into Hollister, California, "Birthplace of the American Biker," for the Hollister Independence Rally held the first week in July. One hundred and fifty thousand motorcyclists rode into Hollister in 2004. Every year 500,000 motorcyclists descend on Daytona, Florida, during Bike Week in March. On the east coast every June more than 300,000 motorcyclists thunder into Laconia, New Hampshire. The sleepy town of Sturgis, South Dakota draws in over 300,000 motorcyclists during their Bike Week in August. Three-hundred and fifty thousand motorcyclists attended the Harley Davidson 100th Anniversary in Milwaukee in 2005. Riding among these motorcyclists, but not with them are one-percent bikers. All the other motorcyclists know who they are by their bikes, tattoos, and three-piece back-patches—colors. They know the one-percenters are to be avoided and left alone. That's the way the one-percenters want it. They live and identify themselves as "outsiders" and engage in a deviant lifestyle that often includes serious criminal behavior, including organized crime—national and international. The bizarre behavior and the mystique surrounding the one-percent bikers has become a part of American popular culture.

ONE-PERCENT BIKERS: AMERICAN POPULAR CULTURE

One-percent biker clubs, particularly the Hells Angels Motorcycle Club (HAMC), are part of American popular culture. Biker movies include classics like the seminal cult biker film, *The Wild One,* starring Marlon Brando and Lee Marvin; *Hells Angels on Wheels,* starring Jack Nicholson with Hells Angels leader Sonny Barger as a "technical advisor"; and the enormously successful cult classic *Easy Rider,* starring Peter Fonda, Dennis Hopper, and Jack Nicholson. In 1983, the HAMC produced their own film/documentary, *Hell's Angels Forever,* starring the Hells Angels, including Sonny Barger, with appearances by Jerry Garcia, Bo Diddley, and Willie Nelson. Documentary films such as the Arts and Entertainment Network's *Secret Life of Outlaw Bikers, In Search of History: Hell's Angels; Road Warriors: The Biker Brotherhood;* MTV's *Road Hogs;* and the Discovery Channel's *Choppers* and *Hells Angels* portray one-percent biker clubs as mythic figures not criminals and violence prone individuals.

Biker music is popular. Steppenwolf introduced the biker anthem, *Born to be Wild* in the movie *Easy Rider.* In addition, ZZ Top, Lynyrd Skynard, Marshall Tucker, Molly Hatchet, Billy Gordon, .38 Special, The Doors, Billy Idol, The Allman Brothers, Stevie Ray Vaughan, Bruce Springsteen, David Allen Coe, and Willie Nelson are considered biker rock bands or musicians. Charismatic Angel leader Ralph "Sonny" Barger is a media celebrity and best selling author. Barger's autobiography, *Hell's Angel: The Life and Times of Sonny Barger and the Hells Angels Motorcycle Club,* was a national best seller. He has since published two biker novels. Nevertheless, Barger is also a convicted felon, ex-con, former cocaine addict, and one-time drug dealer. Hells Angels celebrity and HBO actor Chuck Zito's autobiography, *Street Justice,* was also a best seller. The forward was written by actor Sean Penn and pictures of Zito with Muhammad Ali, John Belushi, Pamela Anderson, Joan Jett, Hulk Hogan, Arnold Schwarzenegger, and Charlie Sheen appear in the book. Zito appears arm in arm with former President Bill Clinton on the dust cover. Like Barger, Zito is a convicted felon, an ex-con, and a violence-prone individual.

PREVIOUS WORKS ON BIKER CLUBS

Popular Literature

Journalistic Accounts

The majority of the literature on one-percent biker clubs are journalistic accounts of their exploits and/or crimes (Auger, 2001 (Canada); Bowe, 1994 (U.S.); Charles, 2002 (U.S. and England); Detroit, 1994 (U.S.-California); Kingsbury, 1995 (U.S.);

Members of the Hells Angels motorcycle clan arrive for the 1983 premiere of the movie *Hell's Angels Forever* in New York City as a crowd gathers on the sidewalk. *Photo courtesy of AP Photo/Corey Struller.*

Lavigne, 1987a, 1987b, 1996, 1999 (World); Lowe, 1988 (Canada); Mello, 2001 (U.S.); Reynolds, 2000 (U.S.); Sher and Marsden, 2003 (Canada); Simpson and Harvey, 2001 (Australia); and Thompson, 1966 (U.S.-California)). These accounts discuss the criminal behavior of the following one-percent clubs and chapters: Bandidos and Commancheros Motorcycle Clubs (Australia); Hells Angels MC (Anchorage; Cleveland; and Charleston (South Carolina) chapters; California Hells Angels MC chapters in Oakland, Orange County, San Bernardino, San Francisco, Sacramento, and Ventura; and Canadian Hells Angels MC chapters in Alberta, British Columbia, Ontario, and Quebec; Outlaws MC (Orlando and Louisville chapters), Pagans MC (Daytona Beach chapter), Canadian chapters of the Rock Machine MC, Rockers MC, and Satan's Choice MC ; and the Warlocks MC (Philadelphia chapter).

Lavigne's books provide an eclectic, although sensationalized and biased—calling the Hells Angels "white trash on wheels" in one (Lavigne, 1987) and a global menace to all races and cultures in another (Lavigne, 1999)—coverage of the HAMC criminal activities worldwide. Lavigne also discusses other motorcycle clubs/gangs: the Pagans, the Bandidos, and the Outlaws. Beare and Stone (1999) of the Law Commission of Canada criticize his works for implying that "biker gangs are a sort of new, ultra-powerful successor to the Mafia, with similar structure and business interests" (p. 17). They go on to say that Lavigne confuses the biker gang's structure with a business organization. In other words, Lavigne confuses individual behavior with collective behavior (or club/chapter). We will return to this issue later when we discuss club-sanctioned criminal actions. Nevertheless, there is no doubt that Lavigne sensationalizes biker criminal activity.

Lowe's and Mello's books are passionate accounts of bikers who have been supposedly imprisoned for crimes they did not commit—Lowe (six Canadian Satan's Choice MC members sentenced for murder) and Mello (Outlaw MC member on Florida's death row for murder). The six Satan's Choice members probably did not commit the murder, but, as the book points out, they were present when the murder of a rival biker club member was committed, knew the identity of the killer (a fellow Satan's Choice member), but refused to identify the killer because of a sense of brotherhood. Lowe also describes the 1970s movement of Satan's Choice into drug selling because "the beer drinking days were over." A similar phenomenon was occurring in the United States at the same time. The subject of Mello's book, Outlaws MC member Crazy Joe Spaziano, was a former Hells Angels and had been involved in a number of serious criminal activities before his indictment, charge, and conviction of the rape/murder charge that put him on death row.

Photodocumentaries

There have been two photodocumentaries of the Outlaws Motorcycle Club and one on the Hells Angels Motorcycle Club. The first, *The Bikeriders*, by Danny Lyon, is a classic work on the Outlaws MC that was first published in 1968. Before it was republished in 2003, copies were selling for $1,000 and up and were bringing more than that on eBay auctions. Lyon, a 23-year-old University of Chicago student and veteran of the Southern civil rights movement, joined the Chicago Outlaws in 1965 and spent the next two years taking pictures of the club. His work is important for several reasons: (1) it is the only objective work done by a one-percent biker club member in the early period of club development; (2) one can see the changes that have occurred in the biker culture since the early 1960s. Lyon rode a Triumph motorcycle. No one-percent biker club member would be allowed to ride a foreign-made bike today. Lyon's pictures also show a time when the one-percent biker clubs, particularly the Outlaws and the Hells Angels, were more brothers than enemies. One picture shows a Hells Angels member wearing his colors riding behind an Outlaws member wearing his colors. Today, the two clubs are bitter enemies who are constantly at war and frequently kill each other. Lyon reports that in the early 1970s the Outlaws split between the beer drinkers and the pot smokers and the founder of the Outlaws, John Davis, was killed by a "pot smoker" in a fight for club leadership. Lyon says he was a member of "the old Chicago Outlaws" (Lyon, 2003:3). This was also about the time that the Outlaws and the other biker clubs moved into drug trafficking and began their expansion and take-over ("patch-over") of other biker clubs.

The second book of photographs on the Outlaws MC is *One Percent,* by Michael Upright. Upright is a professional photographer who took black- and-white pictures of the Outlaws in various locations throughout the United States from 1992 to 1995. Upright says that it took more than a year before he was accepted "or ignored" by the bikers (1999:5). The monograph presents pictures of Outlaws leader Harry "Taco" Bowman leading his troops. Bowman was later indicted for federal racketeering charges, fled, and became a fugitive on the FBI's Top 10 Wanted list. He was captured and tried, and later sentenced to life in prison without parole. In the book, there are also two pictures showing bikers wearing Outlaws rockers (top and bottom patches) but not Outlaws colors (Charley-skull on crossed pistons) in between. The author of this book was told by an Outlaws member that the club in the photo (from England) who later patched over to the Outlaws.

A book of photographs of the Hells Angels Motorcycle Club in England was published in 2004 (Shaylor, 2004). The photographer, Andrew Shaylor, traveled all over England from 2000 to 2003, visiting almost all of the 16 charters Hells Angels (chapters), although several of the charters would not allow photographs. The majority of the HA members he met were family men over age 30 who held regular jobs and came from a working-class background. Some had been to prison, and a few were ex-military. The book contains a brief write-up of the history of the HAMC in England and a photograph of the first charter establishing two chapters in England—Big Deathhead to Peter Jackson in Wimbledon and Small Deathhead to Peter "Buttons" Welsh in London—on July 31, 1969. The charter was signed by the nine California chapter presidents, including Ralph "Sonny" Barger.

Autobiographies

Several members or ex-members of one-percent biker clubs have written, or told their stories to others who have written autobiographies of their lives (Barger, 2000; Levingston, 2003; Kaye, 1970; Mandelkau, 1971; Martineau, 2003; Mayson, 1982; Paradis, 2002; Reynolds, 1967; Wethern and Colnett, 1978, 2004; Winterhalder, 2005, and Zito, 2002). All of these books, except Paradis's, Levingston's, and Winterhalder's, are from former or present Hells Angels. Levingston's book is about the Oakland, California, East Bay Dragons MC and the black biker set. Paradis's (Rock Machine MC leader) book is about the bloody war between the Canadian Rock Machine MC and the Hells Angels. The book by Winterhalder, aka Connecticut Ed, is the only book written about the Bandidos MC. Martineau's book is the autobiography of Serge Quesnel a Canadian Hells Angels contract killer. Reynolds's, Wethern's, Kaye's, and Mandelkau's books discuss the formative years of the Hells Angels.

At least two recent books have been written by retired law enforcement officials, describing their investigations of biker gangs (Stephenson, 2004; Murphy, 1999). Ron Stephenson is a retired Detective Superintendent from the Australian NSW Police Force. He was in charge of the Milperra (Australia) Massacre investigation between the Bandidos and Commancheros. According to Stephenson, the massacre was set in motion by an argument over drug dealing. The Commancheros' club rules prohibited "selling, distributing, or using drugs." Anyone violating the rule would be thrown out of the club. Several members resigned because of the rule and traveled to Houston, Texas, to meet with leaders of the Bandidos MC to establish a chapter in Australia and engage in cooperative drug dealings. The Bandidos agreed. When the renegade Commancheros returned to Australia and set up a Bandidos chapter other Commancheros members joined them, setting in motion the events that resulted in the bloody shootout and deaths. Mark Murphy is a retired Royal Canadian Mounted Police Corporal. He describes the handling of a Mafia contract killer informant who was also an ex–Satan's Choice MC member. His book is not very complimentary of the RCMP and their efforts against organized crime. According to Murphy, RCMP brass are more interested in their careers than combating organized crime. In spite of the author's obvious bias against RCMP brass, the book provides valuable insights into the connections between Traditional Organized Crime and one-percent biker gangs in Canada.

Scholarly Literature

In addition to the limited number of articles (19) in the scholarly literature, and a smaller number in the professional literature, there have been three scholarly books on one-percent bikers. The first *Bikers: Birth of a Modern Day Outlaw,* by Maz Harris, was published in 1985. The late Maz Harris (killed in a motorcycle accident in 2000) was president of the Hells Angels chapter in Kent, England. Harris was also a Ph.D. sociologist, and the book was based on his dissertation research into "motorcycle culture." Harris describes the development of the "outlaw" subculture and the Hells Angels Motorcycle Club. The 128-page book has 81 photographs, many of them of early English bikers. Harris says that the "tribes of the biker nation" are international and although they do not share a common language they share a common belief "a belief in freedom and in brotherhood" (Harris, 1985:125). His work downplays the criminal involvement of the HAMC, and is not very objective, but is a good sociological explanation of the subcultural development of biker clubs.

Daniel R. Wolf's, *The Rebels: A Brotherhood of Outlaw Bikers,* was first published in 1991 and republished in paperback three times (1992, 1995, 1999). The late Wolf's book (he was also killed in a motorcycle accident) is based on his 1981 Ph.D. dissertation in anthropology at the University of Alberta written under the name Daniel A. Reshetylo. Wolf rode with a chapter of the Rebels MC in Edmonton, Canada, for more than six years in the middle to late 1970s. His ethnography is recognized as the best and most scholarly work on a one-percent biker club. At the time that Wolf was studying the Rebels, they were a group of tough, impulsive blue-collar outsiders united by a real sense of brotherhood. Many members had committed relatively minor criminal offenses but nothing serious or organized. In the last edition of the book, Wolf writes that affiliation with American originated clubs such as the Hells Angels or Outlaws increased the opportunity to become involved in organized crime activities such as drug trafficking. He points to the Satan's Choice MC's affiliation with the Outlaws as an example. This is what happened to the Rebels after the last edition was published. The Canadian Rebels MC no longer exists; they first affiliated or patched-over to the Hells Angels, but in a rare move, many changed their minds and patched-over to the Bandidos, according to the autobiography of a former Bandidos member (Winterhalder, 2005:76). The first former Rebels–then–Hells Angels member to become a Bandidos member was shot and killed along with a Bandidos hangaround, while leaving an Edmonton nightclub one year later. Police authorities attributed the slayings to a turf battle between the Bandidos and the Hells Angels (Winterhalder, 2005:77). The Angels evidently won the turf war because all the Edmonton Bandidos are now Hells Angels.

Social psychologist Arthur Veno has been studying outlaw motorcycle clubs for almost 20 years. Veno (2002), who holds dual Australian-American citizenship, was born in Burlington, Vermont, and attended high school and college in California. He received his Ph.D from the University of California at Berkeley. He writes that he was present at two significant events in Hells Angels history that made national news: the 1964 Labor Day rally in Monterey, California, when a alleged gang rape of two teenage girls by Hells Angels made national news, and the 1965 confrontation between the Angels and anti–Vietnam War demonstrators in Berkeley, California. Although he mentions a long list of outlaw motorcycle clubs and discusses the history of the HAMC, his book is about Australian clubs. According to Veno, the major Australian clubs are the Hells Angels, the Bandidos, the Rebels, the Coffin Cheaters, and the Gypsy Jokers. There are other home-grown

Australian clubs—Commancheros, Black Uhlans, Odin's Warriors, and the Finks. The Outlaws also have several chapters in Australia. Veno paints a more sedate picture of biker clubs than most do (particularly law enforcement officials), stressing their sense of brotherhood and downplaying their criminal activities. Veno says that the ideals of the clubs are still there—brotherhood, partying, commitment, and riding—but they are changing as a result of outside pressures. According to Veno, the number of clubs are decreasing worldwide as a result of amalgamation, and the number of members is also decreasing. Most experts would agree with him on the first point, but would argue with his "romanticized" view of biker club ideals. The opinions of Australian law enforcement officials, as well as the available evidence, do not support his sedate view of criminal behavior by "bikie gangs" (Australian term).

CRIMINAL ACTIVITY AND VIOLENCE

As we will see, the deviant life style of the one-percent biker clubs/members includes individual criminal acts, group criminal acts, and club- or chapter-sponsored/condoned criminal acts ranging from assaults and murder to drug manufacturing and trafficking. For some clubs and chapters of clubs, crime is a way of life that is organized regionally, nationally, and internationally. In addition, the popular image, culture, and romanticized deviant lifestyle tends to attract individuals with a propensity for crimes and violence. Before sentencing 30 bikers for crimes from manslaughter to murder, one Australian judge asked rhetorically, "why do 'good' people turn to violence in biker clubs?" This same culture attracts men who are racists and misogynists.

This book is the first to examine the reported criminal behavior of the entire spectrum of one-percent biker clubs and members; literally from A to W—Aliens to Warlocks. Other books examine the criminal exploits of one or more of what are called the "Big Five" biker clubs because of their size and sophistication—the Hells Angels, the Bandidos, the Outlaws, the Pagans, and the Sons of Silence—or the sensational crimes of lesser known one-percent biker clubs or club members. This myopic approach leaves unexamined the criminal activities of individuals, groups, and chapters of other clubs. There are numerous one-percent biker clubs with fewer members and less publicity than the Big Five. Some of these clubs, such as the Mongols MC, the Vagos MC, and the Warlocks MC (or members of these clubs) have engaged in serious criminal behavior, including organized crime, and are expanding overseas like the Hells Angels, Bandidos, and Outlaws. Many regional one-percent biker clubs such as the Breed MC, the Aliens MC, and the Warlocks MC in the Northeast operate independently of larger clubs or as puppets for larger biker clubs in their criminal activities. A recent analysis of federal and state court cases by the author revealed that there were 66 different one-percent biker clubs involved in crimes in 44 different states over a 40-year time period. The Big Five were involved in the most cases in the most states. Two Big Five clubs, the Hells Angels and the Outlaws, were involved in the most cases in the most states (20 and 13 states, respectively). Thirty-four of these cases involved RICO (Racketeer Influenced Corrupt Organization)—that is, organized crime—prosecutions of nine different biker clubs. The Outlaws MC, Pagans MC, and Hells Angels MC had the most cases, but less well known one-percent biker clubs such as the Avengers MC, Diablos MC, Dirty Dozen MC, and the Fates Assembly MC were also prosecuted under RICO (Barker, 2006).

BIKER WARS

The one-percent biker clubs, although they share the same biker culture and a romanticized sense of brotherhood, are unable to live with one another without violence. Wars between one-percent biker clubs have occurred in the United States and overseas on a steady basis since the 1950s, as clubs compete with each other for territory, "showing class," and illegal markets. In the early 1960s, the San Francisco and Oakland chapters of the Hells Angels stomped and beat each other. The 1960s, 1970s, and 1980s were especially violent as the one-percent biker clubs expanded throughout the United States and overseas. A March 1971 battle between the Breed MC and the fledgling Cleveland Hells Angels chapter resulted in five dead bikers—four Breed and one Angels. It took 150 police officers with tear gas to stop the bloodletting. In 1973, members of the Storm Troopers MC, now the Durham, North Carolina, Hells Angels, killed two Pagans MC members and wounded five others in a van traveling along I-85 outside Durham. Some sources say that the bloody war between the Outlaws MC and the Hells Angels began in 1974 when three Angels were murdered by Outlaws in Florida. The Pagans MC and the Outlaws MC clashed for the first time at the 1976 Daytona Bike Week and have been bitter enemies since.

The murder and mayhem between biker clubs continues in recent years. In February 2002, members of the Pagans MC and the Hells Angels MC clashed during the Hellraisers Ball, an annual tattoo and motorcycle expo on Long Island, New York, leaving one dead, three wounded by gunfire, and seven stabbed and beaten. Angel celebrities

Sonny Barger and Chuck Zito were signing autographs at the time the fight broke out. Speculation is that the Pagans were there to challenge the Hells Angels movement into Long Island, traditionally Pagans territory, and to kill Barger. Seventy-three Pagans were convicted or pleaded guilty to federal charges stemming from this incident. The battle and the depletion of Pagans members led to an infusion of Hells Angels into the Delaware Valley, particularly Philadelphia. This increased tension between the clubs led to more violence. The April 2002 shootout between the Hells Angels and the Mongols MC at Harrah's Casino in Laughlin, Nevada, during an annual motorcycle rally left three dead and 13 injured. Many of the injured were terrified casino patrons caught up in the biker violence. Harry "Taco" Bowman, the International President of the Outlaws MC, was on the FBI's Most Wanted List 1997-1999 for three counts of murder. One of those murders was of the President of the Warlocks MC.

Unidentified members of the Hells Angels MC arrive at the federal court in Las Vegas. A State Supreme Court review of charges against eight Hells Angels and six Mongols preceded scheduled arraignments of 44 Hells Angels members on separate federal charges of attempted murder and other counts stemming from the same 2002 brawl in a Laughlin hotel-casino. *Photo courtesy of AP Photo/Jae C. Hong.*

With expansion of the U.S. clubs, the murder and mayhem has moved overseas. In 1984, gunfire broke out at a motorcycle swap meet in Milperra, Australia, between chapters of the American-originated Bandidos MC and the Australian Commancheros MC. Seven people, including a 15-year-old girl, were killed. The recent five-year war over drug dealing markets in Canada, between the Quebec Nomads Chapter of the Hells Angels and the Canadian Rock Machine MC (now a chapter of the Bandidos MC), left more than 160 bikers and several innocent civilians dead, including an 11-year-old boy hit by shrapnel from an exploding bomb. The vicious leader of the Quebec Nomads HA chapter had two corrections officers, one a mother of two grown children, murdered in an attempt to intimidate the Canadian criminal justice system. The Great Nordic Bike War between the Hells Angels and Bandidos over drug markets in Denmark, Finland, Norway, and Sweden resulted in numerous deaths and injuries to bikers and innocent civilians. It was fought with RPGs and bombs and involved two shootouts at airports.

The HAMC maintains an AFFA (Angels Forever, Forever Angels) web site as a memorial to Angels who have died since the clubs 1958 founding. The site contains names and pictures of several hundred deceased Hells Angels. Above many pictures are replicas of the Angels version of the U.S. Purple Heart Medal, which has "AFFA" across the ribbon and the Angels Death Head logo on the purple background where George Washington's bust appears on the U.S. Purple Heart Medal. The web site explains that the Angels' medal is awarded to Angels "who have died at the hands of another man." Although several murdered Angels from chapters overseas appear on the web site, no murdered Canadian Angels are listed, including the five members of the North Hells Angels chapter slaughtered by their Canadian HAMC brothers in a feud over drug profits. This was the first time in Angels' history that an entire chapter was marked for execution by other Angels, although it has not been uncommon for Angels to murder Angels.

In spite of the violence against each other, the one-percent biker clubs portray themselves as modern-day outlaws riding iron horses and united by a sense of freedom and brotherhood. They claim to be the victims of media sensationalism and law enforcement harassment. Furthermore, they proclaim that their days of "mugging and thugging" are in the past. There is general consensus among scholars that media sensationalism in the 1960s and 1970s created a "folk devil" image and moral panic about bikers, particularly one-percent bikers, that persists to this day. In fact, a "moral panic" concerning the "biker problem" in Canada followed the death of the 11 year-old boy (mentioned earlier) after a bombing by rival motorcycle gangs (Morsani, 2005). There is also evidence that police harass or profile back-patch- wearing bikers in general. Some police motorcycle clubs/members, like the Choir Boys MC and the Wild Pigs MC, complain that they are harassed by their supervisors and fellow officers. Several court cases have come to the conclusion that there is no doubt that law enforcement agencies and officers "harass" and "profile" one-percent bikers.

Many one-percent biker clubs have made an effort to clean up their image, sponsoring and participating in numerous charitable events, but how much of this charitable work is self-serving public relations is open to question. Spokesmen for the clubs also say they are not responsible for the crimes of some members and point out that the law enforcement agencies that harass them have "bad apples" as well. Recognizing that one-percent biker club members have engaged in drug-related organized crime, club spokesmen say that drug manufacturing and selling by "bad apples" is not organized or endorsed by the clubs. On the other hand, law enforcement officials throughout the world, including Interpol and Europol, refer to one-percent biker clubs as outlaw motorcycle gangs (OMGs) involved in international organized crime. These officials say that one-percent biker clubs are criminal organizations (i.e. gangs) whose members use their membership in a motorcycle club as a basis for criminal activities; they are literally criminals on two wheels.

The debate between these two views is the purpose of this book—to examine whether one-percent biker clubs are really motorcycle clubs or whether they are gangs of criminals united for profit, engaging in organized crime. This book contends that the reality lies along a continuum. Not all one-percent biker clubs or their chapters are involved in organized crime activities, but many are. There are some one-percent biker club members who are law-abiding individuals, but many are convicted felons and career criminals. Some clubs or chapters have or have had leaders who are/were career criminals, and some have not. Criminal behavior is, or has been, a prerequisite for membership in some clubs or chapters of clubs, but for others this is not true.

This book will examine the reported criminal behavior of one-percent biker clubs and identify the clubs whose members have been involved in criminal behavior. We will classify their behaviors on a "Continuum of One-Percent Motorcycle Clubs as Criminal Organizations," ranging from gangs at one end to clubs on the other. Guiding this inquiry is the network approach to organized crime proposed by Klaus von Lampe.

ORGANIZED CRIME

Noted German organized crime researcher Klaus von Lampe says that there are two areas of consensus in the study of organized crime: (1) no one doubts that organized crime exists; however, (2), there is no generally accepted definition of organized crime (von Lampe, 2003). Many researchers now use the concept of "illegal enterprise," which uses the activities and not the structure as a starting point. For instance, Albanese (2004:8) has developed a typology of organized crimes by using activities as the starting point. He classifies organized criminal behavior by: (1) type of activity; (2) nature of activity; and (3) harm (see Table 1.1).

Table 1.1: Typology of Organized Crime Activities

Type of Activity	Nature of Activity	Harm
Provision of Illegal Goods	OC offers goods that a segment of the public wants: drugs, liquor, stolen property.	Consensual. Violence not inherent, but comes with market control. Economic harm.
Provision of Illegal Services	OC offers services that legal society does not fulfill: money, sex, gambling, loan sharking.	Consensual. Violence not inherent, but comes with market control. Economic harm.
Infiltration of Legitimate Businesses	Coercive use of legal businesses for purposes of exploitation.	Nonconsensual activities. Threats, violence, extortion. Economic harm.

Criminal enterprises (organized crime) exist when groups of criminals provide an illegal good or service on an ongoing basis. This would be exemplified by groups such as drug-trafficking organizations (DTOs). Von Lampe says that classifying organized criminal behavior by enterprise/activity avoids the conspiracy theory involved in ethnically defined criminal organizations—which is referred to by Albanese as the "ethnicity trap" (1994). Furthermore, as Van Duyne (2003) and others point out, many researchers and organizations, such as the Council of Europe, the European Commission, and the United Nations, use what is known as the enumeration method to define organized crime. This method contains a listing of mandatory and optional criteria to define organized crime.

The mandatory criteria are:

1. Collaboration of three or more people (group behavior);

2. For a prolonged or indefinite period of time;

3. Suspected or convicted of committing serious criminal offenses;

4. With the objective of pursuing profit and/or power.

The optional criteria are:

1. Having a specific task or role for each participant;

2. Using some form of internal discipline and control;

3. Using violence or other means suitable for intimidation;

4. Exerting influence on politics, the media, public administration, law enforcement, the administration of justice
   or the economy by corruption or any other means;

5. Using commercial or business-like structures;

6. Engaged in money-laundering;

7. Operating on an international level.

The enumeration method contains "fuzzy" or hard-to-define terms, including value terms that are redundant and difficult to measure, such as "serious," "prolonged," or "indefinite."

Another method of identification uses ethnicity to define organized crime; this is what Albanese calls the "ethnicity trap." The efforts to define organized crime relying on ethnically defined criminal organizations such as "Italian Mafia," "Russian Mafia," and so on, leaves out a large number of criminal groups and networks of criminals. In fact, the term "Mafia" has become a metaphor for organized crime and has been applied to Russian, Mexican, and Dixie groups indiscriminately. Obviously, ethnically defined criminal organizations do not fit many organized crime groups and networks that do not share the same ethnic background. Street gangs and biker gangs are but two examples.

Network Approach to Organized Crime

Von Lampe also says that enterprise theory, with its emphasis on market orientation, fails to address "predatory and fraudulent crimes with no primary market orientation [such as investment fraud], and quasi-governmental or parasitic power syndicates that occupy strata above criminal groups [for example, political machines] engaged in illegal business transactions," such as those addressed by Block (1983) in his seminal study of organizing crime in New York from 1930 to 1950. In an effort to deal with the previous criticisms of definitions, Von Lampe proposes a new concept—"criminally exploitable ties"—in describing a network approach to organized crime that provides for a better understanding of the "phenomena subsumed to organized crime" (von Lampe, 2003:10). His analysis assumes that crimes such as drug trafficking, or investment fraud; criminal collectives such as "mafia syndicates"; and criminogenic milieus or systematic conditions, such as corrupt alliances of businessmen, politicians, and public officials, all begin with participants connected through criminally exploitable ties that combine to form criminal networks. These criminal networks are sets of actors connected by ties that in some way or another support the commission of illegal acts. Criminal networks constitute "the least common denominator of organized crime" (von Lampe and Johansen, 2004:167). This leads to the four principles in the network analysis of organized crime.

First Principle
All group crime begins with a dyadic network between individuals with criminally exploitable ties.

According to the *network approach to organized crime*, the basic unit in any form of criminal cooperation is a criminally exploitable tie linking two actors. Each actor in the basic network has latent or manifest criminal dispositions that come together when the opportunities arise and there is a common basis of trust. Each actor could already be an individual criminal actor; however, a network between them will not be formed without common trust. Trust is necessary for two actors to engage in criminal activities in order to minimize the risks involved in illegal transactions. Those risks include the increased risk of detection and prosecution that comes with "partnering up." After all, one has to be sure that the partner is not an undercover officer or an informant, loose-lipped, or in other ways unreliable, because agreements between criminal partners cannot be enforced in a court of law. Of course, this trust can be misplaced or break down under the pressure imposed by law enforcement authorities, but it will have been perceived to be there by both parties when the network began. This leads to the second principle.

Second Principle
Networks between criminal actors will depend on a common basis of trust.

Trust is formed in a number of ways. Trust in the criminal milieu can be based on one's reputation among criminal actors. This common basis of trust can also be found in some sort of bonding relationship, such as ethnicity, kinship, childhood friendship, and prison acquaintanceship. The bonding relationship can be formed by affiliation or membership in secret societies such as the Sicilian Mafia, Chinese Triads, or Japanese Yakuza, or in subcultures that share a specific set of values and a code of conduct much like street gangs and one-percent motorcycle clubs. Groups such as street gangs and one-percent biker clubs are recognizable to each other by reputation or distinctive clothing, behavior patterns, or tattoos. As social groups, they adhere to mutual support and noncooperation with law enforcement. The common basis of trust can also develop over time as actors come together in legal and/or illegal business relationships. These latter ties will not be as strong and intense as those of ethnicity, kinship, affiliation, and membership, and they will often be ephemeral. They also may be more common in certain organized criminal activities such as drug trafficking (see Desroches, 2005).

Figure 1.1: Organized Crime in the United States—Networks

> Organized crime in the United States today is a multi-ethnic enterprise, comprised of many different groups, most of them quite small, which emerge to exploit criminal activities (e.g. frauds, smuggling, stolen property distribution, and so on). Many of these groups are short-lived, comprised of career criminals, who form temporary networks of individuals with desired skills (e.g., forgery, smuggling connections, border and bribery connections, etc.) to exploit a criminal opportunity. These *networks* often dissolve after the opportunity has been exploited, as the criminals seek new opportunities that may employ different combinations of criminals

Source: Albanese, 2004:13. (Italics added.)

Criminal organizations evolve out of group criminal networks—a set of three or more people linked by criminally exploitable ties. They do so by the size and complexity of the networks necessary for some crimes. When the dyadic relationship requires a third person, the nucleus for organized crime appears. Therefore, organized crime begins with a group network—three or more persons linked by criminally exploitable ties. In addition, in order to be organized crime groups, these group networks must engage in ongoing or recurring illegal acts, rather than isolated incidents (Albanese, 2004:11). Obviously, two criminals would not be enough to engage in all the activities necessary in many criminal activities, such as the production and distribution of narcotics or human trafficking. Organized crime requires conspiracies between criminal actors. Illicit goods must be found, grown, or otherwise produced, and transported; customers must be found or identified; law enforcement must be avoided or neutralized; and profits must be laundered. Some criminal activities are spatially separate—regional, national, and transnational; all these tasks require combinations of individuals linked together by criminally exploitable ties—criminal organizations.

Third Principle
A criminal organization consists of a combination of individuals linked through criminally exploitable ties.

Many crimes require organization: drug and weapons trafficking, protection rackets, human trafficking, organized retail theft (ORT), protection rackets, disposing of stolen goods, gambling, prostitution, money laundering, and the production and distribution of pornography. Von Lampe provides a typology of criminal organizations according to the functions they serve and their degree of structural complexity (von Lampe, 2003). Criminal organizations serve one of three functions: economic, social, and quasi-governmental. *Economic criminal organizations* are those set up for the sole purpose of achieving material gain, such as gangs of burglars, robbers, drug traffickers, or an illegal casino. At times, for deviant motorcycle clubs or chapters of these clubs, there is a fine line between economic and social criminal organizations. As we will see, some deviant motorcycle clubs, such as the Canadian Rock Machine MC, were set up for the sole purpose of achieving illegal material gain such as drug trafficking. At times, chapters of many deviant motorcycle clubs have acted as economic criminal organizations. For example, according to Canadian law enforcement officials, the Quebec Nomads HA chapter had $18 million in drug sales from November 10 to December 19, 2000 (Cherry, 2005:168). During that time they sold 1,916 kilograms of cocaine in addition to other drugs.

Social criminal organizations support the economic activities of their members only indirectly. Membership creates and promotes a sense of solidarity and belonging—trust establishes contacts, gives status within a criminal milieu, and provides a forum for sharing information, both criminal and noncriminal—and promotes a deviant ideology. In other words, membership establishes and intensifies criminally exploitable ties and makes possible criminal networks that can extend regionally, nationally, and internationally for some clubs. Some street gangs, including the notorious Crips, have evolved from social organizations. For example, The L.A street gang, Canoga Park Alabama (named after the neighborhood and street it considers its turf), began in the 1930s as a social club for Latino farm workers (Covarrubias and Winton, 2007). The gang evolved into a car club before becoming a street gang involved in drug trafficking. Even the Ku Klux Klan evolved from a social organization formed by Confederate Civil War veterans for the sole purpose of amusement and fraternity (Trelease, 1999). There is no doubt that many biker clubs started out as special interest clubs devoted to partying and riding; their criminal activities were not structured or organized, rather it was confined to individual or small groups of members. That has changed for many clubs or chapters of clubs. The criminal members took and take advantage of the structure and nature of the clubs to further their criminal interests.

A *quasi-governmental criminal organization* affects the economic activities of its members and those of other criminals operating within its sphere of influence by making and enforcing rules of conduct and by settling disputes. Some Cosa Nostra families have operated in this manner (Anderson, 1979). That is, they have imposed and enforced rules of conduct for criminals who operated in a geographic area.

Fourth Principle
A social criminal organization, such as one-percent biker clubs,
indirectly supports the criminal activities of it members.

Following the logic of von Lampe's argument that a social criminal organization supports the criminal activities of its members when
groups of individuals with criminally exploitable ties come together
within a common basis of trust, the focus of study becomes the recruitment process, the socialization process for new members, and the
peer group support that arises for certain forms of criminal behavior.
The symbolic representation of one-percent biker clubs—patches, colors, tattoos, and dress—contributes to the cultural solidarity and support of activities by members (both criminal and noncriminal). We will
examine each of these factors in later chapters as we examine outlaw
motorcycle gangs as organized crime.

Criminal organizations also vary by structural complexity: horizontal differentiation, vertical differentiation, and spatial differentiation. *Horizontal differentiation* refers to the extent that the criminal
organization has subdivided tasks among its members, that is, its
division of labor. *Vertical differentiation* is the extent to which the organization's authority is divided. *Spatial differentiation* depends on the
number of locations in which the organization operates. Motorcycle
clubs are vertically differentiated and vary spatially differentiated
throughout the United States and the rest of the world. In addition,
related to their structural complexity, deviant motorcycle clubs have
written constitutions and by-laws in order to appear outwardly legal
even though their members engage in a variety of criminal activities.
Club spokesmen (there are no spokeswomen) point to these constitutions and by-laws as proof that they are merely clubs who happen to
have a few members who commit crimes.

METHODOLOGY

Research on subjects who belong to deviant groups is difficult
under any circumstances, but such research on outlaw motorcycle
group members is even more difficult and potentially dangerous for the
researcher and the subjects. The usual data collection methods—ques-
tionnaires, interviews, observation—are often not feasible. Studies
of deviant activities that also involve biker groups often exclude them
from study because of the difficulties involved in studying them. In
Desroches' seminal study of drug trafficking, biker gang members
refused to be interviewed (Desroches, 2005). A Canadian study of HIV-
related risk factors among erotic/exotic dancers excluded "women

who dance in bars controlled by motorcycle gangs, commonly referred to as biker bars" (Lewis and Maticka-Tyndale, 1998:2). The clubs do not want to be studied and, because of their criminal activities, maintain strict access to club business to frustrate the information- gathering efforts of law enforcement agencies. Quinn (1983), in his seminal work on "one percenters," found that "[a]s secret societies there are rules, inhibitions, and severe sanctions (i.e., expulsions and death) prohibiting discussions of any and all club affairs with non-members." Another researcher found that "[b]iker gangs are tight-knit, regimented organizations that demand a high degree of conformity to norms [their deviant norms] and exert strong control over individual members" (Desroches, 2005:7). Individual members cannot grant an interview without getting themselves into serious trouble. Furthermore, much of the official information on outlaw motorcycle gangs produced by government agencies such as the Federal Bureau of Investigation (FBI), Bureau of Alcohol, Tobacco, Firearms, and Explosives (ATF), and the National Drug Intelligence Center (NDIC) is considered to be law enforcement–sensitive and not for public dissemination. For these reasons, this book is based on a combination of quantitative and qualitative methods: published sources such as journalistic accounts and autobiographies of former and present members of biker clubs; academic/scholarly works; available law enforcement/government reports; articles from newspapers and biker web sites; and a content analysis of biker court cases—federal and state—from a LexisNexis search. The work is also based on "interviews/conversations" and associations with current and past biker club members; "interviews and associations" with law enforcement officers; Internet web sites of biker clubs and chapters; other materials available on the World Wide Web; and more than 30 years of studying crime, criminals, and organized crime.

SUMMARY

In the remainder of this book it will be argued that deviant motorcycle clubs can be placed on a continuum from gangs on one end to clubs on the other, with social criminal organizations in the middle. Many of these clubs have evolved into social criminal organizations, that is, organizations that support the criminal activity of its members indirectly. This indirect support facilitates the individual and group behavior of its members. In addition, some of these clubs or chapters of these clubs are involved in organized criminal activities on a national and international scale.

On occasion, some one-percent biker clubs act as economic criminal organizations, directly supporting the criminal activities of its members. The nature, structure, and culture (or subculture, if you will) of deviant motorcycle clubs, particularly one-percent bikers, attract individuals with criminal or potential criminal dispositions—criminally exploitable ties—and facilitates and supports the criminal networks that arise in these clubs. The selection process and socialization experiences ensure this for many clubs and chapters of clubs. Patchholders—a term referring to members—often invite for membership and select prospects only those who share their same criminal propensities, sometimes even making the commission of crimes a prerequisite for membership. Biker clubs/gangs as secret societies or subcultures share a specific set of deviant values and adhere to a certain code of conduct that instills in each member a common basis of trust known as brotherhood. The criminal networks that result from members linked together by criminal exploitable ties evolve into criminal organizations. Furthering the development of these criminal networks into criminal organizations for one-percent bikers are the weekly meetings of chapter members, monthly meetings of chapter officers, and yearly meetings of officers worldwide for many clubs. Many outlaw motorcycle gangs (OMGs) are criminal organizations that can, and have, expanded into national and international networks sharing a common affiliation.

REFERENCES

Albanese, J. (2004). "North American Organized Crime." *Global Crime* 6(1):8-18.

Anderson, A.C. (1979). *The Business of Organized Crime: A Cosa Nostra Family.* Stanford, CA: Hoover Institutional Press.

Auger, M. (2001). *The Biker Who Shot Me: Recollections of a Crime Reporter.* Toronto: McClelland & Stewart.

Barger, R., with K. Zimmerman and K. Zimmerman (2002). *Hell's Angels: The Life and Times of Sonny Barger and the Hell's Angel Motorcycle Club.* New York: HarperCollins.

Barker, T. (2006). "Busting Biker Gangs." Paper presented at the Annual Meeting of the Academy of Criminal Justice Sciences, Baltimore, MD, March 2006.

Beare, M.E, and R.T. Naylor (1999). "Major Issues Relating to Organized Crime: Within the Context of Economic Relationships." Nathanson Centre for the Study of Organized Crime and Corruption. Found at: http://www.ncjrs.org/nathanson/organized.htm

Bowe, B. (1994). *Born to be Wild.* New York: Warner Books.

Charles, G. (2002). *Bikers: Legend, Legacy and Life.* London: Independent Music Press.

Cherry, P. (2005). *The Biker Trials: Bringing Down the Hells Angels.* Toronto: ECW Press.

Covarrubias, A., and R. Winton (2007). "From Social Club to Street Gang." *Los Angeles Times,* March 21, 2007. Found at: http://www.latimes.com/news/local/la-me-canoga21mar21,0,7301120

Desroches, F.J. (2005). *The Crime That Pays: Drug Trafficking and Organized Crime in Canada.* Toronto: Canadian Scholars' Press.

Detroit, M. (1994). *Chain of Evidence: A True Story of Law Enforcement and One Woman's Bravery.* New York: Penguin Books.

Harris, M. (1985). *Bikers: Birth of a Modern Day Outlaw.* London: Faber & Faber.

Kaye, H.R. (1970). *A Place in Hell: The Inside Story of 'Hell's Angels'—The World's Wildest Outsiders.* London: New English Library [First published in 1968 by Holloway, USA].

Kingsbury, K. (1995).*The Snake and the Spider.* New York: Dell.

Lavigne, Y. (1987). *Hell's Angels: Taking Care of Business.* Toronto: Ballantine Books.

Lavigne, Y. (1996). *Hells Angels: Into the Abyss.* Toronto: HarperCollins.

Lavigne, Y. (1999). *Hells Angels at War.* Toronto: HarperCollins.

Levingston, T.G.. with K. Zimmerman and K. Zimmerman (2003). *Soul on Bikes: The East Bay Dragons MC and the Black Biker Set.* St. Paul, MN: MBI.

Lewis, J., and E. Maticka-Tyndale (1998). "Final Report: Erotic/Exotic Dancing: HIV-Related Risk Factors 1998. A Report to Health Canada." Grant #6606-5688.

Lowe, M. (1988). *Conspiracy of Brothers.* Toronto: Seal Books.

Lyon, D. (2003). *The Bikeriders.* San Francisco: Chronicle Books.

Mandelkau, J. (1971). *Buttons: The Making of a President.* London: Sphere Books.

Martineau, P. (2003). *I Was a Killer for the Hells Angels: The True Story of Serge Quesnel.* Toronto: McClelland & Stewart.

Mayson, B., with T. Marco (1982). *Fallen Angel: Hell's Angel to Heaven's Saint.* Garden City, NY: Doubleday & Co.

Mello, M. (2001). *The Wrong Man: A True Story of Innocence on Death Row.* Minneapolis: University of Minnesota Press.

Morsani, A. (2005). "Societal Reaction to the Biker Gang War: The Construction of a Moral Panic." Unpublished Master's Thesis. Queen's University Kingston, Ontario, Canada.

Murphy, M.G. (1999). *Police Undercover: The True Story of the Biker, the Mafia and the Mountie.* Toronto: Avalon House.

Paradis, P. (2002). *Nasty Business: One Biker Gang's War Against the Hell's Angels.* Toronto: HarperCollins.

Quinn, J.F. (1983). "Outlaw Motorcycle Clubs: A Sociological Analysis." Unpublished Master's Thesis, University of Miami.

Reynolds, F., as told to M. McClure (1967). *Freewheelin' Frank: Secretary of the Angels.* New York: Grove Press.

Reynolds, T. (2000). *Wild Ride: How Outlaw Motorcycle Myth Conquered America.* New York: TV Books.

Shaylor, A. (2004). *Hells Angels Motorcycle Club.* London: Merrill.

Sher, J., and W. Marsden (2003). *The Road to Hell: How the Biker Gangs Are Conquering Canada.* Toronto: Alfred Knopf.

Simpson, L., and S. Harvey (2001). *Brothers in Arms: The Inside Story of Two Bikie Gangs.* Crows Nest, NSW, Australia: Allen & Unwin.

Stephenson, R. (2004). *Milperra: The Road to Justice.* NSW, Australia: New Holland.

Trelease, A.W. (1999). *White Terror: The Ku Klux Klan Conspiracy and Southern Reconstruction.* Baton Rouge: Louisiana State University Press.

Thompson, H.S. (1966). *Hell's Angels: The Strange and Terrible Saga of the Outlaw Motorcycle Gangs.* New York: Ballantine Books.

Upright, M.H. (1999). *One Percent.* Los Angeles: Action.

Van Duyne, P. (2003). "Medieval Thinking and Organized Crime Economy." In E.C. Viano, J. Magallanes, and L. Bridel, *Transnational Organized Crime: Myth, Power, and Profit.* Durham, NC: Carolina Academic Press, pp. 23-44.

Veno, A. (2002). *The Brotherhoods: Inside the Outlaw Motorcycle Clubs.* Crows Nest, NSW, Australia: Allen & Unwin.

Von Lampe, K. (2003). "Criminally Exploitable Ties: A Network Approach to Organized Crime." in E.C. Viano, J. Magallanes, and L. Bridel, *Transnational Organized Crime: Myth, Power, and Profit.* Durham, NC: Carolina Academic Press, pp. 9-22.

Von Lampe, K., and P.O. Johansen (2004). "Organized Crime and Trust: On the Conception and Empirical Relevance of Trust in the Context of Criminal Networks." *Global Crime* 6(2):159-184.

Wethern, G., and V. Colnett (1978). *A Wayward Angel.* New York: Richard Marek.

Winterhalder, E. (2005). *Out in Bad Standing: Inside the Bandidos Motorcycle Club—The Making of a Worldwide Dynasty.* Owasso, OK: Blockhead Press.

Zito, C., with J. Layden (2002). *Street Justice.* New York: St. Martin's Press.

2

Conventional and Deviant Clubs

INTRODUCTION

The first motorcycles were built in the late 1800s, with the first American production in 1898: the Orient-Aster. Almost immediately, rugged individuals started racing these dangerous and unwieldy machines. In 1903, William Harley and his friends Arthur and Walter Davidson launched the Harley-Davidson Company in Milwaukee, Wisconsin. At first, Harley-Davidson motorcycles were primarily racing bikes, and Harleys dominated the fledgling sport (Fuglsang, 1997). However, by the early 1920s, Harleys became used more as a means of transportation and pleasure than for racing, and they dominated the American market. The Harley-Davidson Company changed the nature of motorcycle riding from primarily racing to an experience enjoyed by a wide range of Americans. Since that time, groups of American motorcycle riders formed together in clubs that can be broadly classified as either conventional or deviant (norm-violating) clubs.

Conventional club members, representing all races and sexes and riding all makes of motorcycles foreign and domestic, behave according to the norms of society and join together based on their common interest in motorcycles, riding together for pleasure and companionship. They join traditional motorcycle associations such as the American Motorcycle Association (AMA). Historically, they come from different social strata and dress differently and act differently from deviant club members. From a sociological standpoint, deviant (i.e., norm-violating) clubs would include clubs that are not AMA-sanctioned; those of all one race, sex, or sexual orientation; or those labeled as outlaw motorcycle clubs (OMCs). Deviant clubs have always represented a small percentage of the motorcycle riding public, but they receive the most attention and publicity.

Drawing particular attention are the one-percent bikers (or one-percenters). Over time, groups of deviant motorcyclists evolved into a subculture of bikers labeled by others and themselves as one-percent bikers. These one-percent bikers make up a small percentage of all deviant motorcyclists. The coinage of the "one-percent" term will be discussed later in this chapter.

It is possible for clubs to be considered a deviant club and not be a one-percent club (e.g., motorcycle clubs based on the same sex, race, or sexual orientation). The web site for BURN MC (Black Urban Ryders Nation) lists 444 black motorcycle clubs/chapters (www.xtremeburn.com). This includes all–black male and all–black female clubs. The Women on Wheels Motorcycle Association lists 120 women's clubs/chapters (www.womenonwheels.com). There are also numerous gay/lesbian motorcycle clubs. The Cavaliers MC (the New Orleans Gay Motorcycle Club) lists 102 gay/lesbian motorcycle clubs in North America and internationally (www.cavaliersmc.com). The largest lesbian motorcycle club, Dykes on Bikes MC, has been in a battle with the U.S. Patent and Trademarks Office for years trying to trademark "Dykes on Bikes" (www.dykesonbikes.org). According to the web site, the Patent Office says the word "dyke" is vulgar.

One-percent biker clubs are deviant clubs known as outlaw motorcycle clubs. The clubs are made up of males (primarily white) who ride "American Iron," mainly Harleys. The one-percenters, for the most part, engage in "in your face" opposition to conventional norms and values, seeing themselves as outsiders and seeing others (nonbikers) as outsiders.

Women ride down Fifth Avenue in the "Dykes on Bikes" contingent of New York City's 2005 Gay Pride Parade. *Photo courtesy of AP Photo/Jennifer Szymaszek.*

The evolution of deviant motorcycle clubs into outlaw motorcycle clubs, and then into a subculture of one-percent biker clubs, is an American phenomenon that had its roots in Southern California.

OUTLAW MOTORCYCLE CLUBS

The first classification of conventional and deviant motorcycle clubs resulted from efforts to standardize and organize racing events taking place in the early history of motorcycling. The Federation of American Motorcyclists (FAM), formed in 1903, held its first organized event in 1908 (Fuglsang, 1997). The two-day endurance run around New York City and Long Island resulted in a Harley-Davidson defeat of 84 other riders on 22 different makes of motorcycles. The FAM held runs sporadically until its demise in 1919. The American Motorcyclists Association (AMA) was founded in 1924 after the 1919 collapse of the Federation. By the 1930s, the AMA had sanctioned/chartered 300 motorcycle clubs (Fuglsang, 1997). These clubs represented the "responsible" motorcycle riders and had strict dress codes (Norris, 1992). Clubs that obtained a charter from the AMA were considered legal clubs; the others were classified as "outlaws" (Wolf, 1999). The "outlaw" label in this case meant non-AMA, not criminal. However, the deviant label had consequences: outlaw clubs were not allowed to participate in AMA-sanctioned events such as mixers, charity events, races, and hill-climbing contests.

At about the same time as the appearance of the outlaw label, groups of motorcyclists who were often more criminal gangs than motorcycle clubs began to appear in the motorcycle-friendly weather of Southern California in the early 1930s. Depression stricken "Okies," looking for work and riding motorcycles because they were cheap transportation, appeared on the scene. Although most were loners who rarely stayed in one town for long, some banded together in the squalid Southern California industrial districts and formed loose-knit motorcycle clubs. Riding together in groups, these outsiders worked menial jobs and lived a deviant lifestyle of drinking and rowdy behavior, with some dealing in stolen motorcycle parts and other criminal pursuits (Yates, 1999; Wood, 2003). Harley-Davidson motorcycles were the most popular and abundant bikes at that time, so Harleys became the motorcycles of choice for these groups—for both possession and theft. Yates (1999) claims that this solidified the Harley-Davidson's identification as an outlaw machine. These outlaw clubs—non–AMA sanctioned and more like gangs than clubs—were also different in dress and behavior from the AMA clubs. Their appearance foreshadowed the development of the outlaw motorcycle clubs and the one-percent bikers.

The steady growth of AMA-chartered clubs and outlaw clubs continued into the early 1940s. At first, outlaw clubs, still in the minority, were not much of a threat to conventional motorcycle clubs or the image of motorcycle riders in general, but this changed in the late 1940s. Following World War II, outlaw clubs began disrupting AMA-sanctioned events and the label "outlaw motorcycle club" took on a new meaning and changed the public image of motorcycle riders. Although no one person was responsible for the change, "Wino Willie" Forkner has come to be representative of the change and the men who brought it about.

The Original Wild One: "Wino Willie" Forkner

In the early 1940s, conventional motorcycle clubs like the 13 Rebels and the Three Points existed in the Los Angeles area (Reynolds, 2000). Club members were riders with wives and kids who wore flashy sweaters and ties and had their bikes tuned for competition racing. A hard-drinking young motorcyclist named Wino Willie Forkner joined the 13 Rebels and rode with them for two years before the attack on Pearl Harbor. The young Forkner, who was to become a legend in outlaw motorcycle history, acquired his nickname at the age of 12 because of his affinity to red wine. After Pearl Harbor, the dipsomaniac Forkner joined the Army Air Corp and was soon manning a .50-caliber machine gun on a B-24 Liberator for the next 30 months (Reynolds, 2000). During that period, Wino Willie flew numerous missions in the South Pacific, made corporal, and lost his stripes because of a drunken episode in which he trashed a bar and got thrown in jail. In the summer of 1945, the hell-raising Wino Willie returned to California and re-joined the 13 Rebels, most of whom had spent the war years working in the area's aircraft manufacturing plants. It was not long before their conventional lifestyle and Willie's clashed.

Forkner, according to his widow, Teri, was like many of the returning veterans "back from the war and letting off steam" (Bill Hayes Video Interview: The Original Wild Ones, 2003). "Letting off steam" meant riding their bikes and drinking together in an attempt to recreate the camaraderie and excitement they had experienced in battle. In the summer of 1946, Forkner and his drinking buddy and fellow 13 Rebels' member, Blackie, were "letting off steam" in their favorite watering hole, the All-American Bar, when they decided to show up at a 13 Rebels–sponsored quarter-mile race in San Diego after an all-night drinking session (Reynolds, 2000:34-36). Forkner and Blackie sat in the stands and watched what they thought was a boring race. Thoroughly plastered and frustrated, Wino Willie decided to liven things up. He drove his bike through the wooden gate leading from the parking lot onto the track. The drunken Forkner burst onto the track in a shower of shattered wood and loud applause from the audience who shared his view of the race. Forkner roared down the straightaway and made four laps around the track before losing control and turning his bike over. The subdued whirling dervish was promptly arrested and hauled off to jail. After a weekend in jail, Forkner pleaded guilty to trespassing and being drunk and disorderly. He hitchhiked back to Los Angeles and faced an enraged group of 13 Rebels members. The club members demanded his 13 Rebels sweater and threw him out of the club. The unrepentant Forkner reportedly returned the sweater after defecating on it (Reynolds, 2000:36). Wino Willie's legend and the evolution to one-percent biker clubs had begun.

The Boozefighters Motorcycle Club (1946)

The angry Wino Willie decided to put the 13 Rebels and the raceway fiasco behind him by drinking and sulking at the All-American Bar (Reynolds, 2000:36-38). He began drinking with three former servicemen, including one who had lost both legs during the war. As the alcohol flowed and the night went on, the four bikers decided to form a new motorcycle club, but they could not come up with a name. Overhearing the animated discussion, an All-American regular named Walt Porter lifted his head off the bar and said, "Call it the Boozefighters." The four bikers thought that was a perfect name. During the coming weeks, Wino Willie and his fellow bikers recruited 16 other members. All were World War II veterans except a teenager named Jim Morrison (not, of course, the Morrison of Doors fame). Forkner declined to be president, and C.B. Clauson, a former paratrooper, was elected president. The Boozefighters even applied for AMA membership, but were turned down by the AMA president, who allegedly said: "No goddamn way I am giving a name like that a charter" (Forkner, 1987). By 1947, three chapters of the Boozefighters MC had formed in Los Angeles, San Pedro, and San Francisco.

The Boozefighters MC was one of the first—but not the only—outlaw (non–AMA sanctioned) club formed by ex-servicemen "letting off steam." World War II veterans joined outlaw clubs and called themselves the Galloping Gooses (supposedly taken from the nickname for the middle-finger salute), the Pissed Off Bastards of Bloomington, Satan's Sinners, and the Market

A Boozefighters back patch. The Boozefighters MC was one of the first outlaw clubs formed by ex-servicemen. *Photo courtesy of the Boozefighters Motorcycle Club and Bill Hayes.*

Street Commandoes. Conventional clubs used simple and innocent-sounding names like the Road Runners, the Glendale Stokers, and the Side Winders. On occasion, these conventional clubs engaged in reckless street races, but their behavior was harmless compared to the sometimes violence-prone behavior of the new clubs (Yates, 1999). To further distinguish themselves from AMA club members who wore ties and racing caps, the outlaw veterans were unkempt in appearance and rowdy in behavior. With these groups, the stage was set for the creation of a new label—outlaw motorcycle clubs. One event is considered to be the incident that changed the social definition of outlaw clubs: The Hollister Motorcycle Incident/Riot in 1947. Yates (1999) claims that it was at Hollister that outlaw motorcycle clubs made their national debut.

Hollister Motorcycle Incident/Riot (1947): Birthplace of the American Biker

The events that took place in the small California town of Hollister during the 1947 July 4th weekend would lead to a staged photograph, which inspired a short story that led to a movie, which influenced a genre of biker movies and media publicity that ultimately constructed a new social definition of outlaw bikers. Fuglsang (1997) opines that "the events [with the media's help] of Hollister began a long process that transformed a small group of Southern California bikers and free spirits into a national scourge" (p. 5). Although there are numerous versions of what took place during that weekend, Reynolds's account, relying on the observations of those present (including Wino Willie) appears to be accurate (Reynolds, 2000:45-58). The AMA had been conducting "gypsy tours" since their inception. These events were long-range rides to motorcycle rallies across the United States. In 1947, the West Coast town of Hollister, California, was chosen as the site for a gypsy tour and would draw in bikers from across the country. Hollister was [and still is] a big motorcycle town in the 1940s, with 27 bars and 21 gas stations. However, the town only had six police officers. Hollister held its first gypsy tour in 1936 and held regular motorcycle races and hill climbs. The residents were not expecting any trouble at the 1947 rally.

Members of all three Boozefighters MC chapters made plans to attend the motorcycle rally. The Los Angeles members, including Wino Willie, met on Thursday evening at the All-American to prepare for the ride to Hollister. Preparation included drinking at the All-American, riding to Santa Barbara for more drinks, and then riding to San Luis Obispo, where they became too drunk to go on. The Los Angeles Boozefighters "slept it off" in a bus terminal for three hours and roared off to King City, where they stopped at a liquor store to finish "preparing" for the ride into Hollister. By the time they arrived in Hollister, several thousand [actual number unknown] motorcyclists were already there and thoroughly "prepared." It wasn't long before intoxicated bikers turned the blocked-off main thoroughfares into drag strips and stunt-riding exhibitions. Many of the local residents joined in the drag racing and merry making. The local bars were making a killing and not complaining.

During the weekend, the nearby Bolado Racetrack was filled to capacity as the scheduled races went on, but the hard-core hell raisers, which included members of the three Boozefighters chapters and the Pissed Off Bastards of Bloomington (POBOB), were driving the town's six police officers crazy. Soon the jail was filled with drunken motorcyclists, including Wino Willie. Wino Willie was arrested for inciting a riot when the police mistakenly thought he was trying to incite the crowd into breaking the arrested bikers out of jail (Bill Hayes Video Interview: The Original Wild Ones, 2003). He was actually talking the mob out of the jail break.

While the commotion was going on, a photographer for the *San Francisco Chronicle* who was there to cover the gypsy tour decided to take a picture of a drunken motorcyclist. For some unknown reason, he staged a photograph even though there were plenty of drunken motorcyclists available to photograph. The photographer, Barney Peterson, and a colleague sat a Harley-Davidson motorcycle on top of a pile of beer bottles and persuaded an intoxicated biker in a leather jacket coming out of a bar to sit astride the bike (see Figure 2.1). The picture never appeared in the *San Francisco Chronicle,* but it would later become one of the most famous pictures in motorcycle history after it was picked up by the Associated Press and printed in *Life* magazine.

Figure 2.1: Eyewitness Account

> The day after everyone had left, near my store there were two guys taking a photograph. They brought a bunch of empty beer bottles out of alley and put them all around a motorcycle and put a guy on it. I'm sure that's how it was taken because they wanted to get up high to take the shot and they borrowed a ladder from me. That photo appeared on the cover of *Life* magazine. [photo appeared on page 31 of *Life's* July 21, 1947 issue].

Source: Hayes, 2005:181 (Ron Yant, Hollister appliance store owner).

On Sunday night the thoroughly exhausted and disgusted Hollister police officers called for help from the California Highway Patrol (CHP). Forty CHP officers arrived at dusk and were met by hundreds of drunken motorcyclists. The majority of the motorcyclists were combat veterans like the Boozefighters and the POBOBs and were used to following orders. The CHP lieutenant in charge ordered his men to break out the tear gas guns, and they began moving the drunken but compliant bikers toward the end of town. The lieutenant spotted a group of musicians unloading their equipment for a dance at the American Legion Hall and ordered them to set up in the street on a flatbed truck and play for the crowd. The crowd started dancing and continued dancing into the night under the watchful eyes of the CHP. While the drunken bikers danced, the local Chief of Police went to all the bars and had them close at midnight, two hours early. The "riot" was over, but the exaggerated and distorted publicity of the incident was just beginning. This distorted publicity would create a new moral panic and "folk devil"—the biker.

Moral Panics and Folk Devils

"Moral panic" and "folk devil" are terms that were first defined by Stanley Cohen (1972) in his seminal work *Folk Devils and Moral Panics: The Creation of the Mods and Rockers*. He described the media's exaggerated and sensationalized coverage of the Mods and Rockers (British rowdy juveniles identified by their dress). A moral panic is created when false or exaggerated perceptions of some behavior or groups of persons, particularly minority groups or subcultures, lead to the conclusion that the behavior or the group is particularly deviant and poses a threat to society. That is not to say that the behaviors or groups are not deviant or do not pose a threat, but only that this threat is oversensationalized, often leading to changes in the law and dealing with the groups too harshly. One can argue that the media's response to 9/11 and the so-called "War on Terror" have created new folk devils—terrorists—and a new moral panic that has led to new laws such as the USA PATRIOT Act, which some believe goes too far and is being used against individuals who have no ties to terrorism.

Nevertheless, there have been numerous examples of folk devils and moral panics created by sensationalized media coverage in recent years, including school shootings, such as the Columbine High School massacre, that led to "zero tolerance" against imagined deviance by some students; daycare sexual abuse in the 1980s, leading to the conviction of several innocent child care providers; child care pornography on the Internet, leading to state laws declared unconstitutional by the U.S. Supreme Court; sexual pedophile laws that in an attempt to protect innocent children have led to several named laws that put restrictions on all types of sexual offenders, even those convicted of statutory rape or urinating in public. Moral panics have also been created over violence in video games like the playing of Dungeons and Dragons and other role-playing games. The same-sex marriage debate is currently a media and political issue that may lead to moral panic.

Cohen (1972:9) opined that certain youth cultures, such as the Teddy Boys (UK), the Mods and Rockers (UK), the Hells Angels, the Skinheads, and the Hippies, created moral panics with their deviant and delinquent behavior, and groups of people, such as communists, blacks, foreigners, immigrants, satanic worshippers, homosexuals, and bikers after the "Hollister riot," have been socially constructed into folk devils.

Bikers as Folk Devils

Reynolds (2000) says that the Hollister incident would have been forgotten except for the picture and caption that appeared in the July 21, 1947, edition of *Life* magazine.

Parts of the short article that accompanied the picture were true—bikers did race up and down Main Street, fights broke out, at least one biker did ride into a bar, some furniture was broken, 49 did get arrested, and 19-year-old Jim Morrison, the only nonveteran Booze-fighter, was arrested for indecent exposure as he urinated in a truck's radiator in a drunken attempt to cool it down. However, there was no riot, and there were not 4,000 members of a motorcycle club. In fact, no motorcycle club of the time had 4,000 members. Even the write-up itself, an extreme exaggeration, could not raise to the level of a riot. The "so-called Battle of Hollister was at best a skirmish and at the least a glorified drunken binge"

The staged photograph at the Hollister Motorcycle Incident that set the tone for viewing bikers as folk devils. The picture appeared in the July 21, 1947, edition of *Life* magazine.

(Yates, 1999:17). What may be the ultimate irony of this staged picture is that it is so famous and received so much publicity, but it is only one of three pictures that appeared in the "Picture of the Week" section of that *Life* magazine. The first picture in the series of pictures showed four dead black prisoners lying on the ground of a Georgia prison camp. According to the article, on July 11, 1947, 27 seven black prisoners in the Thalman, Georgia, camp refused to work until they could air their grievances to a visiting prison inspector. The warden ordered that they be fired on, resulting in seven dead and eight injured. This picture and the Georgia prison incident received no more publicity, but the Hollister incident would reappear again in outlaw motorcycle history.

Riverside Motorcycle Riot (1948)

Drunken motorcyclists, whether outlaw club members or not, were not through disrupting AMA-sponsored events. According to Reynolds, during a Labor Day gypsy tour rally in Riverside, California, in 1948 more than 1,000 drunken motorcyclists recreated the scene that had occurred at Hollister—this time with violent consequences. While they were drag racing and partying, an Air Force officer and his wife, trying to get through, honked at the pack of drunks blocking the street. The mob smashed the car windows, punched the driver, and manhandled his frightened wife (Reynolds, 2002:60). While this was occurring, one of the riders wiped out his bike, killing his girlfriend, who was riding with him. Boozefighters were in the area but not involved in the incident. However, local papers carried pictures of two Boozefighters drinking beer and sitting on their bikes. The caption under the picture read that they were members of the same group who "started the Hollister Riot the previous year" (Reynolds, 2000:60).

Hayes (2005) gives an entirely different account of the Riverside riot. Quoting the sheriff at the time, he says that there were no traffic accidents in the city of Riverside that July 4th weekend, and that most of the arrests that occurred were downtown when the motorcyclists were out of town participating in AMA events. The sheriff goes on to say "that the nation-wide sensational publicity given the 4th of July week-end in Riverside, California was neither honest nor factual" (Abbott, 1948, in Hayes, 2005:44-45). Furthermore, the picture of the Boozefighters appearing in the newspapers had actually been taken a year earlier at Hollister. Nevertheless, the national story coming on the heels of the Hollister "riot," whether it was true or false, led to a motorcycle short story that would create a genre of low-budget exploitation biker movies.

Cyclist's Raid

In 1951, *Harper's Magazine* published a short story by Frank Rooney titled "Cyclists Raid." The story was an exaggerated account of the Hollister incident and would have been forgotten except for the movie it inspired—*The Wild One.* The short story's plot is about an unnamed motorcycle gang taking over and terrorizing a small rural town somewhere on the West Coast. The assault by the leather-jacketed motorcyclists leads to the accidental death of the daughter of a hotel owner. Filmmaker Stanley Kramer read "Cyclists Raid" and decided to make a movie based on the story. He, writer Ben Maddow, and film star Marlon Brando spent three weeks interviewing ex-Boozefighters (Stidworthy, 2003). The resulting screen adaptation of the short story was the first of a genre of biker movies.

THE WILD ONE: FIRST OF THE BIKER MOVIES

The 1954 movie *The Wild One,* starring Marlon Brando, was based on the fictionalized account of the Hollister "riot" that appeared in *Harper's Magazine* in 1951. In the movie, Brando as Johnny, the leader of the Black Rebels Motorcycle Club, leads a group of nomadic bikers into a conservative rural town. The macho, leather-clad bikers terrorize the local "squares" with their outrageous behavior (Osgerby, 2003). Lee Marvin, leather-jacketed and riding a chopped Harley, plays Johnny's arch-rival and leader of the biker club, the Beetles. After the film's release, hundreds of American bikers would emulate Brando and Marvin in dress and behavior. Arthur Veno says that motorcyclists across the Western world "saw the Hollywood version of an outlaw motorcycle club rebel" and copied their attitudes, clothes, disrespect for society, and the way they treated women (Veno, 2002:30). According to Veno, motorcycle clubs in England, Australia, Canada, South Africa, New Zealand, Germany, Denmark, and Italy mimicked their behavior.

The Wild One was the first of a wave of movies that portrayed bikers as the new American outlaws. All these low-budget biker movies had basically the same plot: individualistic bikers—new outlaws—battling a corrupt, unfeeling, and conformist society (Wood, 2003). They were exploitation films based on sensational print media stories, and they were successful because "outlaw motorcycle gangs were a hot topic with many titillating and exploitable elements" (Syder, 2002:12). The most commercially successful biker movie was the cult classic *Easy Rider* (1969), starring veteran biker actors Peter Fonda and Dennis Hopper. The characters played by Fonda and Hopper traveled the country as hippies on bikes, visiting communes, taking LSD, and eventually getting murdered by hippie-hating southern rednecks. The one-percent biker clubs were evolving at the same time as the biker movies.

HELLS ANGELS MOTORCYCLE CLUB AND THE ONE-PERCENTERS

A larger-than-life wooden likeness of actor Marlon Brando is set up in front of Johnny's Bar and Grill during the annual Fourth of July rally in Hollister, California. The Brando movie *The Wild One* made Hollister famous. *Photo courtesy of AP Photo/Gilroy Dispatch, James M. Mohs.*

The history of one-percent bikers is ultimately a narrative of the Hells Angels Motorcycle Club (HAMC). The name "Hell's Angels," although now copyrighted (without the apostrophe) by the Hells Angels Motorcycle Club (HAMC), dates back at least to World War I. There was even an AMA-sanctioned Hell's Angels riding club in Detroit in the late 1920s. The name was first used in movies in a 1930 Howard Hughes film starring an 18-year-old Jean Harlow. The film was about two brothers who left their studies at Oxford to join the Royal Air Force and fight the Germans in World War I. A squadron of General Claire Chennault's famous "Flying Tigers" in China used the name as did at least 12 different bomber squadrons in World War II (Reynolds, 2000). Its use as the name of a motorcycle club appears to be as happenstance as the naming of the Boozefighters MC.

One year after the Hollister incident, the World War II veterans outlaw club, the Pissed Off Bastards of Bloomington, had disbanded, partly because of the bad publicity from the Hollister incident. Reynolds says that Arvid Olsen, a former squadron leader with the "Flying Tigers," suggested the name "Hell's Angels" for a new motorcycle club that he, Otto Friedl, and several other former POBOBs members decided to form in 1948 in San Bernardino, California. Olsen gave the idea of a name but did not join the new club (www.hells angels.com/history.htm). The new members chose as a logo a grinning skull wearing a pilot's helmet with attached wings. A decade later the name and the logo would be adopted by a group of motorcycle-riding young toughs in Oakland, completing the one-percent bikers progression.

During the next decade, Hells Angels Motorcycle Clubs formed throughout California as nomadic members moved from one city to the next: in 1954, San Francisco (former members of the Market Street

Commandos—World War II veterans); in 1956, North Sacramento; and in 1957, Sacramento (Reynolds, 2000:107-108). The 1957 Sacramento Hells Angels chapter was formed out of a mid-1950s chapter of the Hell Bent for Glory Motorcycle Club started by two teenage toughs, James "Mother" Miles and his younger brother Pat. The publicity surrounding the 1966 funeral of "Mother" Miles, the largest in Sacramento history, included a picture in *Life* magazine. These Hells Angels chapters operated autonomously and independent of each other, often not even knowing of the others. One man, Ralph "Sonny" Barger, is credited with bringing the chapters together and creating the largest motorcycle club in the world.

Ralph "Sonny" Barger

Ralph "Sonny" Barger, the son of an alcoholic father and a reportedly negligent mother, is often referred to as the founder of the HAMC. As we have seen, though, this is not accurate. The charismatic Sonny Barger, although the most well-known Hells Angel with his own web site, was only 10 years old when the first HAMC chapter was founded in 1948. According to his best-selling autobiography, he grew up in the blue-collar jungle of Oakland, California and joined the Army in 1955 with a fake birth certificate (Barger, 2000). Less than a year later, the Army discovered his actual age and discharged him. When he returned to Oakland, there were conventional and deviant motorcycle clubs in the city. According to Barger, there were numerous motorcycle clubs, like the Oakland Motorcycle Club, that were family clubs, and there were also "freewheeling clubs" like the Oakland Panthers. He joined the Panthers but soon left because they did not provide enough action. He looked for a more action-oriented club to join.

Once more, serendipity played a part in the history of the HAMC. Barger found a new wild bunch of motorcyclists with whom to ride. One of his new riding buddies "wore a modified Air Force-like patch he'd found in Sacramento, a small skull wearing an aviator cap inside a set of wings" (Barger, 2000:30). The young "outlaws" thought the patch was cool and decided to name their club Nomad Hell's Angels after the patch. In April of 1957, they had patches made based on the design (which later became the copyrighted HAMC death head). Sometime later, Barger met another motorcyclist wearing the very same Hells Angels patch. This Angel filled Barger in on the history of the club, including the other chapters and the rules, regulations, and procedures of being a Hells Angels chapter. Angels from the SoCal (Southern California) chapter visited the quasi-Hells Angels in Oakland. A series of meetings later and the Oakland Chapter of the Hells Angels Motorcycle Club came into being. In 1958, Sonny Barger

Ralph "Sonny" Barger, center, president of the Oakland chapter of the Hell's Angels, reads a statement during a news conference in 1965. Barger announced they would not show up for the Vietnam Day Committee's march on the Oakland Army Terminal. *Photo courtesy of AP Photo.*

became president of the Oakland Chapter; he then became President of the national HAMC and changed the HAMC forever. Although the basic organization was in place when Barger took over as Oakland president, under his leadership and guidance new rules were added pertaining to new members, club officers, and induction of new chapters. With Barger at the helm, the HAMC would expand into the largest motorcycle club in the world. However, there were many bumps along the way, including movement into drug dealing, the adoption of the one-percent label, adverse publicity, and the Altamont Speedway homicide.

Oakland HAMC Chapter: The Early Years

The young toughs who formed the Oakland Hells Angels were not the same as the veterans who formed the early clubs. Outlaw clubs like the Boozefighters were formed by World War II veterans, whereas later clubs, particularly the one-percent bikers, were not veteran-centered. For example, George "Baby Huey" Wethern, a high school dropout who received an undesirable discharge from the U.S. Air Force, became the vice president of the Oakland Angels in 1960 (Wethern and Colnett, 1978). Wethern, like many of the early Oakland Angels who were veterans like Barger, were not comparable in military service to those who formed the first HAMC in 1948. They were not veterans "returning from war and letting off steam." They were young toughs with questionable military service.

Wethern describes the early Angels as "basically honest blue-collar or unskilled workers looking for excitement" (Wethern and Colnett, 1978: 50). The Angels at that time were a nascent version of what von Lampe refers to as a social criminal organization that indirectly supports the criminal behavior of its members (see Chapter 1). Many of the members, although possibly basically honest, shared criminally exploitable ties. This was to become clear in a few years as the Hells Angels moved into drug dealing. In addition to discussing the Angel's drug dealing, Wethern describes an ominous HAMC event—the first club-sanctioned execution of a member in 1968. Paul A. "German" Ingalls, a 21-year-old transfer from the Omaha Hells Angels chapter, was force- fed "reds" [barbiturates] until he went into a coma. Ingalls was tried, convicted, and executed by his "brothers" for committing a capital offense—stealing the president's (Sonny Barger) coin collection (Wethern and Colnett, 1978:154-155).

One-Percent Bikers

"We're the one-percenters, man—the one percent that don't fit and don't care . . . we're royalty among motorcycle outlaws," claimed a Hells Angel (quoted in Thompson, 1966).

Wethern describes a historic meeting that was "sort of like the Yalta conference" in 1960, held at the home of Frank Sadilek, the president of the San Francisco Hells Angels chapter. At the meeting were Hells Angels leaders from across the state and former warring California biker club leaders—of the Gypsy Jokers, Road Rats, Galloping Gooses, Satan's Slaves, the Presidents, and the Mofos. The purpose of the meeting was to discuss police harassment, but discussion soon turned to recent hostile comments by the AMA.

"To draw a distinction between its members and us renegades, the AMA had characterized ninety-nine percent of the country's motorcyclists as clean-living folks enjoying pure sport. But it condemned the other one percent as antisocial barbarians who'd be scum riding horses or surfboards too" (Wethern and Colnettt, 1978: 54). The clubs decided to accept the one-percent label as a tribute and not an insult and adopt the "1%" patch to identify themselves as righteous outlaws. Wethern and Sonny Barger were the first to get "1%" tattoos.

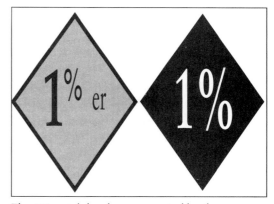

The 1% patch has been accepted by the one-percenters as a badge of honor, and is often represented in tattoos sported by biker club members.

HAMC in the Mid-1960s

The HAMC began to receive a lot of adverse publicity during the mid-1960s, culminating in the Altamont homicide. The long- haired, leather-jacketed, Nazi symbol-wearing outcasts on their chopped motorcycles were thrust into the national limelight by the alleged rape of two Monterey, California, teenagers in 1964 (Thompson, 1966; Reynolds, 2000; Veno, 2002). On Labor Day, Angels from throughout California went on their annual run to Monterey. While they were in a local bar, two girls and five teenage boys started hanging around with them. Later that night, sheriff's deputies responded to a call to some sand dunes where the Angels were camping. When the deputies arrived, they found the young girls hysterical, one naked and the other wearing a ripped sweater. The girls, 14- and 15-years-old, claimed that they had had been assaulted by up to 20 Hell's Angels. Four Angels were arrested. The event hit the national headlines. Hunter S. Thompson, the gonzo journalist and author of the classic and seminal work on the Oakland Hells Angels, says this event made the Hells Angels national celebrities (folk devils). Later, the girls admitted that they and their teenage friends had willingly followed the Angels from the bar to their camp to drink wine and get high. Three weeks later the case was dismissed for lack of evidence, but the dismissal did not receive national publicity. Legend has it that the Angels first moved into drug dealing to pay legal fees associated with their defense.

The California attorney general, Thomas Lynch, responding to pressure from the Monterey "rape," contacted state law enforcement agencies and asked for data on the Hells Angels. In 1965, the "famous" Lynch report was released. Although the report was largely fiction compiled from questionable police files, it again thrust the Hells Angels into national limelight as stories of their alleged debauchery appeared in *Time, Life,* and *Esquire.* Movie director Roger Gorman, sensing opportunity, quickly put together (in 15 days at a budget of $360,000) another biker film, *The Wild Angels,* starring Peter Fonda and Nancy Sinatra in 1966 (Osgerby, 2003). Gorman even hired a group of Ventura, California Hells Angels as extras. The film was "shocking" in its violation of social taboos, including images of men kissing each other, wild partying—drinking and taking drugs—in a church, scenes of sexual violence, a swastika draped over a coffin under a crucifix, and bikers smashing pews and roughing up a priest—all to the sound of wild bongos. It was widely panned by the movie industry but became a huge commercial success, setting the stage for even more successful biker movies such as *Easy Rider* mentioned earlier.

ALTAMONT SPEEDWAY: ONE-PERCENT BIKERS ON DISPLAY

The popularity of the biker movies declined at the same time that the image of the Hells Angels and one-percent bikers became clear—at the Altamont Speedway on December 6, 1969. The Rolling Stones, described at that time as the greatest rock-and-roll band in the world, were finishing a tour of the United States. The band had been criticized for the high prices charged for their performances during the tour and decided to thank the public and assuage their guilt by giving a free concert in San Francisco at its conclusion (Baers, 2002). The event was plagued with problems from the outset. It was first scheduled to be held in Golden Gate Park, but the large number of people expected led the San Francisco City Council to turn down the permit four days before the concert. Sears Point Speedway, outside San Francisco, was then chosen. While the scaffolding, generators, and sound equipment were being assembled at Sears Point, the owners demanded an exorbitant bond to protect them from liability, so the deal fell through. Less than 48 hours remained before the announced concert date when the Altamont Speedway owner, Dick Carter, volunteered his property for free, thinking that he would receive a vast amount of publicity for his benevolence. He was right, but it wasn't the publicity he expected. December 6, 1969, was to become the most violent day in rock history and become hailed as the real and metaphorical end to the 1960s counterculture (Baers, 2002). The true viciousness of the Hells Angels was also exposed that day at Altamont, revealing them to be "really as dangerous as everyone said they were" (Morton, 1999).

The Rolling Stones hired the Hells Angels Motorcycle Club to act as security for the event. The rock group had previously used the London, England, Hells Angels chapter for security at a free concert without any problems. The relatively harmless London Angels shared only the name with their alcohol-drinking, marijuana-smoking, and acid-dropping "brothers" in California. The California Angels believed that the way to handle security was to beat the crowd with pool sticks, throw full cans of beer at them, or drive motorcycles into the crowd. Violence began immediately. During the first set by Santana, inebriated Angels began provoking fights with the enthusiastic and also inebriated audience. Whenever anyone ventured too close to the stage, the Angels whacked them with pool cues or drove their bikes at them. Jefferson Airplane began their set as the Angels arranged themselves on stage. Several Angels jumped off the stage into the crowd and began beating and stomping perceived troublemakers. Singer Marty Balin, knowing several of the Angels personally, jumped off the stage to stop the violence. He was knocked unconscious and stomped repeatedly. The Angels calmed down under the influence of the mellow country rock of the Flying Burrito Brothers, but they continued drinking, smoking marijuana, and dropping acid, setting the stage for the final act.

The Rolling Stones waited for an hour and a half before taking the stage. They wanted to make their entrance as dramatic as possible, but it was a serious mistake. The crowd grew restless, and the Angels continued to get stoned. When the band took the stage, small fights began to break out in front of the stage. Although what happened next is a matter of controversy, it was recorded on film for the documentary *Gimme Shelter*. A young black man, 18-year-old Meredith Hunter, was spotted by the racist Hells Angels with a young white girl. According to Baers, the Angels, after spotting Hunter, jumped off the stage and began savagely beating, stomping, and stabbing him (Baers, 2002). Hunter drew a gun in self-defense. The gun was taken away from him, and the crazed Angels continued their assault and would not let anyone come to Hunter's aid until he bled to death. The Rolling Stones carried on with their song and when they were finished they fled to a waiting helicopter.

Sonny Barger in his autobiography provides a different, but no less violent account of the events on December 6, 1969, at Altamont Speedway. He says that he and the Oakland Hells Angels arrived late in the afternoon, some three hours after the concert started (Barger, 2000). The crowd parted and let them ride to within four feet of the front of the stage. Barger says that there had been several fights before they arrived—one being the incident in which singer Marty Balin had been knocked unconscious. Barger explains this incident as being the result of Balin disrespecting an Angel. According to Barger, while he and the rest of the Angels sat on stage drinking beer waiting for the Rolling Stones to come on, "some of the people who had been pushed around got mad and started throwing bottles at us and started messing with our bikes" (Barger, 2000:164). Barger and the Hells Angels jumped into the crowd, "grabbed some of the assholes vandalizing our bikes, and beat the fuck out of them" (Barger, 2000:164). Shortly after this incident Barger says that a topless fat girl tried to get on the stage and he walked over and kicked her in the head. Barger then says that Keith Richards of the Rolling Stones announced to the crowd that the band was going to stop playing if the violence did not stop. Barger says that " . . . .I stood next to him and stuck my pistol into his side and told him to start playing his guitar or he was dead. He played like a motherfucker" (Barger, 2000:165).

Singer Mick Jagger watches while Hells Angels cross the stage during the Altamont Rock Festival melee to aid fellow motorcyclists (top) and drag onstage an unidentified person assaulted during the concert (bottom). The Rolling Stones hired the Hells Angels to police the festival on December 6, 1969. *Photo courtesy of AP Photo.*

Barger also offers little sympathy for Meredith Hunter, who he says rushed the stage with a gun in his hand. Barger claims that Angels "bravely moved quickly toward the gunman." Hunter got up on the stage, was knocked off, and the gun fired, hitting an Angel. Because the Angel was a fugitive and only received a flesh wound, they did not take him to a doctor or emergency ward. Barger says he didn't see the stabbing; Hunter was already stabbed when Barger got to him, so the Angels picked him up and turned him over to the medics. Whether or not one accepts Barger's account of the stabbing (viewing the *Gimme Shelter* documentary does not support much of his account), his version of the actions of the Hells Angels on that fateful day reveal them to be very violent individuals ill-suited to provide security at any public event.

The gun disappeared after the stabbing and was recovered several days later by Barger and sent to attorney Melvin Belli's with the fingerprints wiped off it (Reynolds, 2000). San Francisco Hells Angel Allen Passaro, age 22, was charged with stabbing Hunter five times and brought to trial. The film clip for the documentary was played for the jury several times. The documentary does show Hunter with a gun in his hand, but it does not show him on the stage or firing the gun. In any event, the jury found Passaro not guilty, leading the Angels to boast that they were bigger than the law. Passaro was found dead years later floating in a ravine, but not before being charged with participating in a criminal enterprise (HAMC) through a pattern of racketeering activity.

Just how ill-suited these violent Angels were for security duties is revealed in a speech given by a psychoanalyst who had worked with Allan Passaro (the psychoanalyst does not give Passaro's name, but it is clear that it is he) in the early 1960s at Hope House, a community mental health center, in New York's East Village (Lasky, 2002). Among those treated at Hope House were a group of really "bad boys" who were members of the New York Chapter of the Born Killers Motorcycle Gang (believed to be a pseudonym for the Aliens MC) who had their clubhouse nearby. These gang members were notorious for their criminal behavior and acts of sadism and violence, including one of them tearing the throat out of the Hope House pet, a kitten, with his teeth. Lasky says that the members of the Born Killers gloried in "terrorizing anyone who was not a Born Killers member; that included both the street kids and the staff of Hope House" (Lasky, 2002: 4). One particular member of the Born Killers (presumably Passaro), although exceptionally violent and sadistic, entered into a six-week period of "twice weekly supportive psychotherapy" on the condition that it be kept from his buddies. Lasky admits that his patient scared him and was made to lock up his "gun, knife, chains, razor-sharp belt buckle, brass knuckles, and any other weapon" before their sessions. Lasky says that the patient mysteriously disappeared after the six-week period, and Lasky forgot about him until seeing the movie that had been made at the Rolling Stones' Altamont concert. While watching the stabbing of Meredith Hunter, ". . . who do you think I saw doing the stabbing? Right. My former patient" (Lasky, 2002:6).

According to Reynolds (2000), Passaro did not own a motorcycle when he was voted in as a member of the San Francisco Hells Angels. He called a man who had a Harley advertised in the paper, went to see him, beat the man unconscious, and stole the bike. Barger makes it clear earlier in his autobiography that he was aware of the violent nature of the Angels when he comments on their selection as security. "Soon enough, the Stones would find out that California Hell's Angels were a little bit different from their English counterpoints of the day." As Stones guitarist Mike Taylor said, 'These guys in California are the real thing. They're very violent'" (Barger, 2002: 160). The intervening years have not changed them much. Hells Angels and the other one-percent biker clubs are still very violent and criminal.

SUMMARY

Motorcycle clubs came into being soon after the first motorcycles were manufactured. Riders soon joined two kinds of clubs—conventional and deviant—and began to label one another. The American Motorcycle Association (AMA) labeled all nonmembers as outlaw clubs, and the media—print and entertainment—exaggerated the behavior of these outlaws, creating a moral panic and a new folk devil: the biker. It was not long before the most deviant of the clubs latched onto the derogation expressed by the AMA and the media-fabricated image and accepted it as their own. The one-percenters were righteous outlaws and proud of it. The outrageous behaviors and "in your face" actions of these roving, free-wheeling bands of hooligans on two wheels set them apart from society and other motorcycle clubs. The most notorious band of one-percent bikers, the Hells Angels, revealed how far the evolution of deviant motorcycle clubs had come on December 6, 1969, at Altamont Speedway. That fateful day was a foreshadowing of the evolution of one-percent motorcycle clubs into gangs and organized crime—national and international.

REFERENCES

Baers, M.J. (2002). "Altamont." *St. James Encyclopedia of Popular Culture.* Found at: http://www.findarticles.com, accessed 8/11/2003.

Barger, R. with K. Zimmerman and K. Zimmerman (2000). *Hell's Angels: The Life and Times of Sonny Barger and the Hell's Angels Motorcycle Club.* New York: HarperCollins.

Cohen, S. (1972). *Folk Devils and Moral Panics: The Creation of the Mods and Rockers.* Oxford: Martin Robertson.

Forkner, W. (1987). *Easyriders.* Video interview. Cited in Reynolds, T. (2000). *Wild Ride: How Outlaw Motorcycle Myth Conquered America.* New York: TV Books.

Fuglsang, R.S. (1997). "Motorcycle Menace: Media Genres and the Construction of a Deviant Culture." Unpublished Ph.D. Dissertation, University of Iowa.

Hayes, B. (2005). *The Original Wild Ones: Tales of the Boozefighters Motorcycle Club.* St. Paul. MN: Motorbooks.

Morton, J. (1999). *Rebels of the Road: The Biker Film.* In J. Sergeant and S. Watson, eds., *Lost Highways: an Illustrated History of Road Movies.* London: Creation (pp. 55-66).

Lasky, R. (2002). "Psychoanalytically Informed Interventions in Violence: Four Case Studies." *Journal for the Psychoanalysis of Culture and Society.* Found at: http://www.highbeam.com/library/doc3.asp?ctrlInfo=R

Osgerby, B. (2003). "Sleazy Riders." *Journal of Popular Film and Television.* 31(3):98-110.

Reynolds, T. (2000). *Wild Ride: How Outlaw Motorcycle Myth Conquered America.* New York: TV Books.

Stidworthy, D. (2003). *High on the Hogs: A Biker Filmography.* Jefferson, NC: McFarland & Company.

Syder, A. (2002). "Ripped from Today's Headlines: The Outlaw Biker Movie Cycle." *Scope: An Online Journal of Film Study.*

Thompson, H.S. (1966). *Hell's Angels: The Strange and Terrible Saga of the Outlaw Motorcycle Gangs.* New York: Ballantine Books.

Veno, A. (2002). *The Brotherhoods: Inside the Outlaw Motorcycle Clubs.* Crows Nest, NSW, Australia: Allen & Unwin.

Wethern, G., and V. Colnett (1978). *A Wayward Angel.* New York: Richard Marek.

Wolf, D.R. (1999). *The Rebels: A Brotherhood of Outlaw Bikers.* Toronto: University of Toronto Press.

Yates, B. (1999). *Outlaw Machine: Harley-Davidson and the Search for the American Soul.* New York: Broadway Books.

3

One-Percent Clubs—The Outsiders

INTRODUCTION

As stated earlier, riding among the four million or so motorcyclists in the United States—but not with them—are the one-percent bikers. All the other motorcyclists know who they are by their bikes, tattoos, and three-piece patches, known as "colors." They know the one-percenters are to be avoided and left alone. That is the way the one-percenters want it, and they will use violence to maintain the boundary between them and outsiders. Hells Angel celebrity Chuck Zito says that the message of anyone wearing the Hells Angel's mark to "citizens" and average motorcycle riders is "Do not fuck with me" (Zito, 2002). Their scary appearances and provocative behavior are intended to send a message to the "fools out in public" not to mess with them. Fear and intimidation are important territorial defenses used by one-percent bikers to prevent intrusions by outsiders such as curious citizens looking to be social, sidewalk commandoes acting tough, or other bikers who are warring with their club.

One percenters, as they call themselves, are a deviant subculture of bikers who only fit in with their "outlaw" clubs and saloon society milieu (Barker, 2004, Quinn, 1987, Thompson, 1966). As previously stated, the one percenters adopted their identity from being excluded and denied membership in traditional motorcycle associations, such as the American Motorcycle Association (AMA); they are true "outsiders," as identified by Becker (1963)—judged by others as deviant and judging others (i.e., citizens/nonbikers) as deviant. In addition, as stated, the history of the one-percent biker clubs is ultimately a narrative of the Hells Angels Motorcycle Club (HAMC). The HAMC is the largest one-percent biker club in the world. They are the most notorious and receive the most media attention. However, there are numerous other one-percent biker clubs in the United States and throughout the world (see Barker, 2004; Interpol, 1998; Lavigne, 1999; Quinn, 2001; RCMP, 1999). Several biker web sites provide listings of one-percent biker clubs. White Trash Networks, a web site dedicated to brotherhood and American iron, lists 134 motorcycle clubs. Sixty-six of these are one-percent biker clubs or chapters of one-percent biker clubs (www.bikernews.net/1perlink.cfm). "Outsider's 1%er news lists 34 1% clubs or chapters" (www.outsidersmc.info/). Numerous one-percent clubs maintain websites, listing chapters and news. Nevertheless, one-percent biker clubs are a homogeneous group. They are macho white males, who predominately come from a lower-/working- class background, ride "American iron" (Harleys, Indians, and Buells) and engage in a deviant life style that often includes serious criminal behavior and support for members who commit criminal behavior.

ONE-PERCENT CLUBS: CHARACTERISTICS

Clubs for White Males

One-percent biker club members are white males who have reached their maturity—21 years old. The age requirement is incorporated in the by-laws and rules of many clubs (see Lavigne, 1999; Wolf, 1991; and Appendix A for examples of by-laws and rules). The age requirement is a reflection of the importance of the club bar in the lower-class saloon society milieu of one-percent clubs (discussed later). Biker clubs are, in the words of Sonny Barger, "elite men's clubs "(Barger, 2000:103). Women ride on the backs of their motorcycles but are excluded from membership. Women do not participate in club business, other than as money-makers, and they do not attend meetings. Females are allowed into this male subculture because of affective, economic, and sexual ties to a male club member (Quinn, 1987). There were women members of the Hells Angels in earlier years, but when Sonny Barger took over as president of the Oakland chapter he put a stop to females becoming members. However, as he said, "[w]henever there's Hell's Angels, you can be sure there's girls, old ladies, and good-time broads" (Barger, 2000:97). This appears to be a true for all biker clubs, even though ethnographic accounts document that women are often subjected to physical and sexual abuse in the one-percent biker subculture (Guisto, 1997; Hopper and Moore, 1990; Quinn; 1987; Watson, 1980; Wolf, 1991).

Figure 3.1: The Boozefighters By-Laws of 1946

11.	There will NEVER be any women in any way affiliated in any way shape or form with the Boozefighters Motorcycle Club or its subsidiaries.

Source: Hayes, 2005:275.

Females in the Biker Subculture

Watson (1980) conducted a three-year participant observation study (1977-1980) of three outlaw clubs—two local and one national—in the Tennessee-Kentucky area. His main concern was to compare Walter Miller's focal concerns of lower- class gang delinquency to the values that arise in outlaw motorcycle clubs, but he also reported on females associated with the clubs. Women were viewed with contempt and regarded as necessary nuisances. Watson says that the status of women in the biker subculture was not much different from their status in the lower-class culture from which they came. They had low self-concepts compatible with their status as bikers' old ladies. Even though one-percenters did not hide their contempt for females, there was an adequate supply of women, who were primarily looking for excitement. The females were often as tough and hard-bitten as the bikers and worked "to keep up their mate and his motorcycle" (Watson, 1980:42).

James Quinn was active in the saloon society milieu for nine years (1970-1979) and was a member of the Pagans Motorcycle Club for two of those years (1973-74) (Quinn, 1983, 1987). In addition, he had close associations with members of the Warlocks, Scorpions, Devil's Disciples, Outlaws, and Hells Angels and was involved in a club-operated drug ring. His study of gender roles and the norms governing them in one-percent biker clubs is among the first of its kind in the scholarly literature. Using a triangulation methodology— informal interviews with law enforcers, current and former bikers, and current and former female consorts; review of journalistic and scholarly articles; and participant reflection—he identified three distinct status roles for females in the biker subculture: mamas, sweetbutts, and old ladies. Mamas were the lowest female status in the subculture. Basically they were viewed as the property of the chapter as a unit and available to any member of the club who desired their sexual services. In return, the club provided her the mama with shelter, transportation, and protection. Sweetbutts were younger than mamas and generally served as a biker's regular sex partner and/or income source. They worked as prostitutes or in topless bars, massage parlors, and similar establishments in the saloon society and were an important part of the biker's income. A sweetbutts was not as close to the club member as his old lady and thus were fair game as sexual partners for other members. On the other hand, old ladies were the exclusive "property" of one biker. Other club members would not "mess" with her without the permission of her old man. Old ladies also worked as prostitutes and saloon society sex workers, providing all their earnings to their old man. Other females helped or worked for the biker subculture. Women associates working in law enforcement agencies and other public bureaucracies, such as motor vehicle registration, provided information to bikers. Women also acted as spies for biker clubs, spying on other clubs, law enforcement, or possible crime targets. Quinn says that sincere and loving relationships between women and bikers were the exception rather than the rule in the biker subculture where women are expendable commodities.

Hopper and Moore (1990) participated and studied outlaw motorcycle gangs in the southeast—Mississippi, Tennessee, Louisiana, and Arkansas—for more than 17 years. They also used a triangulation methodology that consisted of informal interviews, participant observation, and retrospective participant observation by one of the authors who was president of the Satan's Dead, an outlaw club on the Mississippi Gulf Coast during the 1960s (Hopper and Moore, 1990). They reported on the place of females in the biker subculture, the motivations and backgrounds of these women, how these women compared to street-gang girls, and how the place of women changed over the 17 years of study and the reasons for that change. Hopper and Moore found the same three female statuses—mamas, sweetbutts, and old ladies—as did Quinn (1987). Another status they found was that of "sheep." A sheep was a woman who was brought with an initiate when he was going through the initiation ritual. She was a gift to the club and available to all members during the initiation—"pulling the train." Mamas and sometimes old ladies had to "pull the train" vaginally, orally, or anally as a penalty for some infraction, such as disrespect to a biker or not fulfilling his needs—not cleaning his motorcycle or letting his beer run dry. Sexual rituals such as "pulling the train" or deviant sexual acts (e.g., oral sex, anal sex) served also to prevent male or female law enforcement officers from infiltrating the clubs.

The women studied by Hopper and Moore were money- makers for the club and their biker. Their primary occupations were prostitution and topless and nude dancing. However, a few held down "square" jobs as secretaries, factory workers, sales persons, and so on. No matter what the job, the money made by the women was turned over to the club or their biker. The women gave three reasons why they choose to participate in the biker subculture. Some women choose the biker sub-culture for the same reason as male bikers: they loved motorcycles, rid-ing motorcycles—even on the back, and living the biker lifestyle. Others appeared to be drawn to macho men, such as bikers. Lastly, and maybe the main reason, was that many of the women had low self-esteem. Many believed that they deserved to be treated as people of lit-tle worth. Many of these women with low self-esteem came from lower-class family backgrounds that were abusive and dominated by alcoholic parents.

Hopper and Moore found that the roles of women in the biker sub-culture changed during the 17 years of their study as the biker sub-culture changed. When the outlaw gangs first arrived on the American scene, the members were "hell-raising" young men engaged in hedo-nistic pleasures. The females who associated with them were primar-ily partners in their search for hedonistic sexual pleasures, often wanting deviant sex as much as the men. When the motorcycle gangs developed an interest in legal and illegal sources of income, the women became less of a sexual object and more of a "money-maker." Hopper and Moore conclude that women may have become more important as money-makers, but their status in relation to the male biker never changed; they were still expendable commodities in the male chauvinist biker subculture.

Wolf's classic study of the Rebels Motorcycle Club, a Canadian out-law biker club, includes a discussion of women and the outlaws (Wolf, 1991). Wolf rode with the Rebels for six years in the late 1970s, gath-ering data for his Ph.D. dissertation in anthropology. The Rebels were a group of working-class young men who found their identity in motorcycles and the outlaw biker lifestyle. They engaged in deviant behavior—drinking; drugs, primarily marijuana use; and minor crim-inal behavior—but were not involved in major organized criminal activities. Wolf says that when he rode with the Rebels "laws were side-stepped, bent, and broken, but rarely for profit" (Wolf, 1991:268).

The Rebels were macho, conservative male chauvinists who saw females as subservient to men in general and to themselves in partic-ular. Wolf says that, as a group, bikers are more chauvinistic than other males. Females who associated with these outlaws fit into three roles: broads, mamas, and old ladies. Broads, roughly equivalent to the sweetbutts identified by Quinn and Hopper and Moore, were unat-tached single women who were mostly transient visitors in the biker subculture. They socialized with members over drinks at the club bar; "got it on," often "pulling the train" at a club party; or were one-night stands. Wolf says that there were always plenty of broads attracted to the macho biker lifestyle, "taking a walk on the wild side." Because of constant police surveillance, club members tried to ensure that these "sweet things" were old enough to give consent in the legal sense.

Mamas had established social-sexual relationships with the club. Wolf says they were rare, and all the Canadian clubs did not have them. The Rebels had only one in four years. However, some mamas did contribute all or part of their earnings as waitresses, secretaries, or dancers to the club.

Old ladies were the largest number of women associated with the Rebels and represented the most dominant female force in the outlaw club subculture. Old ladies had established a personal relationship with a particular member, either as a girlfriend, live-in partner, or wife. Sixteen of the 24 Rebels had old ladies: 14 involved cohabitation, five were married, and three had children with their old lady. Wolf himself even had an old lady. Even though this relationship (old lady/biker) appeared to be sincere and loving, the women were still in a subservient role. When asked what they would do if they had to choose between their old lady and the club, several of the Rebels chose the club. Wolf makes no mention of the old ladies as money-makers for the Rebels or employment as sex workers. This is probably true because the Rebels had not progressed to the point at which illegal sources of money were the major income for the members. They were at that time still a club and not a gang.

Betsy Guisto's (1997) study is a unique ethnography of outlaw bikers and their old ladies. Giusto is "an insider, a one- percenter's old lady, who, together with her biker old man, conducts fieldwork among her sources, the club members [three Houston, Texas, outlaw biker clubs] with whom she has had rapport for almost two decades" (Giusto, 1997:vi). The study is a folklorist collection of source narratives for her Ph.D. dissertation in English. Two of the three clubs, the Conquistators and the Banditos [sic: Guisto uses this spelling for the Bandidos throughout the work] are one-percent biker clubs. Guisto is not a typical old lady in the one-percent biker subculture because of her middle-class background and college education, but she readily admits her admiration for the one-percenter community and says she was drawn to it because . . ."I have always felt a strong attraction toward walking on the wild side, and the one-percenter lifestyle embodies the height to which wild can go" (Guisto, 1997:42). However, her behavior was typical for the deviant biker lifestyle. She says that she learned to curse, do drugs, drink, and have sex while attending college and continued in that behavior during her 20 years in the biker lifestyle.

Guisto met Carl, her old man, in California after graduation from college. He was a biker, riding a Harley and she was impressed with his looks and macho demeanor. He taught her to ride, and it was not long before she had her own Harley. He soon indoctrinated her into the biker attitude toward women and told her he was intolerant of any female whining and complaining. She never rode her Harley around the other one-percent bikers because they took that as an insult; "women were supposed to be on the back." She also said Carl also would not let her get a "boob job" or work in a whore house (she was curious and several of her friends worked in one). At one point, she and Carl sold drugs in California. They got married before moving to Texas in 1980, where they became totally immersed into the biker lifestyle.

Carl joined the Conquistadors in Texas. Most of the members had old ladies working as prostitutes or as topless dancers and several girlfriends on the side. Guisto says that in the one-percenter lifestyle women are necessary but expendable and interchangeable. According to Guisto, there are also certain unwritten laws for one-percenter old ladies to follow:

1. When you are away from your old man, do not attempt to call or track him down;

2. When partying, do not get "stinking drunk" or mouthy;

3. Be somewhat mechanically inclined. That is, love Harleys and know how to work on them or drive them. If the old man goes to jail, the old lady can drive the bike.

4. When partying, when you're on a run, at someone's house, at a bar, and there are no drugs available, do not go nuts trying to find some: "Go with the flow."

Guisto says that even though old ladies are girlfriends and wives of bikers, they are often considered second-class or "other- class" by their biker old men. Patchholders are responsible for their old ladies' behavior (see Bandidos Don't's).

Figure 3.2: Bandidos Don't's

Don't's
Thing's that will cost you your patch:.
You don't lie.
You don't steal.
That includes Ol' Ladies as well.

Source: Appendix A, By-Laws—Bandidos Motorcycle Club, 1999.

In general, she says bikers consider females as being on a lower evolutionary scale. In spite of this, there seems to be a lot of old ladies who want to be told what to do and dote on their men (Guisto, 1997:202).

Historically, women in the biker subculture are not only treated as second-class members, but they are also subjected to acts of violence and domestic assault. Hells Angels celebrities Sonny Barger and Chuck Zito have both had domestic violence complaints filed against them by their wives. In 2002, Barger was charged with aggravated assault after breaking his wife's rib and back and lacerating her spleen (Sher and Marsden, 2006). The next year, his daughter Sarah told police, after Barger assaulted her and her mother, "He hit my mom all the time. He's going to kill her" (Sher and Marsden, 2006:189).

Blacks in the One-percent Biker Subculture

With a few exceptions, blacks are excluded from membership or riding with one-percent biker clubs. However, there are at least five black or interracial one-percent biker clubs. The Oakland, California, East Bay Dragons Motorcycle Club is an all-black club (Levingston, 2003). The Hells Lovers Motorcycle Club is a nationwide one-percent black club (Winterhalder, 2005). The Wheels of Soul Motorcycle Club's web site says that they are an outlaw motorcycle club founded in 1976 and "is the only one of its kind . . . we have a make-up of black, white, Latino, and Asian members" (www.mosmc-trenton.com/history.htm). The other interracial one-percent biker club is the Ching-a-Lings Motorcycle Club in Queens, New York.

Chuck Zito—media celebrity, actor, bodyguard to stars, and former president of the Hells Angels New York City Chapter—was a member of the Ching-a Lings before joining the Hells Angels (Zito, 2002). According to a State of New Jersey Commission of Investigation 1989 Report, the black Ghetto Riders Motorcycle Club of Camden County was formed in the late 1970s and has approximately 30 members and 20 associates (www.mafianj.com/mc/sg.shtml).

A possible explanation for the exclusion of blacks is that one-percent bikers are white supremacists and or racists. Lavigne (1987) claims that the Hells Angels are white supremacists and that Angel chapters in the southern United States are allied with the Ku Klux Klan. He cites as evidence of the latter statement the involvement of North Carolina Hells Angels chapters with the Klan. The National Gang Crime Research Center (NGCRC) includes motorcycle gang members among the category "White Racists Extremists Gang Members" (WREGs), along with groups such as the Aryan Brotherhood, Aryan Nation, Ku Klux Klan, neo-Nazis, and Skinheads (McCurrie, 1998). One law enforcement source says that outlaw motorcycle gang members have performed security details at Klan rallies (MAGLOCLEN, 2003: 18). The same source said that 22 percent of their members reported that there is a relationship between outlaw bikers and white supremacist groups (MAGLOCLEN, 2003: 18). Skinhead groups were the most often mentioned. Hopper and Moore (1990), report that the white motorcycle gang members they encountered in the 1980s were members of the Aryan Brotherhood. They had become members of the Aryan Brotherhood while serving time in prison. Outlaw motorcycle gang members in California have been found to have ties to PEN1 (Public Enemy Number 1), a skinhead group, and the Aryan Brotherhood (California Department of Justice, 2004). A publication by Paladin Press says the white supremacy beliefs of outlaw motorcycle gangs parallel those of the Ku Klux Klan and the Nazis (Anon., 1992). They report that these same beliefs can be seen in the tattoos, patches, and pins—Nazi swastikas, white-power fists, and white-supremacy pins. Michael Upright, a professional photographer, took black and white pictures of the Outlaws Motorcycle Club in various locations throughout the United States from 1992 to 1995. In his photographs are pictures of 19 outlaws with a patch containing a swastika (Upright, 1999). Upright's photos also show women wearing shirts stating "Property of Outlaws." Danner and Silverman (1986) report that the conservative values and attitudes they found among their sample of incarcerated bikers are consistent with racism. Furthermore, journalistic accounts of bikers are replete with racist attitudes and statements.

All members of one-percent biker clubs may not be racists and white supremacists, but the by-laws of these groups concerning membership often dictate that blacks may not become members, or the manner of selection for membership works against blacks because of the large number of racists in the club (becoming a member discussed fully later). The San Francisco Hells Angels chapter's rules and by-laws for the 1960s had the following membership restrictions: "No niggers, no cops, or ex-cops" (Lavigne, 1999: 491). In his classic work on the early Oakland Hells Angels, Hunter S. Thompson explained why blacks did not become members (Thompson, 1966). He observed a "Negro named Charley" who had been riding with the Oakland Angels for some time and asked several members if Charley would ever get in the club.

Gary Piscottano, a corrections officer from Northern Correctional Institute who was fired for his association with the Outlaws Motorcycle Club, shown in 1980 in his garb as a Ku Klux Klan leader. *Photo courtesy of AP Photo/Journal Inquirer.*

Hell I admire the little bastard," said one, "but he'll never get in. He thinks he will, but, he won't . . . shit, all it takes is two blackballs [votes], and I could tell you who they'd be by just looking around the room (Thompson, 1966:304).

According to Lavigne (1999), more recent Hells Angels rules also restrict membership:

Proposed United States Rules Update:
25. No niggers in the club. Cops or ex-cops (p. 500).

Hells Angels Canadian By-laws:
No member of African descent (p. 501).

Hells Angels World Rules:
Revised March 11, 1998
August 3, 1986—No cops or ex-cops in the club.
August 3, 1986—No niggers in the club.
August 3, 1986—No snitches in the club (p. 506).

There has been at least one black Canadian who was a member of the Hells Angels organization—a member of puppet gang—because of his drug-dealing abilities and usefulness as a hit man, but he was not allowed to become a patched member or ride with the club in the United States (Sher and Marsden, 2003). In addition, the traditionally homophobic Hells Angels had a homosexual Canadian member (Sher and Marsden, 2003).

Other biker clubs, particularly the Big Five—Hells Angels, Outlaws, Bandidos, Pagans, and Sons of Silence—have similar membership restrictions in their constitutions and by-laws. During the trial of Harry "Taco" Bowman, former regional president and national vice president before becoming the International President of the Outlaws Motorcycle Club (1984-1997), the Outlaws constitution was admitted into evidence. The constitution stated that only white males ("no niggers") could become members (*United States v. Harry Bowman*, 2002). However, the Bandidos Motorcycle Club has had at least one black member in the past. Betsy Guisto (1997) documents the case of "Spook," the one and only black to become a member of the club. That would not likely happen today. A musician who played in a band that performed at a Houston, Texas, Bandidos club bar told me the story of the reception they received when a black musician temporarily replaced one of the members of the band. They were told in no uncertain terms that a "nigger" was not allowed in the bar.

Clubs for the Lower/Working Class

On occasion, there have been one-percent biker members who have been highly educated, including having Ph.D.s, and worked in middle- and upper-class professions (Harris, 1985). Some authorities on biker gangs, particularly law enforcement officials, claim that biker gangs have become more sophisticated, better-dressed, and better-educated (Tretheway and Katz, 1998). A detective with the Edmonton, Canada, police testified that there were lawyers in the Canadian Hells Angels (Alberta Judgments [1988], No. 725). According to Quinn (1983), middle-class and even upper-class members joined the clubs after the height of the Vietnam war—1967. These instances were exceptions rather than the rule, however, as many of the bikers of that period were "chronically unemployed due to alcoholism, club- or bike-oriented activities, or individual predisposition" (Quinn, 1983:63). Wolf says that in his 10 years as an active biker he never met a biker that originated in the upper-middle or middle class, and few held professional, managerial, or administrative positions (Wolf, 1991:30). More recently, the notorious Arizona Hells Angels have as members a pilot for America West, a stockbroker, and a manager of a car dealership (Sher and Marsden, 2006). The stockbroker, Paul Eischeid, is also a killer currently on the run for a brutal murder of a 46-year-old single mother of six while he was high on methamphetamine. As stated earlier, some biker gangs are social criminal organizations in which the "club" brings together members with latent criminal exploitive ties or creates a situation where even noncriminals support their fellow members who are engaged in crime.

This U.S. Department of Justice "wanted poster" reads: Eischeid may present a studious, friendly disposition, but he is a member of the Hells Angels outlaw motorcycle gang who is charged with participating in the fatal stomping and stabbing of an innocent female victim. He is charged federally with drug trafficking and violation of the RICO statutes. His arms, chest, and back are covered with numerous, full-color tattoos and he may wear glasses. A reward of up to $25,000 is offered for information leading directly to Eischeid's arrest.

Nevertheless, the journalistic accounts of biker clubs in Australia, Canada, the United States, and the United Kingdom (Auger, 2001; Bowe, 1994; Charles, 2002; Detroit, 1994; Kingsbury, 1995; Lavigne, 1987, 1996, 1999; Lowe, 1988;

Lyon, 2003; Mello, 2001; Reynolds, 2000; Shaylor, 2004; Sher and Marsden, 2003; Simpson and Harvey, 2001; Thompson, 1966; Upright, 1999), autobiographies of one-percent bikers or ex-one-percent bikers (Barger, 2000; Harris, 1985; Levington, 2003; Kaye, 1970; Mandelkau, 1971; Martineau,; Mayson, 1982; Paradis, 2002; Reynolds, 1967; Wethern and Colnett, 1978; Zito, 2002), and the limited scholarly works (Barker, 2004; Danner and Silverman, 1986; Hopper and Moore, 1990; Montgomery, 1977; Quinn, 1987, 2001; Veno, 2003; Watson, 1980; Wolf, 1991) all overwhelmingly demonstrate that the one-percent biker subculture is composed of white males from the lower/working class.

THE MOTORCYCLE: AMERICAN IRON

The motorcycle for the biker is much more than a means of transportation. It is his most cherished possession and his sense of identity. Wolf says that a biker is "a man who has turned to a machine to find himself" (Wolf, 1991:31). The man-machine relationship provides meaning and pleasure and creates emotional experiences that are worth living for. Bikers live to ride and ride to live. For the outlaw biker, there is a cult-like involvement with the outlaw machine—the Harley-Davidson (Yates, 1999). Harleys are motorcycles of the social rebels, while foreign motorcycles, particularly what they call "Jap crap," are motorcycles for the establishment—the outsiders.

Figure 3.3: What Is a Harley?

> To some, a Harley is just another motorcycle. To a biker a Harley is magical, for only a true biker can bring a Harley to life, and in return, only a Harley can bring life to a biker.

Source: Wolf, 1991:37 (Lawman, a biker from Texas).

A one-percent biker must possess and ride a Harley or other "American iron" with a minimum of 700cc engine, depending on the club. The clubs by-laws and rules usually specify that members ride Harleys and provide for expulsion if the machine is not kept in riding order during the riding season. A one-percent biker is also required to ride on specified annual runs, usually on Labor Day and July 4 (unless he is in the hospital or in jail). The Cadillac of motorcycles for a one-percent biker is an older Harley that has been modified, that is, "chopped." Some clubs, including the Hells Angels, now specify that the bike must be American iron, allowing for Indian and Buell motorcycles. Riding any Japanese or other foreign-made motorcycle is grounds for expulsion from the club. Riding American iron, particularly Harleys, is another boundary marker between the one-percent bikers and other motorcycle riders (Wolf, 1991).

SUMMARY

One-percent biker clubs are homogeneous groups of outsiders who are viewed as deviant by others and view others as deviant. These groups of predominately lower- or working-class white males ride American-made motorcycles and engage in a deviant lifestyle that includes serious criminal behavior. Many members have criminally exploitable ties in common when they join and form networks of individuals with criminal dispositions while in the club. They exclude blacks from membership in their clubs because of racist attitudes that are expressed in their rules and by-laws or in their membership voting patterns. The conservative views common to their class background do not encourage racial tolerance. Bikers view women as property and subservient to males. The Bandidos even place restrictions on the old ladies' "property patches" and when they are worn.

Figure 3.4: Bandidos Property Patch

> One Property Patch per member. If she rides her own bike it is NOT to be worn while riding with or around Patchholders or Prospects. It should not be worn in public without her old man in view.

Source: Appendix A, By-Laws—Bandidos Motorcycle Club, 1999.

Women who participate in their subculture do so as sex objects, money-makers, or old ladies. The old ladies are the highest female status, but they are also viewed as property and subservient to their old men bikers. A biker has two possessions—his bike and his women—in that order of importance (Veno, 2003). In many gangs, women are held in virtual slavery and bought and sold by members who use them as a source of income (see *United States v Starrett et al.*, 1995). Females have to accept their lower status to remain in the biker subculture. In many clubs, old ladies wear clothing with "Property of [club name]" emblazoned on them. Women are also used as accomplices or facilitators of crimes, such as stealing credit profiles to use in identity thefts while working in banks or mortgage companies. Some work in state motor vehicle departments where they have access to sensitive information that can be used for criminal activities or to check for the identification of undercover police officers.

REFERENCES

Alberta Judgments (1988). *Alberta Provincial Court, Calgary, Alberta Pepler Prov. Ct. J.* August 26, 1988. Found at: http://www.tamerlane.ca/library/cases/firearms/ kings_crew.html

Anon (1992). *An Inside Look at Outlaw Motorcycle Gangs.* Boulder, CO: Paladin Press.

Auger, M. (2001). *The Biker Who Shot Me: Recollections of a Crime Reporter.* Toronto: McClelland & Stewart.

Barger, R., with K. Zimmerman and K. Zimmerman (2000). *Hell's Angels: The Life and Times of Sonny Barger and the Hell's Angels Motorcycle Club.* New York: HarperCollins.

Barker, T. (2004). "Exporting American Organized Crime: Outlaw Motorcycle Gangs." *Journal of Gang Research* 11(2):37-50.

Becker, H.S. (1963). *Outsiders: Studies in the Sociology of Deviance.* New York: The Free Press.

Bowe, B. (1994). *Born to be Wild.* New York: Warner Books.

California Department of Justice (2004). *Organized Crime in California: Annual Report to the California Legislature 2004.*

Charles, G. (2002). *Bikers: Legend, Legacy, and Life.* London: Independent Music Company.

Danner, T.A., and I.J. Silverman (1986). "Characteristics of Incarcerated Outlaw Bikers as Compared to Nonbiker Inmates." *Journal of Crime and Justice* 9:43-70.

Detroit, M. (1994). *Chain of Evidence: A True Story of Law Enforcement and One Woman's Bravery.* New York: Penguin Books.

Guisto, B. (1997). *Mi Vida Loca: an Insider Ethnography of Outlaw Bikers in the Houston Area.* Unpublished Ph.D. dissertation. University of Houston.

Harris, M. (1985). *Bikers: Birth of a Modern Day Outlaw.* London: Faber & Faber.

Hayes, B. (2005). *The Original Wild Ones: Tales of the Boozefighters Motorcycle Club Est. 1946.* St. Paul, MN: Motorbooks.

Hopper, C.B., and J. Moore (1990). "Women in Outlaw Motorcycle Gangs." *Journal of Contemporary Ethnography* 10(4):363-387.

Interpol (1998). *Motorcycle Gangs. International Criminal Police Review* 469-471: 195-204.

Kaye, H.R. (1970). *A Place in Hell: The Inside Story of 'Hell's Angels'—The World's Wildest Outsiders.* London: New English Library.

Kingsbury, K. (1995). *The Snake and the Spider.* New York: Dell.

Lavigne, Y. (1987). *Hell's Angels: Taking Care of Business.* Toronto: Ballantine Books.

Lavigne, Y. (1996). *Hells Angels: Into the Abyss.* Toronto: HarperCollins.

Lavigne, Y. (1999). *Hells Angels at War.* Toronto: HarperCollins.

Levingston, T.G., with K. Zimmermah and K. Zimmerman (2003). *Soul on Bikes: The East Bay Dragons MC and the Black Biker Set.* St. Paul, MN: MBI.

Lowe, M. (1988). *Conspiracy of Brothers.* Toronto: Seal Books.

Lyon, D. (2003). *The Bike Riders.* San Francisco: Chronicle Books.

MAGLOCLEN (2003). *Outlaw Motorcycle Gangs* (July).

Mandelkau, J. (1971). *Buttons: The Making of a President.* London: Sphere Books.

Martineau, P. (2003). *I Was a Killer for the Hells Angels: The True Story of Serge Quesnel.* Toronto: McClelland & Stewart.

Mayson, B., with T. Marco. (1982). *Fallen Angel: Hell's Angel to Heaven's Saint.* Garden City, NJ: Doubleday & Co.

Mello, M. (2001). *The Wrong Man: A True Story of Innocence on Death Row.* Minneapolis: University of Minnesota Press.

Paradis, P. (2002). *Nasty Business: One Biker Gang's War Against the Hell's Angels.* Toronto: HarperCollins.

Quinn, J.F. (1987). "Sex Roles and Hedonism Among Members of 'Outlaw' Motorcycle Clubs." *Deviant Behavior* 8:47-63.

Quinn, J.F. (2001). "Angels, Bandidos, Outlaws and Pagans: The Evolution of Organized Crime Among the Big Four 1% Motorcycle Clubs." *Deviant Behavior* 22:379-390.

Reynolds, F., as told to M. McClure (1967). *Freewheeling Frank: Secretary of the Angels.* New York: Grove Press.

Reynolds, T. (2000). *Wild Ride: How Outlaw Motorcycle Myth Conquered America.* New York: TV Books.

RCMP (Royal Canadian Mounted Police) (1999). *Outlaw Motorcycle Gangs Around the World* 61(7-12):51-57.

Sher, J., and W. Marsden (2003). *The Road to Hell: How Biker Gangs Are Conquering Canada.* Toronto: Alfred Knopf.

Shaylor, A. (2004). *Hells Angels Motorcycle Club.* London: Merrell.

Sher, J., and W. Marsden (2006). *Angels of Death: Inside the Biker Gangs' Crime Empire.* New York: Caroll & Graf.

Simpson, L., and S. Harvey (2001). *Brothers in Arms: The Inside Story of Two Bikie Gangs.* Crows Nest, NSW, Australia: Allen & Unwin.

Thompson, H.S. (1966). *Hell's Angels: The Strange and Terrible Saga of the Outlaw Motorcycle Gangs.* New York: Ballantine Books.

United Sates v. Harry Bowman (8/20/2002), No. 01-14305). Found at: http://www.law.emory.edu/ 11circuit/aug2002/01-14305.opm.html

Upright, M.H. (1999). *One Percent.* Los Angeles: Action.

Veno, A. (2003). *The Brotherhoods: Inside the Outlaw Motorcycle Clubs.* Crows Nest, NSW, Australia: Allen & Unwin.

Watson, J.M. (1980). "Outlaw Motorcyclists: An Outgrowth of Lower-Class Cultural Concerns." *Deviant Behavior* 2:31-48.

Wethern, G., and V. Colnett (1978). *A Wayward Angel.* New York: Richard Marek.

Winterhalder, E. (2005). *Out in Bad Standing: Inside the Bandidos Motorcycle Club-The Making of a Worldwide Dynasty.* Owassso, OK: Blockhead City Press.

Wolf, D.R. (1991). *The Rebels: A Brotherhood of Bikers.* Toronto: University of Toronto Press.

Yates, B. (1999). *Outlaw Machine: Harley Davidson and the Search for the American Soul.* New York: Broadway Books.

Zito, C., with J. Layden (2002). *Street Justice.* New York: St. Martin's Press.

4

Becoming a Member:
Righteous Biker to Patchholder

INTRODUCTION

The basic unit of the biker subculture is the club bar. The club bar is the meeting place for deviant and conventional bikers and has a particular significance for outlaws and one-percent bikers. It is here that the process begins in determining whether the motorcycle club/chapter evolves into a criminal organization. However, few bikers live the outlaw life style, and very few of them that do go on to become one-percent biker club members. And for those who do want to join a one-percent club, it is not easy. One becomes a one-percent biker within the club activity and linguistic interchange between club members. First, the potential member has to make contact with the one-percent bikers and the club and receive an invitation. Initial contact takes place in the saloon society milieu that is the biker's world. This most often occurs at the club bar. One-percent biker clubs have designated club bars, typically working-class bars, where the boundary between the outsiders (citizens, and other non-club-affiliated bikers) and club members comes together. This is where the recruitment process begins. After being invited, the potential member must undergo a four-stage process that may lead to becoming a member or patchholder (see Table 4.1). It is not an automatic process; many invited to begin do not complete the process.

Table 4.1: Four Stages in Becoming a Patchholder

Stage	Purpose
Righteous Biker	Necessary but not sufficient first stage
Friend of Club/hang around	Form affective bonds with members
Striker/Prospect/Probate	Probationary period. Socializing, learning and testing stage.
Initiation/Patchholder	Membership

Source: Adapted from Wolf, 1991:34.

The process outlined is for "righteous" bikers (i.e., those who are committed to the biker lifestyle) who are not already patched. The candidate must go through the necessary socializing and testing experiences to become a member or demonstrate that he or she has what it takes to be a club member. According to the literature and other sources, the process is the same for all biker clubs (see Veno, 2003, pages 42-60, for a description of the process in Australia). However, the name of the stages or the time spent in each stage often varies by club. The Bandidos MC by-laws prescribe a six-month minimum for a hang-around and a one-year minimum probationary period [striker] for first time patchholders (see Appendix A). For some already- patched bikers, the process may be altered or the times in any given stage may be shortened. In addition, for actions against rival clubs such as bombing their clubhouse or the murder of a rival club member, patch-holder status may be granted immediately (see Figure 4.1). On occasion, under special circumstances—expansion of territory or drug markets—individual club members or whole clubs may be "patched over" to another club without going through the first two stages. Quinn (1983) reports that in the 1975 merger of the Devil's Disciples with the Outlaws, members of the Devil's Disciples simply traded in their old patches for Outlaw patches. Those not wanting to patch-over to the Outlaws moved to California and reformed under the protection of the Hells Angels.

Clubs also have associates who are not members but are very important because of what they do for, or supply to, the club or individual patchholders. Associates are common for many organized crime organizations. Traditional organized crime groups such as the Chicago Outfit have at least 10 associates for each "made" member (Lindberg et al., 1998). Oftentimes, associates are persons who because of ethnicity, race, employment (e.g., past or present law enforcement officers are not eligible for Hells Angels membership), or other reasons are not eligible for club membership. Associates are particularly important for the illegal activities of individual members, group of members, and chapters because they provide an informal and loosely organized network of persons with whom to do business that the members know and trust. Associates will handle the retail sale of drugs, leaving the wholesale distribution to club members. Many associates act as smurfs, that is, persons who deposit illegal gains in legitimate financial institutions—doing the money laundering. If the associates are caught in an illegal transaction, the club can deny that the smurfs are club members. In a large Canadian drug-trafficking case, a Hells Angels associate handled the negotiations with Colombian traffickers, including traveling to Colombia as a representative of the club (Desroches, 2005:183). He is also suspected in the murder of two Angels, one who was erroneously suspected of being untrustworthy and the other for becoming addicted to cocaine and heroin—a club no-no. In one recent New York RICO prosecution, a criminal defense attorney made frequent trips to Arizona to transport methamphetamine that had been purchased in Mexico back to New York (*U.S. v Moran et al.,* 2005). The particular attorney was deeply involved in all of the drug-trafficking activities of the New York Hells Angels and their puppet clubs—the Red Devils and the Highwaymen.

Figure 4.1: Patch for Murder

Jay "Jaybird" Dobyns killed a member of the Mongols MC club, a bitter rival of the Hells Angels MC. He threw the victim's body in a ditch and took digital photographs of the body and the blood-soaked leather jacket bearing the Mongols MC insignia. Two days later, in Prescott, Arizona, he showed the pictures and the jacket to members of the Hells Angels and was granted membership without the required year-long probation [striker/prospect]. One of the Angels grabbed Dobyns and hugged him, saying, "How does it feel to be a Hells Angel?" There was a problem for the Angels. Both Dobyns and the very much alive man lying in the ditch covered with cow's blood were Special Agents with the Bureau of Alcohol, Tobacco, and Firearms, working undercover. The resulting undercover investigation would lead to 16 Arizona Hells Angels and associates indicted for racketeering, conspiracy, murder, and drug dealing

Source: Wagner, 2005.

THE CLUB BAR

Numerous bars and restaurants are not receptive to bikers because of the real and perceived problems associated with the deviant lifestyle of the one-percent biker clubs, particularly their penchant for violence (see Figure 4.3). For that reason, many bars exclude patchholders, those in biker attire, or groups riding motorcycles from the premises or refuse to serve them or offer less-than-friendly service. This has led to lawsuits and complaints by individual bikers, biker groups, and one-percent clubs (Leo, 2001). It has also led to several hundred Internet web sites listing "biker-friendly" bars and restaurants by state (see Figure 4.2). There is at least one book, *Hartmann's Chicagoland Guide to Biker Bars,* listing biker bars in the Chicago area (www.chicago bikerbars.com). There are also individual bars and restaurants throughout the United States and Canada that advertise on the Internet that they are biker-friendly (see Topsiders Club: Biker Bar, www.topsiders-club.com/). The one-percent biker clubs choose a club bar from among these biker-friendly establishments.

Figure 4.2: Biker-Friendly Bar Sites

State sites:
North and South Carolina (www.carolinamcevents.com/bbrest/bbrest.html);
Pennsylvania (www.myauntedna.com/biker_bars.htm);
West Virginia (www.westvirginia.com/bars.html)

Multiple-state sites:
(www.etattoos.net?Biker_Bars.htm, www.powerhogs.com)

City sites:
Chicago (www.chicagobikerbars.com/3sons/index_4.htm);
Sturgis, South Dakota (www.sturgis.info/Bars.htm)

Country sites:
United States and Canada (www.bikernews.org).

Figure 4.3: Lynn, Lynn, the City of Sin

(Popular ditty and what appears on Hells Angels stickers)

Lynn, Massachusetts, affectionately known as the City of Sin, was the scene of an assault of an off-duty police lieutenant by two Hells Angels in a known HA club bar. The two Angels "sucker punched" the cop and stomped him on the floor while he was eating lunch with friends. No one in the bar intervened to help the officer, and patrons prevented his friends from coming to his aid while the assault took place. The bar later lost its licenses and the two Angels are waiting trial for assault.

Source: Casey, 2004.

The one-percent biker clubs can only perpetuate themselves by crossing the boundaries between themselves and outsiders—non-club members (Wolf, 1991:180-209). They cross these boundaries by designating a bar in their declared territory the club's bar and using it as a regular drinking spot and rendezvous point. The club bar complements the clubhouse where the formal functions and social activities take place and where outsiders are excluded except by invitation. Obviously, all the club members know its location, and other members of the biker saloon society also know which bars are designated club bars and the clubs to which they belong. Traveling bikers learn of friendly bars and restaurants off the Internet, in their favorite watering holes before leaving their home area, or consult a *Bikers Atlas* (www.powerhogs.com). Traveling one-percent bikers must also know the location of safe bars. One-percent bikers will not go to another area without knowing the location of their other chapters' club bars or where friendly clubs' bars are located. Wandering into a warring club's bar risks serious injury or death. Many one-percent biker clubs maintain monthly newsletters—for members only—on their web sites that list changes in club bars among the shared information. Motorcyclists riding foreign bikes ("rice burners" and "Jap crap") avoid the bars designated as club bars or those frequented by only Harley-riding bikers.

Club members pull tables together, effectively marking off a portion of the club bar. The area is for the exclusive use of members, friends of the club, invited unaffiliated righteous bikers, old ladies, invited unattached females, known associates, and friendly patchholders from other clubs. No one is allowed to enter this section without invitation and permission from club members. The club management and bouncers will assist club members in marking off this territory to help avoid trouble. Club members control the behavior of their members and assist management if needed. The club bar is an important part of the patchholder's presentation of self to other members and outsiders, and their behavior is generally dominated by hard beer drinking and boisterous behavior (Wolf, 1991:180-209). Invited righteous bikers also demonstrate their class to club members. In the club bar, potential members "exhibit their personal prowess, demonstrate their commitment to the ideals of the biker subculture, and experiment with forming ties with club members" (Wolf, 1991:181). It is in this milieu that some righteous bikers enter into the membership process.

FOUR STAGES IN BECOMING A MEMBER

First Stage—Righteous Biker

Figure 4.4: What is a Biker?

> (Most agree that a biker is usually a man—tough, paid his dues, ready to fight, hard drinker, doper, and shitkicker. He can mellow as he ages, but not by much. He's got to teach his sons to be bikers. This is done by modeling the role. He's usually working class, often poor, sometimes rich, and he made it the hard way. He is proud of this. His identity is tied into biking. He reads the biker rags, studies the specs of the new bikes, schemes to own them, and spends much of his life involved in bike business. He wrenches [works on his bike]. Every biker worthy of his name can tear his bike down and rebuild it.

Source: Joans, 2001:65.

In her ethnography, *Bike Lust: Harleys, Women, and American Society,* Barbara Joans, an anthropologist who rides a Harley-Davidson Lowrider, succinctly and accurately defines a biker as described in the academic, popular, and autobiographical literature. As Joans and others familiar with the biker's world point out, a biker is more than a person who rides a motorcycle. A biker is a male whose main interest in life is motorcycles and motorcycling (Veno, 2003). His bike is the defining component of his life. Bikers read biker magazines, attend rallies, ride on runs, and attend meetings on biker issues such as helmet reform laws. They wear the clothes of the bike world and sport the tattoos. They know bikes and work on bikes. Their looks, demeanor, and attitude identify and set them apart from mainstream society. They have chosen a life-world that revolves around riding a motorcycle, but all of that does not assure them entry into a one-percent biker club, if that is what they want.

Being a biker is a necessary but not sufficient status to be invited to begin the process or "hang around" with club members. One must be recognized as a "righteous" biker or demonstrate that one can become a righteous biker—committed to the biker lifestyle and the mutual support ethic—to even be considered (Veno, 2003). First, a righteous biker is riding a Harley or another brand of American Iron. It is their most prized—maybe their only—possession. Biking for them is a lifestyle that includes values, norms, and a specialized argot. The righteous biker must ride the right machine and love biking, but to be considered for a club he must be willing and capable of entering into the brotherhood of one-percent bikers. The overriding value of one-percent bikers is brotherhood—the mutual support ethic. The principles upon which brotherhood are based are loyalty, masculinity, discipline, independence, and courage (Veno, 2003). The righteous biker must exhibit these to be considered for membership. Brotherhood is a social network, shared to some extent with and among all righteous bikers, but that sense of brotherhood is, according to club members, strongest among club brothers. It is this spirit of trust among brothers that makes the formation of criminal dyadic, group, and organization networks within one-percent biker clubs possible.

Figure 4.5: Code of Brotherhood

Brotherhood is love for members of the club . . . You know there's going to be a brother there to give you a hand when you need it. There's going to be a brother there to loan you five bucks for gas when you want to go for a ride. There's going to be a brother there to talk to when you need someone to talk to . . . You never have to worry because there's always going to be someone there to back you, and you know it.

Source: Adapted from Wolf, 1991:96 (Onion, Rebels MC).

The Hells Angel celebrity Chuck Zito says that bikers [one-percent bikers] have their own brotherhood that includes a passion for riding motorcycles and an outlook on life that is hard to explain (Zito, 2002). That sense of brotherhood, he says, includes their own rules, their own code of ethics, and their own definition of right and wrong. Their subcultural code does not allow redress of wrongs through the criminal justice system. Zito also says that the Hells Angels are "an international brotherhood . . . the world's largest extended family (Zito, 2002:117). However, there is often trouble in the family. In the Netherlands 15 Hell s Angels members were tried for killing three other chapter members, including the chapter's president (Anon. 1, 2005). The killings allegedly took place in the clubhouse and were in retaliation for a 300-kilogram cocaine theft from a Colombian drug gang.

Whether or not this idealized expression of brotherhood is more rhetoric than reality is an empirical question that will be examined later, but there is little doubt that it is an important value for one-percent bikers and a recurring theme in their culture. If the righteous biker has impressed the members of the club, he may be given the opportunity to proceed to the next stage, at which he begins to form the bonds of brotherhood with club members (Wolf, 1991:60-87).

Second Stage—Friend of the Club/Hang-around

"Friends of the club" fall into two categories: those who have no intention of becoming members, and those who have expressed an interest in joining the club. The first category includes people who have no intention of becoming members but want to establish friendship ties to the club or individual club members (Wolf, 1991). These friends of the club may later become known as associates of the club and even participate in the illegal activities of the club or individual members (i.e., after they develop trust relationships with individual or groups of members). The second category includes those who have expressed an interest in joining and have been told to hang around until "we get to know you." In any event, the process to become a friend of the club is the same for both categories.

To enter the world of one-percent bikers, a righteous biker must establish a friendship bond with a member and have that member sponsor him. This is the initial screening process and can have consequences, good and bad, for the sponsor. If the sponsor finds and puts forward righteous bikers who are good friends and later become class members or worthy associates, his reputation is enhanced among his brothers. However, if the sponsored friend turns out to be without class, a less-than-righteous biker, a doper, or an undercover cop, the sponsor's reputation will suffer and he may lose his patch or get stomped or killed, depending on the circumstances.

The sponsor brings the name of the potential friend up in a weekly meeting and makes his case for the guest. Following approval of the members, the guest is extended an invitation to become a friend of the club. Depending on the club, the by-laws prescribe the vote required for an invitation. Wolf, who rode with the Rebels, said that two negative votes overruled an invitation in that club. Other clubs require 100-percent approval. Friends of the club will be invited to attend club parties, runs, and other club activities, but because the friend is not a member, he cannot vote, attend meetings, or become involved in club business. For many friends of the club, the relationship stays at this level. However, people in the second category of friends of the club—those wanting to join—may be invited to begin the slow assimilation process of becoming a striker/prospect/probate. .

Many clubs require that the biker fill out an application form so they can perform background checks (Veno, 2004:55). William Queen, an undercover ATF agent who joined the Mongols Motorcycle Club, says that the three-page form was as extensive as any he filled out in law enforcement (Queen, 2000). Queen had to supply social security number, driver's license, veterans administration records, telephone numbers and addresses for relatives, high school records, and W-2s for five years (Queen, 2005). The Mongols gave the application to a private investigator to check him out. In spite of this, the ATF agent became a patched member, secretary-treasurer, and vice-president of his chapter. Veno (2003:55) cites the case of an Australian club that uses voice-stress testers when interviewing nominees. If everything checks out, their sponsor must again bring up the prospective member at a weekly meeting for approval by the membership. If approved, the striker will be given the club's bottom rocker, which he sews on his leather or denim vest and begins the striker/prospect stage.

Third Stage—Striker/Prospect/Probate

The striker period is a socializing process (see Figure 4.6). One- percent club bikers use it as a learning and testing period to ensure that the prospect adheres to the three core values of outlaw bikers—(1) love of biking, (2) love of brothers, and (3) love of club (Wolf, 1991). It is an intense process requiring close personal interaction between the striker and other club members; therefore, clubs will only have one or two prospects at any given time (Wolf, 1991). Depending on the club, the striking period will last from three months to two years and will always include the summer riding season. A series of testing situations determine how well the prospect lives up to the core values of the outlaw biker's world.

Figure 4.6: Purpose of Prospecting

Prospecting is not an initiation as you would find in a fraternity. It is instead a period of training that is sustained until the prospect, in every sense, conducts himself as a Patchholder. It's a time in which:

The man's attitude is conditioned so that he displays a sense of responsibility and respect toward the patchholders of the club, without which he will not develop a sense of brotherhood.

He is educated in basic MC [motorcycle club] protocol and etiquette.

He is given time to develop the habits that are basic to good security and good communication.

To get the man into the habits of participating.

To give his family time to adjust to the demands of the club.

To experience and learn an essential degree of humility.

To become accustomed to trusting the judgment, at times blindly, of those patchholders who will someday be his brothers.

Source: Adapted from Hangaround/Prospect Information document of a Big Five Motorcycle Club. Must remain anonymous.

Love of Biking

The striker has already demonstrated that he is on the surface a righteous biker. He had to do that to be invited to be a friend of the club. Now, he is going to be evaluated on his commitment to biking. Strikers are required to have their bikes up and running during the entire prospect period, and they have to attend every meeting, party, bike event, or gathering of any kind where club patchholders are present (see Bandidos By-laws in Appendix A). The prospect will make every national and regional club run and attend every funeral. During these situations, his potential brothers are evaluating his riding behavior, the number of miles he puts on his speedometer, the weather conditions under which he will ride, and his overall mechanical skills. The striker must be capable of taking care of his bike. One-percent bikers do not call AAA for a tow or to change a tire. They do not put their bikes in the local garage for maintenance. Patchholders will help the striker or teach him how to make major repairs or modifications. That is part of the brotherhood, but the striker must show his commitment to biking by knowing the basic aspects of motorcycle maintenance.

Love of Brothers and Love of Club

The learning and testing process for the core values of love of brothers and love of club are intertwined. The first act of love of club the striker must demonstrate is the pledging of his bike and title during the striking period (see Bandidos by-laws in Appendix A). It shows that he loves the club more than his identity by offering his most prized possession as proof of his commitment to becoming a member. Should he fail to complete the striking period, his chances of losing his bike are real and virtually certain.

Individual chapters usually range from six to 25 members, with 30 as maximum. Having at least six members ensures that there are enough members to protect the chapter's territory, and having no more than 25 members allows for face-to-face personal relationships among members. The learning and testing process for a striker is the responsibility of all club members as well as the sponsor. In addition, because each member is going to vote on the prospect, the striker is expected to get to know and interact with each member on a personal basis (Wolf, 1991:101).

The club tests the striker's willingness to follow orders from his brothers through a series of duties he must perform. He is responsible for cleaning the clubhouse and making sure that the refrigerator is fully stocked with beer. In addition, the striker stands guard at the clubhouse and makes periodic security checks during meetings. During club runs, the prospect sets up tents, gathers firewood, and keeps the fire going. He may even drive the "crash truck," which carries the beer, spare motorcycle parts, weapons, and dope. Strikers are the designated gofers at all club functions and the club bar. The striker must perform these duties willingly and without complaint—patchholders are always right. Some clubs require or have required strikers to commit criminal acts during the striking period to demonstrate commitment and eliminate the possibility of bringing an undercover cop into the club (see Veno, 2003). Others, according to biker and law enforcement sources, require that a striker must have his sponsor's or the chapter president's permission to engage in criminal activities.

The interpersonal relationship between striker and club members creates a group social network in which the striker learns the code of brotherhood and love of the club and, in some clubs or chapters, the basis for trust in criminal activities as either a participant or supporter. Formal club events, such as meetings, runs, and funerals, and informal relations with members at the club bar (e.g., riding, partying, working on bikes, performing club duties, and drinking together) come to dominate the striker's world.

The frequent, intense, and exclusive relations with club members leave little time for anyone else but his brothers. He soon withdraws from all social contacts with non-club members and loses his social identity. Being a brother is his whole social world. He is and always will be a club member. The one-percent biker's clubs express this theme in sayings and tattoos such as: "Angels Forever, Forever Angels"; "Bandidos Forever, Forever Bandidos"; "Outlaws Forever, Forever Outlaws"; "Pagans Forever, Forever Pagans"; and so on.

Those strikers/prospects that successfully progress through the prospecting stage are brought up for a vote to become members—patchholders. Depending on the club, the vote to become a member must be unanimous or no more than two negative votes (see Lavigne, 1999; Veno, 2004; Wolf, 1991).

Fourth Stage—Initiation-Patchholder

The actual initiation ritual varies by club and has been the subject of controversy and myth since the 1950s. The accounts, appearing primarily in the popular literature, describe activities that range from sexual depravity to murder (see Figure 4.7). Some law enforcement authorities repeat these accounts as fact in their training seminars as they attempt to portray one-percent bikers as demonic sex perverts. Hells Angels authors such as the late Dr. Maz Harris, Sonny Barger, and Chuck Zito dismiss these accounts, at least for the Hells Angels, as myths (Barger, 2000; Harris, 1985; Zito, 2002). Barger and Zito say that there is no initiation beyond that of serving as a prospect. However, they do not describe the actual ceremony when the prospect is given his colors. Veno speculates that the clubs themselves may be the source of these initiation myths to cause "in your face" outrage among the outsiders (2003:59). Wolf (1991) says that the Canadian clubs he was familiar with held "initiation nights," "colors parties," or "initiation runs" when the prospect was given his colors.

Some bizarre initiation rites have occurred. A video of a late 1960s or early 1970s Hessians MC initiation shows initiates lying on the ground while others urinate on them, and it appears that one or more of the initiates engages in oral sex with a young women (Centaur Productions, 2005). Quinn (1983) reported that initiates "may be forced to cook and eat excrement or drink from a boot filled with urine, vomit and beer." Wolf describes an initiation he attended where two Rebel prospects were roughed up, stripped, and then staked, spread-eagle, to the ground. They were then smeared with a concoction of "engine oil and transmission fluid, grease and urine, STP and shit" (Wolf, 1991:113). The members then stood around them drinking beer and urinating on them before throwing them in a lake. He also relates the account of a Satans Choice prospect who engaged in a gang sodomy of a woman during his initiation. Other Satans Choice members told of being thrown in a frozen lake, passing out, and being dragged back by a rope tied around them or having to fight another member. William Queen, a Special Agent for the Bureau of Alcohol, Tobacco and Firearms, working undercover became a patched member of the Mongols Motorcycle Club. He says that the night he was initiated the club president handed him his top rocker and the rest of the members poured 50-weight motorcycle motor oil and beer all over him. He says "It was a mess, but I was happy I made it" (Queen, 2000). The nature of the rituals is not as important as the process they represent.

The initiation process is important to the club and the striker. For the striker it is the end of a series of transformations in his personal status and identity. He began as a citizen; then, he separated himself emotionally and symbolically when he became a righteous biker. From there the righteous biker became a friend of the club, was invited to become a striker, and now will be initiated into the "club and the lives of his brothers as a patchholder" (Wolf, 1991:110). It is important for the club because it reaffirms their identity as patchholders, clearly identifies the boundaries between the club and the outside world, and ensures that the club perpetuates. When the club loses its identity—its patch—it ceases to exist. One-percent bikers are aware of clubs that have lost their patches to other clubs or that have been assimilated—patched over—by other clubs. As mentioned earlier, the Rebels with whom Wolf rode were assimilated by the Hells Angels.

Figure 4.7: Dangerous Motorcycle Gangs

INITIATIONS

Each gang has its own requirements, which run from the low college type stunts to the most outrageous, disgusting, and shocking acts one could think of. Rituals range from stopping a women in public and demanding she take off her underpants and hand them to you, to laying on the ground face down while fellow bikers urinate, defecate, and vomit on your original colors. Some clubs may just pour grease and oil all over you, while others may require you to submit to the sexual pleasure of the club mascot, which in most cases is a dog.

Source: Anon.2, 1992.

PATCH/COLORS

The three-piece patches worn by the club member on the back of his cutoff vest are called "colors," and they are the official club insignia. The top and bottom sections are called rockers. The top rocker is the name of the club. The bottom rocker is the location of the chapter. The club logo is between the two rockers (The Fat Mexican for the Bandidos).

SUMMARY

Only righteous bikers are considered for membership in one-percent biker clubs/gangs. Those invited to become members must go through a rigorous process to prove their worthiness—righteous biker, friend of the club, striker, and patchholder. The "newbie" must demonstrate his class and adherence to the code of brotherhood at each stage, and at each stage the club will vote on the possible new member's progression. For those that endure the time-consuming process, if they receive chapter approval they become patchholders.

Bandidos biker gang jackets display the club's colors at a news conference in Winnipeg. The jacket on the right indicates the probationary status of the owner. *Photo courtesy of AP PHOTO/CP, John Woods.*

REFERENCES

Anon. 1 (2005). "15 Hells Angels on Trial for Triple Murder." *Expatica News,* January 21, 2005. Found at: http://www.expatica.com/source/site_article.asp?

Anon. 2 (1992). *An Inside Look at Outlaw Motorcycle Gangs.* Boulder, CO: Paladin Press.

Barger, R., with K. Zimmerman and K. Zimmerman (2002). *The Life and Times of Sonny Barger and the Hell's Angels Motorcycle Club.* New York: William Morrow.

Casey, J. (2004). "Off-duty Lynn Police Officer Attacked; Hell's Angel Member Held." *The Daily Item,* November 27, 2004. Found at: http://www.thedaily itemoflynn.com/news/view,bg?articleid=7725

Centaur Productions (2005). *Hessians MC: Hessians West Coast.* DVD.

Harris, M. (1985). *Bikers: Birth of a Modern Day Outlaw.* London: Faber & Faber.

Leo, J. (2001). "Hell's Litigious Angels." *U.S. News & World Report.* Found at: http://www.highbeam.com/library/doc3.asp?ctr1Info

Lindberg, K., J. Petrenko, J. Gladden, and W.A. Johnson (1998). "Traditional Organized Crime in Chicago." *International Review of Law Computers & Technology* 12 (1): 47-73.

Queen, W. (2000). ABCNEWS.com. "William Queen Interview." Found at: http://http://more.abcnews.go.com/onair/2020/transcripts/2020_000918_queen_trans.html

Queen, W. (2005). *Under and Alone.* New York: Random House.

Quinn, J.F. (1983). *Outlaw Motorcycle Clubs: A Sociological Analysis.* Unpublished Master's Thesis, University of Miami.

Veno, A. (2003). *The Brotherhoods: Inside the Outlaw Motorcycle Clubs.* Crows Nest, NSW, Australia: Allen & Unwin.

Wagner, D. (2005). "Hell's Angels: The Federal Infiltration." *The Arizona Republic,* January 23, 2005. Found at: http://www.azcentral.com.com/arizonarepublic/news/articles/o123hellsangels23.html

Wolf, D.R. (1991). *The Rebels: A Brotherhood of Outlaw Bikers.* Toronto: University of Toronto Press.

Zito, C., with J. Layden (2002). *Street Justice.* New York: St. Martins Press.

5

The Deviant Clubs: Big Five, Major Independents, and Others

INTRODUCTION

There is no accurate count of the number of one-percent biker clubs and their chapters in the United States or the world. The National Alliance of Gang Investigators' Associations estimates that there are more than 300 one-percent biker clubs in the United States (www.nagia.org). Some clubs have web sites that include a listing of chapters, but this is subject to their control, and many chapters are not listed. Membership is an even more debatable statistic. Law enforcement authorities have made membership estimates of some clubs when they have prosecuted them in affidavits, indictments, and testimony. These official estimates appear accurate for some clubs but not for others. A problem with law enforcement estimates is that they are made based on confidential government sources, so we do not know how the calculations were made. It is difficult for academic criminologists to estimate the true numbers because of the limited scholarly research conducted on these deviant groups. Although the actual size of this "secret" subculture is the subject of guesswork, one can make a "best guess" estimate of membership by using the numbers mentioned earlier—six minimum and 25 maximum—for a chapter. In spite of the vagueness of the membership numbers, there is general agreement among the authorities and biker experts that five clubs—Hells Angels,

Bandidos, Outlaws, Pagans, and Sons of Silence—are the largest in membership and numbers of chapters in the United States.

THE BIG FIVE ONE-PERCENT BIKER CLUBS

Hells Angels Motorcycle Club (HAMC)

The Hells Angels Motorcycle Club (HAMC) is by all accounts the most prominent and numerous international motorcycle club. Law enforcement estimates put their membership at 2,000 worldwide and 700 in the United States (unnamed BATF Special Agent). The club is also known as "Local 81" after the placement of the letters H (8) and A (1) in the alphabet, and "The Big Red Machine" and the "Red and White" after the color of their patches. Supporters and known associates are allowed to wear Local 81, Big Red Machine, and Red and White patches and other support gear but not Hells Angels (without the apostrophe), which is a registered name worn only by patched members. Their puppet clubs (discussed later) are the only one-percent biker clubs that are allowed to wear red and white patches; anyone else wearing the same color patch is subject to losing it after a stomping. The club's logo, the winged "death's head," is also protected by copyright and can only be worn by patchholders. The HAMC will sue and have sued to protect their copyrights.

Sonny Barger has a personal attorney who is also the Hells Angels intellectual property lawyer. It is this attorney's job to protect the club's two registered trademarks. In doing so he has sued or threatened to sue Gotcha Sportswear, Marvel Comics, and a pornography producer who made a film called *Hell's Angel: Demon of Lust* (McKee, 2001). Marvel Comics published a comic book titled *Hell's Angels* and ignored the cease-and-desist letter. The Angels filed a suit in federal court, and the federal mediator sided with the Angels. The comic book's name was changed to *Dark Angel,* and Marvel gave the Hells Angels $35,000, which was donated to Ronald McDonald House Charities. Gotcha Sportswear was sued for putting a death's head logo on surfer hats. Currently, the Hells Angels are suing Walt Disney Corporation, claiming that their logo and name have been used in a film script without their permission.

As detailed earlier, the first Hells Angels chapter was formed in San Bernardino, California, on March 17, 1948, by World War II veterans who were former members of the Pissed Off Bastards of Bloomington (POBOB). The present day Hells Angels were formed in Oakland, California, in 1957 by Ralph "Sonny" Barger and his gang of young toughs, without them knowing that other Hells Angels chapters existed. Within the next 10 years the Oakland chapter became the mother chapter, disbanding or taking in the other Hells Angels chapters. In 1966, the Hells Angels incorporated as a club "dedicated to the promotion and advancement of motorcycle riding, motorcycle clubs, motorcycle highway safety and all phases of motorcycling and motorcycle driving" (Lavigne, 1996:1). After their incorporation, the HAMC began moving out of California. Today, they are the largest one-percent biker club in the world.

The actual number of Angel charters [chapters] is unknown and probably unknowable by outside sources. The official HAMC web site lists 30 charters in the United States and states that not all the charters are listed. Arthur Veno, an Australian expert on outlaw motorcycle clubs and the self-proclaimed "only academic in the world who has made it [the study of outlaw motorcycle clubs] their focus," says there are 100 HAMC chapters (65 in North America and 35 in other countries) (Veno, 2002). The "best guess" estimate—six minimum to 25 maximum—using Veno's figures would put the membership of the HAMC at 600—2,500 members.

Pallbearers from regional chapters of the Hells Angels Motorcycle Club carry the casket of former Salem, Massachusetts, Hells Angel leader Alan Hogan. *Photo courtesy of AP Photo/Ed Wray.*

The HAMC's first expansion outside the United States occurred in 1961 when a chapter was established in Auckland, Australia. The first European chapter was established in London in 1969, followed by Zurich in 1970, Hamburg in 1973, and Paris in 1981 (Haut, 1999). At the present time, the HAMC lists chapters in 23 countries (United States, Canada, Brazil, Argentina, South Africa, Australia, New Zealand, Spain, France, Belgium, Holland, Germany, Switzerland, Lichtenstein, Austria, Italy, England/Wales, Finland, Norway, Denmark, Greece, Bohemia/Czech Republic, and Portugal) and two hang-around chapters in Russia and Chile (hells-angels.com/charters.htm).

Canadian and Australian HAMC chapters are particularly problematic in terms of crime. Canadian authorities consider the Hells Angels to be one of the most powerful and well-structured criminal organizations in Canada (CICS, 2000). There were organized biker gangs in Canada since the early 1930s, but biker gangs were not a problem until the Hells Angels arrived (Alain, 1995). Lavigne (1987:235) says that the "Quebec Angels are the most vicious and conscienceless bikers in the world." In Australia, the Hells Angels have been a crime problem for more than 20 years. Since the 1980s, HA chapters and their puppet gangs have been involved in narcotics, prostitution, major armed robberies, movement of arms and explosives, fencing, and assaults and murders (Reid, 1981). The Melbourne Chapter of the HAMC has had strong connections to the Oakland Hells Angels chapter since as early as the late 1970s. According to law enforcement sources, outlaw motorcycle gangs (OMGs), particularly the Hells Angels and the Bandidos, are a major organized crime problem in Australia. This led to the formation of Panzer, a National Task Force, to deal with them (www.nca.gov.au/html/pg_TskFce.htm).

Bandidos Motorcycle Club

The Bandidos Motorcycle Club was formed in Houston, Texas, by the late Donald Eugene Chambers and other disillusioned Vietnam veterans in the late 1960s. Supposedly, Chambers, a former Marine and Vietnam veteran, chose the club colors—red on gold—to represent the Marine Corps colors. Law enforcement sources say he formed this one-percent biker gang to control drug trafficking and prostitution in Texas (von Lampe's economic criminal organization). Club members say that the club was formed because of an interest in motorcycles and partying. Whatever the reason for its founding, it was not long before the club and its members, including Chambers, were involved in criminal activities. In 1974 Chambers and several other members of the Bandidos were convicted of killing two brothers who had sold them baking powder instead of "speed" (*Donald E. Chambers v. State of Texas,* 1974). A Bandidos prospect who had dug the grave for the two brothers turned them in and testified against his fellow gang members.

Since the 1970s the Bandidos Nation has been called the fastest-growing OMG in the United States by the National Alliance of Gang Investigators' Associations (NAGIA). According to their national web site, the Bandidos Nation has 72 chapters in 14 states (Alabama-3, Arkansas-1, Colorado-2, Hawaii-1, Louisana-3, Mississippi-2, Montana-2, Nevada-2, New Mexico-11, Oklahoma-3, South Dakota-2, Texas-30, Utah-2, Washington-8, and a Nomads Chapter that claims "everywhere" as its location) (www.bandidosmc.com). The web site says that "more are coming." The Nomads chapter is reportedly made up of long-time members who act as a security element, taking care of counterintelligence and internal discipline. The "best guess" estimate would put U.S. membership at 438 to 1,825.

The Bandidos Nation lists 81 chapters in 12 countries outside the United States: Australia-12, Bangkok-1, Channel Islands, Denmark-11, Finland-3, France-7, Germany-31, Italy-2, Luxembourg-1, Norway-5, and Sweden-4. As discussed in Chapter 1, the Bandidos had chapters in Canada but police pressure and their turf wars with the Hells Angels led to them shutting down. The "best guess" estimate would put membership outside the United States ranging from 486 to 2,025 members and worldwide membership at 924 to 3,850, making them larger than the HAMC. At least one law enforcement source says that they are now larger than the Angels (Queen, 2005). However, the HAMC admits that all chapters are not listed, and the author of this book is aware of HA chapters that are not listed on the web site.

The Bandidos and the Outlaws Motorcycle Clubs are considered affiliated clubs. They list each other as links on their web sites, and they socialize together. There are law enforcement reports that the Outlaws and the Bandidos have had an alliance since 1978 (Southeastern Gang Activities Group, 2000). This same source says that the Outlaws provide the Bandidos with drugs for resale and that the clubs participate in joint criminal ventures and own property and legitimate businesses together. The two clubs are also united in their hatred for the Hells Angels.

Outlaws Motorcycle Club

According to their national web site, the Outlaws Motorcycle Club is the oldest and first one-percent motorcycle club, disputing the claims to this made by their bitter rival, the Hells Angels (www.outlawsmc. com/history.html). They claim to have been established in 1935 as the McCook Outlaws Motorcycle Club, "out of Matilda's Bar on Route 66 in McCook, Illinois outside Chicago." Quinn (1983:85) claims that in 1946, the fledgling Outlaws petitioned for a charter from the Hells Angels only to have their petition permanently tabled. He says that this disrespect led to the hatred between the clubs. In 1950, the club's name was changed to the Chicago Outlaws. In 1963, the Outlaws MC became an

The Outlaws MC's colors feature what is affectionately known as "Charlie," a white skull with crossed pistons on a black background. A similar image is visible on Marlon Brando's black leather jacket in the movie, *The Wild One*. *Photo courtesy of Bill Hayes.*

official member of the One-percent Brotherhood of Clubs, the first true one-percent club east of the Mississippi. The web site states that in 1965 the club became the "Outlaws Motorcycle Club Nation."

Since their 1935 beginning in McCook, Illinois, the Outlaws have grown into one of the largest motorcycle clubs worldwide. Law enforcement sources say that the Outlaws are the dominant outlaw motorcycle gang in the midwestern United States (NAGIA, 2005). The Outlaws list 80 chapters in 20 states (Alabama-1, Arkansas-1, Colorado-1, Connecticut-2, Florida-13, Georgia-6, Illinois-12, Indiana-3, Kentucky-4, Maine-1, Massachusetts-5, Michigan-6, New Hampshire-2, New York-2, North Carolina-5, Ohio-6, Oklahoma-1, Pennsylvania-5, Tennessee-5, and Wisconsin-10). The "best guess" estimate puts U.S. membership at 480 to 2,000. Worldwide the Outlaws list 116 chapters in 14 countries outside the United States: Australia-14, Belgium-8, Canada-9, England-20, France-2, Germany-34, Ireland-4, Italy-5, Norway-3, Poland-6, Russia-3, Sweden-3, Thailand-2, and Wales-3. According to their official web site, the Outlaws established chapters in Moscow, Russia, evidently to compete against the HAMC chapter. Using the "best guess" estimate, membership outside the United States ranges from 696 to 2,900, making a combined total ranging from 1,176 to 4,900 (again larger than the estimate for the HAMC). There is continual warfare between the clubs in cities and countries where the HAMC and the Outlaws both have chapters.

Pagans Motorcycle Club

The Pagans Motorcycle Club is an enigma among the one-percent biker club/gangs and the most secretive. One source claims that the club was formed by Lou Dobkins (a biochemist at the National Institute of Health) in 1959 in Prince George's County, Maryland (en.wikipedia.org/wiki/Pagans_MC). According to Wikipedia (the free Internet-based encyclopedia), the original Pagans Motorcycle Club was not a one-percent biker club when founded. The original 13 members wore white denim jackets with Surt, the pagan "fire giant" carrying a flaming sword, logo on the back. The original members rode Triumph motorcycles. By 1965, this benign motorcycle club had evolved into a fierce one-percent biker club with ties to organized crime groups such as the Mafia. The Pagans became an extremely violent club when John Vernon "Satan" Marron took over as president in the early 1970s (Lavigne, 1987). The club expanded by the 1980s into 900 members in 44 chapters from New York to Florida (South Eastern Gang Activities Group, 2000; Jenkins, 1992, Lavigne, 1987). Most of the chapters are in the northeastern part of the United States—New Jersey, New York, Pennsylvania, Delaware, and Maryland—although there are, or have been, chapters in Florida, Ohio, North Carolina, South Carolina, Virginia, and West Virginia. Twenty-five percent of Ohio law enforcement officials responding to the latest survey by the National Alliance of Gang Investigators Association (NAGIA) report Pagan presence in their areas (NAGIA, 2005:28).

In June 2005, 125 federal and local law enforcement officers raided six houses in northeastern Ohio belonging to the Order of the Blood, a criminal network financed and managed by the notorious white supremacists the Aryan Brotherhood and the Pagans Motorcycle Club (Holthouse, 2005). They seized 60 weapons, including 13 fully automatic machine guns and large quantities of methamphetamine, cocaine, heroin, and oxycodone. The NAGIA also reports that the Pagans

Members of the Pagans Motorcycle Club wait for a priest to conclude a 1970 service for Philip J. Knoetgen. The Pagans later conducted a service of their own for Knoetgen, known to them as "Brother, Injun Joe." *Photo courtesy of AP Photo.*

have a presence in Nevada and Washington (NAGIA, 2005:33). In the 1980s there was a chapter in Kentucky.

Pagans membership appears to be dropping since the 1970s, as a result of law enforcement pressure, competition from other biker gangs (particularly the Hells Angels), and internal dissension. Seventy-three Pagans MC members were arrested after a bloody battle between them and the Hells Angels MC at a bike show in Plainview, New York (Kessler, 2002). The battle left one dead, three wounded by gunfire, and seven stabbed and beaten. Three of the Pagans national leaders, members of the Pagans Mother Club—national leadership group, were arrested and later pleaded guilty to several federal charges (Kessler, 2002). In all, 73 Pagans were convicted or pleaded guilty to federal charges and received sentences ranging from 27 to 63 months. The fight was in retaliation for the HAMC patching-over the Pagans in New York. The battle and the depletion of Pagans members led to an infusion of Hells Angels into the Delaware Valley, particularly Philadelphia. The Hells Angels moved into Philadelphia and patched-over Pagans members in this traditional Pagans stronghold, setting off a war between the two clubs that has left at least one dead so far (Gibbons and Anastasia, 2005).

Three high-ranking Pagans members defected and patched-over to the Hells Angels when the South Philadelphia chapter president was in prison (State of New Jersey, 2004). At the present time, the Philadelphia Hells Angels chapter has been disbanded, and all but three members have turned in their colors, leaving the appearance that for now the Pagans have won the war. The Pagans and the Outlaws seem to be involved in a turf war nonetheless. Several members of the Breed patched-over to the Outlaws and established a chapter in the Philadelphia suburb of Kensington (Caparella, 2006). New Jersey authorities say that the Pagans are building up their membership by patching-over members of their puppet gangs and establishing a Central Jersey chapter (State of New Jersey, 2004:88). The Outlaws MC, in an obvious attempt to counter the expansion of the HAMC, have established five chapters in Pennsylvania. The Pennsylvania-based Warlocks reacting to perceived Pagans weakness have established two chapters in South Jersey. Nevertheless, the Pagans remain as one of the largest one-percent biker clubs in the United States. New Jersey law enforcement authorities estimate that there are 300-400 Pagans, with 40 to 60 members in three chapters in New Jersey (www.mafianj.com/mc/pagans.shtml).

The Pagans have the general reputation among bikers as being very reclusive and having little to do with other clubs. Their proclivity for violence reinforces this reputation. In addition, their heavy involvement in criminal activities, particularly organized crime, would define them as economic criminal organizations organized for profit and not a criminal social organization supporting the criminal activities of their members. The Pagans MC does not have any international chapters or a national web site, although there is a web site for jailed Pagans and one for "Conan 13 1%er," Pagan's MC New York (www.hometown.aol.com/JAILEDPAGANS/). The web site for jailed pagans has the pictures of several burly, thick-armed Pagans covered with tattoos. The web site also lists e-mail and conventional mail prison addresses. Conan's web site (hometown.aol.com/pagansmc13ny/) states that he was the National Sergeant-at-Arms of the Pagans Motorcycle Club and is in his seventh year of a 16-year sentence at the federal penitentiary in Lewisburg, Pennsylvania. The "13" he wears and uses in his name signals that he was a member of the Pagans Mother Club.

Sons of Silence Motorcycle Club

Although there is little information about the formation of the Sons of Silence Motorcycle Club, it appears that the club was formed in Colorado in the late 1960s (1968) with chapters in Fort Collins, Greeley, and Niwat (Abbott, 1999; Foster, 1999; Kilzer, 2001). The group's national headquarters is in Colorado Springs, and there are at least three chapters in Colorado—Colorado Springs, Commerce City, and Denver (Abbott, 1999). Law enforcement sources (BATF) have stated that the Sons of Silence has 14 chapters in seven states and Germany, with 175-200 members (Kilzer, 2001). In 2001, a Sons of Silence MC World Map showed chapters in nine states: Colorado, Iowa, Indiana, Illinois, Minnesota, Kansas, Louisiana, North Dakota, and Germany. In addition, the club now has at least one chapter in Florida. The 2005 Sons of Silence New Year's Bash in Sarasota, Florida, was hosted by the Sons of Silence Sarasota Chapter (Bragg, 2005). Therefore, one would assume that there are more chapters and members than previously reported. The National Alliance of Gang Investigators' Association (NAGIA) says that there are also Sons of Silence chapters in Arkansas, Kentucky, and Louisiana (NAGIA, 2005:22).

The Sons of Silence have tenuous relationships with several of the other Big 5 clubs. The Bandidos have had a chapter in Denver since the early 1990s. The two clubs are on "friendly terms" and list each other on their web sites, but the Hells Angels—enemies to both clubs—patched-over a local Denver motorcycle club and established a chapter in Denver, causing concern about a biker war (Foster, 1999). In 1980 the national vice president of the Sons of Silence killed the national vice president of the Outlaws in Indianapolis (Foster, 1999). In an interesting turn of events, on June 19, 2003, members of the Hells Angels, Outlaws, and Bandidos attended the funeral of Leonard "JR" Reed, who was the Sons of Silence president for 22 years (www.biker life.com/notices.html). According to the article (posted on biker-life.com), Reed was well respected by the other clubs and had been seen as a peacemaker. The Sons of Silence and the Iron Horsemen—an independent club—are affiliate clubs. The Sarasota New Year's Bash was celebrated both clubs (Bragg, 2005).

Figure 5.1: Promise to Momma

One of the hardest things for undercover officers to do is avoid taking drugs during their infiltration of a biker gang without raising suspicion that they are cops. In the late 1990s two ATF agents infiltrated the Sons of Silence, eventually becoming patched members. One of the agents told the bikers that he had been an addict and his mother saved him and made him swear that he would never use drugs again. She died shortly after he made the promise and he had "Never Forget" tattooed on his arm as a reminder of the promise to his mother. The bikers believed him.

Source: McPhee, November 20, 1999.

Major Independents

There are clubs that operate in areas where there are no Big Five clubs, or in the same general areas with permission of the dominant Big Five club. These are on friendly or tolerated terms with the larger clubs but remain independent of them. Other independent clubs, such as the Mongols, operate in the same areas as the larger clubs due to their ferocity and willingness to use violence in their challenge. Independent clubs will often be tolerated or on "friendly" terms with one club yet at war with another. For example, in Virginia the Florida-based Warlocks, an independent club, are on "friendly" terms with the Hells Angels but at war with the Pagans. The Mongols are on friendly terms with the Pagans, Bandidos, and Outlaws but are at war with the Angels. The major independent clubs, in terms of chapters, membership, and geographical expansion, are the Warlocks, the Mongols, and the Iron Horsemen. There are also smaller independent clubs, such as the Avengers, the Breed, and Renegades, that operate in limited geographical areas and have tenuous relationships with larger clubs. Two of the three major clubs—Mongols and Warlocks—have chapters outside the United States and make claims to being included in the Big 5. All three have been involved in organized criminal activities.

The Warlocks Motorcycle Club

There are at least three one-percent biker clubs with the name Warlocks—two in the United States and one in Australia. There is also a Warlocks MC in Detroit that is not a one-percent biker club. In the United States there is a Florida-based Warlocks MC and a Pennsylvania- based Warlocks MC. They are not affiliated with each other.

Pennsylvania Warlocks MC

Bowie (1994:21-22) says that the Pennsylvania-based Warlocks came into being in the summer of 1967 when a group of Philadelphia "young toughs" formed the club and elected a president, vice president, secretary, treasurer, and sergeant-at-arms. They formulated rules and chose as their insignia a multicolored caricature of a harpy—mythical minister of divine vengeance. They declared themselves to be a one-percent club and wore the one-percent diamond on their denim vest. Three tattoos were mandatory—a swastika, a naked lady, and the words "BORN TO LOSE." Members had to be male, between 18 and 35, own a Harley, and have committed a felony—theft, rape, or murder—to be considered for membership, making this clearly an economic criminal organization. Membership was confined to those with identifiable criminal exploitable ties.

The club has been a significant crime problem in the Delaware Valley since the 1970s. The Pennsylvania Crime Commission (1980) reported that the regional Warlocks and the national Pagans were the major motorcycle clubs in the southeast region of Pennsylvania. Both clubs were known for their violence and acted as enforcers for La Cosa Nostra families. The report listed 22 Warlocks members by name. One of those listed, Bobby Nauss, was a 1970s serial killer, drug dealer, and the subject of a book and an HBO movie (Bowie, 1994).

The Pennsylvania-based Warlocks also have several chapters in New Jersey (State of New Jersey, 2004). A 1989 New Jersey Commission of investigation report put the membership range from 60 to 136 with chapters in Philadelphia—the mother club, southern New Jersey, and Delaware County, Pennsylvania.

Florida-Based Warlocks MC

According to their national web site, the Florida-based Warlocks MC was founded aboard the aircraft carrier *USS Shangri-La* in the Mediterranean Sea in the summer of 1966 (www.warlocksmc.net/about.html). The 12 original members chose the orange Phoenix bird as their logo. Each of the members was to establish a chapter in their hometown when they retired from the Navy. Only one of the retired sailors made good on their promise to establish a chapter, however: Grub from Orlando, Florida. He founded the first chapter in Jacksonville Beach, Florida, and soon moved it to Orlando, where it is now the mother chapter.

Law enforcement sources (BATF) report that the Florida-based Warlocks have 15 chapters worldwide—13 in the United States, one in England, and another in Germany (BATF Search Warrant Affidavit, 2003). In the Unites States the chapters are divided into three regions—Northern, Central, and Southern. The Northern Region chapters are located in Brooklyn, New York; Martinsburg, West Virginia; Mt. Jackson, Virginia; and Charlottesville, Virginia. Central Region chapters are in Florence, Columbia, and Greenwood, South Carolina. The Southern Region chapters are located in Cocoa, Orlando, Seminole, Brooksville, and Melbourne, Florida. The same source estimates that there are approximately 137 members (BATF Search Warrant Affidavit, 2003). The "best guess" estimate puts the membership from a low of 90 to a high of 375.

The Warlocks, even though they have extensive membership applications and background checks and a membership process of hang-around, probate, and then membership, have been penetrated several times by undercover law enforcement officers. In the latest case, two Bureau of Alcohol, Tobacco, and Firearms special agents became patched members; one became his chapter's Road Captain, an appointed officer position (BATF Search Warrant Affidavit, 2003). In 1991 during an investigation dubbed Operation Easy Rider, four undercover federal agents (BATF) and a Volusia County, Florida, deputy sheriff became patched members. One of the agents became president of the Fort Lauderdale Warlocks chapter, which he set up on instructions from the Warlocks national president. The agent recruited the other undercover agents to join him. They became an all-police one-percent biker club. This was not the first all-cop one-percent biker club. In the early 1970s the Long Beach, California, Widow Makers Motorcycle Club was made up of six undercover ATF agents (Queen, 2005). This was the first undercover operation on biker gangs on the West Coast.

The Warlocks and the Pagans and the Outlaws are bitter enemies. In 1991, the International Outlaw President, Harry "Taco" Bowman, murdered the National Warlocks President.

The Mongols MC

The Mongols started as a Chicano prison gang in East Los Angeles in the early 1970s and formed an alliance with La Eme, the Mexican Mafia. Many of these early members had never owned or ridden a motorcycle. It appears that the Mongols were formed to be and still are an economic criminal organization organized for profit through criminal activities. The club is still predominately Hispanic, with a large number of former street gang members according to an ATF agent who became a patched member and rose to the rank of secretary-treasurer of the San Fernando Valley chapter (Queen, 2005). The Mongols are a particularly violent motorcycle club due to the large number of former gangbangers in their chapters. They have a higher percentage of convicted felons and murderers in their ranks than any of the other clubs (Queen, 2005). Former Minnesota Governor Jesse Ventura was a member of the Mongols in the early 1970s when he was stationed at the naval facility at San Diego but

As Minnesota Governor, Jesse Ventura yells to the crowd at the People's Inauguration in Minneapolis. Ventura was a member of the Mongols Motorcycle Club in the early 1970s. *Photo courtesy of AP Photo/Jim Mone.*

claims that he did not participate or hear of their criminal activities (Queen, 2005).

Their official web site of the Mongols MC lists 62 chapters in six states and Mexico—California-48; Oklahoma-5; Colorado-1; Arizona-1; Montana-1; Nevada-5; and Mexico-1. Queen claims that there is also a chapter in Georgia. The Mongols and the HAMC fought a 17-year war in California about wearing "California" on the bottom rocker of the three- piece patch. The Hells Angels originally would not allow any other club to wear the California rocker, but they gave up the fight and said the Mongols had earned the right (Queen, 2005). The Mongols agreed not to establish a chapter in San Bernardino (Berdoo), the founding site of the Hells Angels. The Mongols have not established a chapter, but members live in Berdoo and fly their colors there, which is considered an act of major disrespect to the Angels. The two clubs are still at war. A recent altercation took place at Harrah's Casino in Laughlin, Nevada, on April 27, 2002, resulting in the deaths of one Mongols member and two Hells Angels as well as numerous injuries. In May 2005, the president of the Hells Angels San Diego chapter was sentenced to 57 months in federal prison after pleading guilty to racketeering charges for conspiring with other HA members to kill Mongols (AP, August 16, 2005). An ominous indication of future trouble between the two clubs is the announcement on the Mongols web site that a chapter in Oakland, California (home of the HAMC mother chapter) is coming soon (www.mongolsmc.com/cali.html). Queen (2005) says that there are approximately 350 members in the Mongols Nation. However, using the "best guess" estimate would put membership in a range from 132 to 1,540 members.

The Iron Horsemen

It is extremely difficult to determine the number of chapters in the Iron Horsemen Nation. Chapters are not listed on their web site, there is no law enforcement estimate of which this book's author is aware, and Iron Horsemen members that the author has contacted will not provide the number (assuming they know it). Their response has been "that is club business." Nevertheless, an examination of a variety of sources (biker web sites, newspapers, court cases, and interviews) has identified 17 chapters in the following states: Ohio-4; Kentucky-3; Indiana-3; Maine-2; Maryland, 1; New York, 1; New Jersey, 1; and Tennessee, 2. The "best guess" estimate would put membership as ranging from a low of 102 to a high of 425. The Iron Horsemen are affiliated with the Sons of Silence MC, but have had confrontations with the Bandidos in Washington and the Black Pistons and the Outlaws in Maine.

Puppet Clubs

There are also "puppet" clubs that do the bidding of the larger clubs, act as potential recruiting sources, serve as cannon fodder in the wars between clubs, and give a portion of their illegal gains to the larger club. The Nomads chapter of the Quebec Hells Angels required a 10-percent tithing or a minimum of $500 from each member of their puppet club, the Rockers (Sanger, 2005). As with associates, puppet clubs will handle the retail sale of drugs, with patched club members handling the wholesale distribution. Puppet clubs also serve to insulate the larger clubs from prosecution. If a puppet club member is caught while committing a crime for the larger club and keeps quiet, he will be rewarded with cash or drugs or allowed to become a prospect for the larger club. Puppet club members are also required to "take the fall" for full-patched members of the larger club when necessary. The Caribbean Brotherhood is a HAMC puppet gang in Curacao that supplies cocaine from the FARC (Revolutionary Armed Forces of Colombia to the Hells Angels in Europe (Sher and Marsden, 2006).

Figure 5.2: Puppet Gangs in Canada

> . . . outlaw motorcycle gangs for example do have a formalized structure for dealing with its support crime groups [puppet gangs]. Essentially, these supportive crime groups are used to train the younger generation, identify those candidates with the potential to become full-fledged members, as well as exclude undesirables. In this kind of relationship, the advantage for the dominant group is that the subordinate one further insulates the dominant group's members from the day-to-day criminal activities that would bring them into direct contact with the authorities and/or their rivals. Other benefits for the dominate group include the payment of money, goods, and services they receive from members of the subordinate group.

Source: CICS, 2005 Organized Crime in Canada, 5 & 6.

The Red Devils MC is well known as a puppet club for the HAMC, and the Black Pistons MC and Forsaken Few are known as puppet clubs for the Outlaws (see Red Devils MC below). The Outlaw Nation and the Bandidos Nation list their puppet clubs on their national web sites. The Bandidos MC web site lists 22 "puppet" clubs in the "Red and Gold World" (referring to their patch colors). Edward Winterhalder, the only ex-Bandidos member to write an autobiography, lists 47 Bandidos "support" clubs in 13 states with 929 members (Winterhalder, 2005).

Figure 5.3: Red and Gold World

Amigos MC	Asgard MC	Bandaloros MC
Blazes MC	Campesinos MC	Commancheros MC
Compadres MC	Companerous MC	Destralos MC
Diablos MC	Gringos MC	Guardian MC
Guerrillos MC	Hermanos MC	Hombres MC
LA Riders MC	Lones MC	Los Mados MC
OK Riders MC	Pistoleros MC	Regulators MC
Zapata MC		

The only support (i.e., puppet) clubs listed on the Outlaws national web site are Black Piston clubs in the United States, Canada, Germany, Britain, Norway, Poland, and Belgium. The Pagans reportedly have the Tribe MC and the Blitzkrieg and Thunderguards MCs as puppet clubs.

Figure 5.4: Red Devils MC

CW [confidential informant] stated that the Red Devils continued and sole purpose is to support the HAMC through several facets, including increased membership, conducting drug and prostitution deb collections, extorting jobs and acquiring and maintaining weaponry and narcots on behalf of HAMC members.

Source: BATF Search Warrant Affidavit, 2003.

BLACK OR INTERRACIAL ONE-PERCENT BIKER CLUBS

There are at least five black or interracial one-percent biker clubs. The Oakland, California, East Bay Dragons MC is all-black (Levingston, 2003). The Wheels of Soul MC's web site says that they are "an Outlaw Motorcycle Club, was founded in 1976 and is the only one of its kind . . . .we have a make-up of black, white, Latino, and Asian members (www.mosmc-trenton.com/history.htm.). The Ching-a-Lings MC in Queens, New York City are interracial. Chuck Zito was a member of the Ching-a-Lings before joining the Hells Angels (Zito, 2002). According to a State of New Jersey Commission of Investigation 1989 Report, the black Ghetto Riders MC of Camden County was formed in the late 1970s and has approximately 30 members and 20 associates (www.mafianj.com/mc/sg.shtml). The Bandidos' "Connecticut Ed" Edward Winterhalder says in his autobiography that there is a black, nationwide one-percent club, the Hell's Lovers (Winterhalder, 2005:289). The author of this book has located chapters in Texas and Wisconsin.

ORGANIZATIONAL STRUCTURE

Wolf (1999:274) describes the community of outlaw bikers as "not predicated on a formal organization." However, they could be described as quasi–formal organizations. They have a (1) club name, which becomes a shorthand statement of corporate identity, (2) a written mandate stating the purpose of association, (3) written statutes outlining criteria of membership, and (4) formal regulatory mechanisms for enforcing those statues—all of which result in (5) a degree of autonomy and sense of exclusivity regarding outlaw club activity (Wolf, 1999:274). The basic organizational structure of a biker club consists of a president, vice-president, sergeant-at-arms, secretary-treasurer, road captain, and patched members. The clubs are more or less participatory democracies, with the officers elected by the membership. It must be remembered that force, proclivity for violence, and murder have played a part in the officer selection in many clubs throughout their history. Nevertheless, the officers fill typical roles found in formal organizations except that of sergeant-at-arms and road captain.

Figure 5.5: Biker Club Chapter Organizational Structure

President

Has claimed the position through force or fear or has been voted in. He has final authority in the club. Has veto power over decisions voted upon by that chapter.

Vice President

Second in command and acts for the president in his absence. Often has been hand-picked by the president. Heir apparent.

Secretary-Treasury

Keeps the chapter roster, maintains their accounting system, takes the minutes, collects dues and fines, pays bills, and collects profits-legal and illegal.

Sergeant-at-Arms

Although all formal organizations might have someone to maintain order during meetings, it is largely a ceremonial role. Not so in biker clubs. The sergeant-at-arms is often the strongest or most violent member. He is completely loyal to the president and will administer beatings or worse for violations of club rules. He is the enforcer for the club, often having killed for the club.

Road Captain

The road captain, unique to biker clubs, is the logistician and security officer for the club on runs and outings. He maps out the route, arranges for fuel and food stops, and often carries money for bail. On occasion, he liaisons with local police to prevent unnecessary stops.

HAMC Structure

All outlaw motorcycle clubs are structurally organized for deci-sionmaking, with a multilevel chain of command. Many clubs, such as the Outlaws and the Mongols, have national officers who decide issues for the club. Some, such as the Pagans and the Warlocks, have a defined group (e.g., Pagans Mother Group, Warlocks Counsel) who make all important decisions affecting the club. Individual chapter pres-idents usually run the day-to-day operations of their chapters. Some clubs, such as the Hells Angels, allow for more chapter autonomy, with important decisions made at regional, national, and international meetings (Search Warrant affidavit Joseph Slatalla, July 2, 2003). This organizational structure is often denied by club leaders in order to prevent them from being declared criminal enterprises at trial, par-ticularly when faced with RICO (Racketeer Influenced and Corrupt Organizations) prosecutions. In 1985 HAMC leader Sonny Barger was called before a federal grand jury in New York and asked questions, some of which related to the HAMC organizational structure (*Appellant v. United States*, No. 85-6528, 1985). Although he was granted statutory immunity, Barger refused to answer 13 questions on First Amendment grounds and was found in contempt of court (see Figure 5.6). Nevertheless, web sites and court testimony show that worldwide HAMC chapters are grouped into regions headed by an executive board elected within the region. The United States is divided into a West Coast region and an East Coast region. Route 81, which extends from North Dakota to Texas, is the dividing line. The two regions meet reg-ularly with an officer from each chapter attending along with a liaison from the other region attending as a nonvoting member. Canada has three regions—West Coast, East Coast, and Central. England, Australia, and Europe have regular officer's meetings. The international meetings are held at during the United States and World Runs, held in different locations each year. International business and critical issues affecting the HAMC worldwide are discussed at these meetings. In the United States the HAMC has regular state meetings to discuss issues within that particular state.

Figure 5.6: Unanswered Questions—Sonny Barger

1. What, if any, offices have you held in connection with the Hells Angel Motorcycle Club?
2. When was the club founded?
3. How many chapters are there in the club?
4. What is the Filthy Few?
5. Does the club have a national treasury?
6. What does "Dequiallo" (patch meaning that wearer has used violence against law enforcement officers) mean?
7. Is there a connection between the Oakland Chapter of the Club and the New York Chapter of the Club? And by connection, I mean, do you have any members in common, or do you communicate on a regular basis?
8. Does the New York City Chapter of the Hells Angels pay any money to the Oakland Chapter?
9. What clubs does the Hells Angels Motorcycle Club consider to be their chief rivals?
10. Isn't it a fact that certain animosity or antagonism exists between the Hells Angels and other motorcycle clubs?
11. Does the Hells Angels Motorcycle Club employ anybody on a paid full-time basis?
12. Are club members required to pay dues to the Club, and if so, how much are the dues?
13. Isn't it a fact that part of the activities of the Club are financed through the distribution of methamphetamines?

The organizational structure, including written constitutions and by-laws, can be helpful to the clubs as they conduct their business and affairs and can be used to argue that they are voluntary associations of individuals united by their love of biking and brotherhood. On the other hand, as stated above, these same trappings of formal organizations can be useful in a prosecution against them as a criminal organization. Billy Queen, the ATF agent who became secretary-treasurer of a Mongols chapter, used the chapter books as a crucial piece of evidence to show that the club was an ongoing criminal enterprise (Queen, 2005).

SUMMARY

All the one-percent clubs identified, including the puppet and black, share certain characteristics. They have formal positions and titles of rank, sets of rules, often published in written constitutions and by-laws; systems of punishment for members who break the rules, ranging from fines to expulsion; and ceremonies or rituals that give the club strength and permanence—induction, probation, and patching. They identify themselves with clothing, attire, tattoos, and demeanor—the only criminal groups other than street gangs and the Japanese Boryoku-dan to do so.

REFERENCES

Abbott, K. (1999). "Dozens Held in Biker Gang Inquiry 42 Indicted in Undercover Investigation; Many Appear in Court after 3-state Roundup." *Rocky Mountain News,* October 9, 1999.

Alain, M. (1995). "The Rise and Fall of Motorcycle Gangs in Quebec." *Federal Probation* 59(2):54-57.

Associate Press (2005). "Local Hells Angels Leader Gets Prison." NBCSandiego.com, August 16, 2005.

Bowe, B. (1994). *Born to Be Wild.* New York: Warner Books.

Bragg, M. (2005). "Sons of Silence New Year's Bash." Found at: http://www.bikernet.com/events/PageViewer.asp?PagelID=370

Caparella, K. (\2006). "Turf Wars Recycled: Now its Pagans vs. Outlaws." *Philadelphia Daily News*, May 8, 2006.

CICS (2000). "Outlaw Motorcycle Gangs." *Criminal Intelligence Service Canada-2000.*

CICS (2005). *2005 Organized Crime in Canada.* Ottawa: Criminal Intelligence Service Canada.

Foster, D. (1999). "Actions Speak Volumes for Sons of Silence Arrests for Guns, Drugs Thwart Biker Gang's Attempt at New Image." *Denver Rocky Mountain News*, October 18, 1999.

Gibbons, T.J., and G.G. Anastasia (2005). "Cycle Club Member Shot Dead in Phila." *Philadelphia Inquirer*, January 15, 2005.

Haut, F. (1999). "Organized Crime on Two Wheels: Motorcycle Gangs." *International Criminal Police Review:* 474-475.

Holthouse, D. (2005). "Smashing the Shamrock: A Massive Federal Indictment Names the Senior Leadership of America's Most Frightening Prison Gang. But Will it Work?" *Intelligence Report.* Southern Poverty Law Center. Fall (2005).

Jenkins, P. (1992). "The Speed Capital of the World: Organizing the Methamphetamine Industry in Philadelphia." *Criminal Justice Policy Review* 6(1):18-39.

Kessler, R.E. (2002). "Feds: Pagans to Take Plea Deal/Nearly All of 73 Bikers to Face Prison for Brawl. *Newsday.*

Kilzer, L. (2001). "Biker Club on Denver Doorstop Hells Angels Form Chapter." *Rocky Mountain News*, June 30, 2001.

Lavigne, Y. (1987). *Hell's Angels: Taking Care of Business*. Toronto: Ballantine Books.

Lyon, D. (2003). *The Bikeriders*. San Francisco: Chronicle Books.

McKee, M. (2001). "On the Side of Angels." *Legal Business* Found at: http://web.lexis-nexus.com.library.eku.edu/universe/document?

McPhee, M. (1999). "Sons of Silence Meet Accuser in Courtroom." *The Denver Post*, November 20, 1999, B-06.

NAGIA (2005). *2005 National Gang Threat Assessment*. Washington, DC: National Alliance of Gang Investigators' Association: Bureau of Justice Statistics.

Pennsylvania Crime Commission (1980). *A Decade of Organized Crime*. Commonwealth of Pennsylvania.

Quinn, J.F. (1983). *Outlaw Motorcycle Clubs*. Unpublished Master's Thesis, University of Miami.

Sanger, D. (2005). *Hell's Witness*. Toronto: Penguin Group.

Southeastern Connecticut Gang Activities Group (2000). *Pagans Motorcycle Club*. Found at: http://www.segag.org/mcgangs/pagan.html

State of New Jersey: Commission of Investigation (May 2004). *The Changing Face of Organized Crime in New Jersey—A Status Report*.

Queen, W. (2005). *Under and Alone*. New York: Random House.

Veno, A. (2003). *The Brotherhoods: Inside the Outlaw Motorcycle Clubs*. Crows Nest, NSW, Australia: Allen & Unwin.

Winterhalder, E. (2005). *Out in Bad Standing: Inside the Bandidos Motorcycle—The Making of aw Worldwide Dynasty*. Owasso, OK: Blockhead City Press.

Zito, C., with J. Layden (2002). *Street Justice*. New York: St. Martin's Press.

6

Evolution from Clubs to Gangs: Outlaw Motorcycle Gangs

"Federal prosecutors, with the help of the FBI, the DEA, and the California law enforcement, decided that there was a criminal enterprise called the Hell's Angels motorcycle 'gang' . . ."

> Ralph "Sonny" Barger, Hells Angels celebrity
> and convicted felon (Barger, 2000: 210).

"It's [Hells Angels MC] more than just a motorcycle club. It's an international brotherhood . . . the world's largest extended family."

> Chuck Zito, Hells Angels celebrity
> and convicted felon (Zito, 2002: 117).

"This ain't no club, Rocky continued. We're outlaws. I've had to do things that would send me to prison for years if I got caught. You ready for that? Would you kill for the Mongols? Because that's what you might have to do. We're outlaws, Billy. You need to know that. You need to be sure. You need to understand what you're getting into."

> Advice from Mongol MC member
> to undercover ATF special agent (Queen, 2005: 51).

INTRODUCTION

The major controversy surrounding outlaw (one-percent) motorcycle clubs is whether they are clubs or gangs—voluntary associations united by the biker lifestyle or criminal organizations (engaging in crime as a cohesive unit). that is, networks of criminals who organize for criminal activities. The organizational and social structure of the clubs can facilitate the operation of the clubs or chapters of the clubs as criminal organizations and make networks of criminals easier to form and safer to operate. Club spokesmen say they are clubs made up of individuals united by their love of motorcycles, biking, and a sense of brotherhood and freedom (see Barger, 2000; Zito, 2002). These same spokesmen readily admit that some members engage in criminal activities, including organized criminal behaviors, but they retort that these behaviors represent the actions of a few individual members and not the clubs—i.e., rotten apples, not rotten clubs. Furthermore, they claim that law enforcement authorities have labeled the clubs as gangs to justify their aggressive actions, including harassment, of the clubs and their deviant lifestyle. There is evidence that police harass or profile back patch–wearing bikers in general. Some police motorcycle clubs and members, including the Choir Boys MC and the Wild Pigs MC, complain that they are harassed by their supervisors and fellow officers. Several court cases have come to the conclusion that law enforcement officers "harass" and "profile" one-percent bikers, ATF special agent William Queen, when he was working undercover as a Mongol, had police officers harass him, pull guns on him, and threaten to shoot him when he was "flying his colors"(Queen, 2005).

Biker club members claim the media sensationalizes the exploits of the few to create a false impression of the clubs (Barger, 2000; Zito, 2002). They argue that well-publicized violent activities and drug manufacturing and selling by "bad apples" is not organized, endorsed, or sanctioned by the clubs. There is general consensus among scholars that media sensationalism in the 1960s and 1970s created a "folk devil" image and moral panic about bikers, particularly one-percent bikers, that persists to this day (Cohen, 1980; Fuglsang, 1997; Harris, 1985; Pratt, 2002; Shellow and Roemer, 1966; Veno, 2003; Wood, 2003; Wolf, 1999). However, an examination of the popular literature, including biker autobiographies, even though it may be sensationalized or biased, provides valuable insight into the clubs-vs.-gangs controversy. This literature becomes even more important because of the dearth of scholarly research on biker clubs/gangs.

BIKER LITERATURE

Angel Autobiographies

One-percent biker clubs, from their inception, have always considered themselves to be different and apart from conventional motorcycle clubs sanctioned by motorcycle associations such as the AMA. Their contempt for society and deviant lifestyle—drinking, drug taking, and deviant sexual activities, outrageous manner of dress, and racist attitudes is what makes them outsiders. However, in the formation stage (1940s to 1960s)—with the exception of occasional acts of violence, including rapes—their crimes were acts against public order rather than organized crime for profit. This changed in the mid-1960s and early 1970s (Barger, 2000; Lowe, 1985; Lyon, 2003; Thompson, 1996). The change is reflected in the autobiographies of early Hells Angels members.

There are eight autobiographies written by Hells Angels or former Angels (Barger, 2000; Kaye, 1970; Mandelkau, 1971; Mayson, 1982; Reynolds, 1967; Wethern and Colnett, 1978; Zito, 2002). Five of these books—the ones by Barger, Kaye, Mandelkau, Reynolds, and Wethern and Colnett—discuss the formative years and the change from clubs to gangs. Mayson's book describes the Angels' criminal behaviors in the late 1970s and expansion into the southern states.

"Freewheeling Frank" Reynolds was Secretary of the San Francisco Hells Angels in the early 1960s. He was the first Angel to "tell" his story. Reynolds's story fits the popular image of bikers that appeared in the media of the 1960s—social misfits driven by freedom of the road, wind whipping through their hair, showing their contempt for society through drinking, drug taking, and deviant sexual activities, including gang rapes. According to Reynolds, drugs were the most important aspect of the lifestyle of the early Angels, and they wore the patch DFFL (Drugs Forever, Forever Loaded). Reynolds says he "never really became a Hell's Angel until I took LSD" (Reynolds, 1967:74). The early Angels were, according to Reynolds, racists warring with "niggers" [sic] and each other. The Frisco and Oakland Angels kicked and stomped each other during a three-year Great War. The Brotherhood that bonded the Angels together was, both then and now, often more rhetoric than reality.

George "Baby Huey" Wethern was a member of the Oakland Hells Angels chapter at the time it was founded and (according to the dust cover of his autobiography) one of the most important drug dealers on the West Coast (Wethern and Colnett, 1978). His autobiography was published in 1978 and republished in 2004. Wethern, a high school drop out, joined the Oakland Angels in 1958 after receiving an undesirable discharge from the U.S. Air Force and became their vice-president in 1960. Wethern describes the early Angels as "basically honest blue-collar or unskilled workers looking for excitement" (Wethern an Colnett, 1978:50). This changed in a few years as drugs replaced brotherhood as a focus. Wethern says that the club social structure made the transition to drug dealing easier. New chapters were established based on whether they could assist the Hells Angels "by providing a drug route link, manufacturing a drug, supplying chemicals or distributing drugs in an untapped area" (Wethern and Colnett, 1978:102). Wethern and Terry the Tramp (an early prominent Angel) controlled the psychedelics, another Angel "scored big mescaline supplies," and Ralph "Sonny" Barger controlled heroin and cocaine (Wethern and Colnett, 1978:109). In order to weed out undercover agents, new members were required to commit criminal acts. Wethern's description of the HAs would make the club at this time in their history an economic criminal organization set up for the sole purpose of material gain. Furthermore, Wethern says that Barger's personal contacts with European Angel chapters helped them set up drug operations overseas, which is further evidence of an economic criminal organization exporting its criminal activity overseas.

Wethern left the Angels in 1969 after shooting his Angels drug-dealing partner during a drug-induced psychotic episode. Later, the Angels buried three bodies (one a suicide and the other two murder victims) on his isolated ranch in 1971. Another Angel who witnessed the murders and burials went to the police for protection, fearing for his life. This set in motion a series of events that led to Wethern going into the federal witness protection program after testifying against his former "brothers." Sonny Barger was acquitted of the murder charges, but was later sentenced to 10 years to life after pleading guilty to four felony drug counts, federal income tax evasion, and gun charges.

Kaye's book, *Place in Hell: The Inside Story of 'Hell's Angels'—The World's Wildest Outsiders*, first published in 1968, is touted as the autobiography of Wild Bill Henderson as told to the author. Supposedly, "Wild Bill" was one of the original founding members of the Hells Angels. However, he is not mentioned in any of the other chronicles, such as Reynolds's, Wethern's, or Barger's. Mandelkau's book, *Buttons: The Making of a President*, published in 1971, is the autobiography of "Buttons" (Peter Welsh), one of the two first English presidents of a Hells Angels chapter. In May 1969, Buttons flew to San Francisco and "prospected" with the Frisco chapter. He returned to England in November 1969 with the official club charter for the Hells Angels— England. The books by Kaye and Mandelkau describe the early deviant lifestyle common to the early Angels—drug taking, sex orgies, and drug dealing. Buttons also relates the account of earning his "brown wings" through the sodomy of a man observed by other Angels: he and a group of Angels sodomized a "drag queen." Others, particularly law enforcement, have alluded to "brown wings," but recent works by Hells Angels members say they never existed. Nevertheless, according to records released under the Freedom of Information Act, FBI agents in their reports to Director J. Edgar Hoover described the Hells Angels as drug addicts and homosexuals, supposedly because of such activities.

Barry Mayson's 1982 autobiography, *Fallen Angel: Hell's Angel to Heaven's Saint,* is the story of the evolution of a "poster child" gangster on two wheels—chapter president, violent individual, drug dealer, and pimp for his own wife—to a "born again" Christian and evangelical minister to bikers. On his web site, Mayson has a picture of a tattoo showing the date of his being "born again" under the tattoo of the Hells Angels logo and his date of initiation into the Angels. A skeptical person might wonder how much the "scared straight" experience the California Angels attempt on his life had on his conversion to religion—what part did Jesus or fear of the Hell's Angels have in his conversion? In any event, the book is important because it provides a first-person account of the expansion of the Hells Angels MC into the Southeastern United States and the Outlaws MC expansion into Atlanta and the drug-dealing activities of these early clubs/gangs. Mayson also describes the resulting wars of the Angels and Outlaws with each other and other one-percent biker clubs over territory and illegal drug markets during this expansion.

Sonny Barger's best-selling autobiography recognizes the "sins and warts" of the Hells Angels Motorcycle Club described in the previous works. Barger says that the HAMC can be broken down according to decades. In the 1950s the club existed to party and ride—freewheeling hell-raisers. Media publicity in 1960s made "folk devils" out of the Angels. The media and movies made "us out to be the wildest motherfuckers to roam the earth since Genghis Khan and his warriors" (Barger, 2000:252). Barger admits that he sold drugs and got into a "lot of shit" in the 1970s—the gangster era, but he says he and the rest of the club paid for their crimes, as well as some they did not commit, in the 1980s—payback time. In the 1990s, according to Barger, the Hells Angels came full circle and started riding and partying together again. Barger never mentions the vicious and criminal Canadian Hells Angels in the 1990s and today, and also fails to mention the 1990s federal and state convictions of numerous Hells Angels and their associates. In fact, he vehemently denies the HAMC's involvement in organized crime.

Although Chuck Zito's autobiography does not discuss the early years of the HAMC, it serves to point out that one-percent bikers, if not organized criminals (Zito claims he was framed by the government for his drug conspiracy conviction) are violent individuals who have little in common with conventional motorcycle club members and share a penchant for violence that is characteristic of gangs. Zito's

(2002) autobiography is a violent read about a violent man who believes in the most elemental version of justice—street justice. Biker justice is violent because "[b]ikers have their own rules, their own code of ethics, their own definitions of right and wrong" (Zito, 2002:80). According to Zito, biker clubs have their own way of settling grievances: "When outlaw motorcycle clubs meet to settle a grievance and they're armed with guns, people can and do get killed [sometimes it is innocent civilians]. It's part of the culture, part of the risk. It's also part of the appeal" (Zito, 2002:90). He and his "brothers" carry guns, knives, and are trained in the martial arts and revel in their ability to beat others—bikers and citizens—who transgress them, according to their definitions of transgressions. The clubs Zito describes are not voluntary associations. They are "gangs" of violent and dangerous adult males. Zito paints a romanticized version of the Angels' international brotherhood by saying that the Hells Angels are "the world's largest extended family." Again, like Barger, he makes no mention of the Canadian Hells Angels "family" members like Maurice "Mom" Boucher, convicted of the murders of two correction officers; Serge Quesnel, Canadian HA hitman of five for the club; or Yves "Apache" Trudeau, HA hitman credited with 43 murders for the club and recently convicted of child molestation of a 10-year old boy (Martineau, 2003; Sher and Marsden, 2003). Trudeau's sentencing judge remarked to him: "You've killed more people than did the Canadian army during the Gulf War. You have a deplorable past and a pitiful future" (Sanger, 2005:333).

Law enforcement agencies were also beginning to recognize that outlaw motorcycle clubs were evolving—or had evolved—into criminal gangs during these formative years and thus began increasing their efforts against them.

EARLY LAW ENFORCEMENT EFFORTS

In the 1970s, the already-established outlaw clubs began to attempt to clean up their public images by decreasing their "in your face" confrontations with citizens, eliminating their Nazi symbols, and punishing members for gang rapes and, through expansion and growing sophistication, escalated their move into diverse criminal operations (Haut, 1999; Reid, 198). Their lower profile attracted less attention from the media. However, some law enforcement agencies began to treat the one-percent motorcycle clubs as organized crime groups. Local law enforcement was moving against the clubs/gangs before federal involvement. In 1976 and 1977, the Orange County, California Sheriffs Office had an undercover female deputy riding with a Hells Angel member

(Detroit, 1994). The undercover operation led to the indictment of 77 bikers, 19 of them Hells Angels, for charges ranging from drug trafficking to murder. The Angels posted a $25,000 reward for the deaths of the deputy and the Angels member with whom she rode. The California Hells Angels even imported a New York Hells Angels contract killer to kill both of them. The deputy left California and located in another state under an assumed name, and the informer later died in a motorcycle accident under suspicious circumstances. Several of the Angels brothers who caused the penetration of the gang were murdered.

The growing threat posed by outlaw motorcycle gangs also began receiving attention at the federal level. In testimony at 1979 congressional hearings on the activities of outlaw motorcycle gangs, Pennsylvania Congressmen Robert Walker stated that: "The problem of motorcycle gangs is pervasive and growing. They pose a serious threat to our society" (Davis, 1982). At the Sixth International Conference on Outlaw Motorcycle Gangs in 1980, an FBI agent reported that the investigation of outlaw motorcycle gangs "is a relatively new area and one in which not too many people have been involved in—at least not in the federal level" (B.W., 1980:1508). The agent also predicted that this would change with the application of RICO to motorcycle gangs, which is exactly what happened.

Interpol recognized the international threat of motorcycle gangs in the early 1980s. A May 1984 Interpol meeting on motorcycle gangs held in St. Cloud, France, was attended by law enforcement representatives from eight countries (Canada, Denmark, France, Federal Germany, the Netherlands, Switzerland, the United Kingdom, and the United States) (ICPO-Interpol, May, 1984). At that time it was reported that only four gangs (Hells Angels, Outlaws, Pagans, and Bandidos) were organized on a national scale in the United States. The Hells Angels were the only motorcycle gang with chapters in 12 countries, but as predicted by Interpol, this would change in the near future.

In the 1980s, state and local law enforcement was also increasing their efforts against motorcycle gangs, particularly HAMC. In 1981,

Weapons and utilities of the Hells Angels, shown during a press conference in Duesseldorf, Germany. They were found during a raid aimed at combating organized crime. *Photo courtesy of AP Photo/Edgar R. Schoepal.*

an investigation by the Fayetteville (North Carolina) Police Department into thefts of Harley-Davidson motorcycles and insurance fraud led to a local Hells Angel chapter (Johnson, 1981). The investigation resulted in arrests in 20 states. Motorcycle clubs other than the HAMC had also evolved into gangs organized for illegal profits in many states. The Ohio Attorney General listed 29 motorcycle gangs, including the Hells Angels, Outlaws, Pagans, Avengers, and Iron Horsemen, operating in Ohio (Organized Crime Consulting Committee, 1986). In 1982, a raid of a drug factory run by the Avengers MC in Ohio found 50 pounds of methqualone powder (Organized Crime Consulting Committee, 1986). The same report stated that 12 homicides in northern Ohio had been linked to the war between the Hells Angels and the Outlaws. A 1982 law enforcement report listed the criminal activities of major motorcycle gangs as: manufacturing and distribution of narcotics, prostitution, weapons-related violations, extortion, murder, arson-for-hire, pornography, protection rackets, loan sharking, interstate transportation of stolen property and stolen vehicles, and insurance fraud (Davis, 1982). The profits from these illegal activities were being invested in legitimate businesses.

The FBI began targeting the outlaw clubs now officially known by law enforcement agencies as outlaw motorcycle gangs (OMGs) in 1981 under its Organized Crime Program and RICO (Racketeer Influenced Criminal Organizations) statute. The RICO law allowed for the prosecution of OMGs following the enterprise theory of investigations, which called for identifying the hierarchy and networks between members. Common to such investigations are the use of cooperating witnesses, informants, undercover agents, and—most importantly—court-approved electronic surveillance. In 1979, federal authorities decided to take action against the Hells Angels as a criminal organization, not as individual criminals. However, they underestimated the Hells Angels and the complexity of making a plausible RICO case that a jury would believe. The first federal action under the RICO statute action against the Hells Angels and Sonny Barger resulted in a nine-month trial and a mistrial. The government tried again, and a second mistrial was declared (Barger, 2000). Later efforts were more successful.

In 1981, the FBI raided a Hells Angels arsenal in Cleveland, Ohio, and found a large quantity of explosives and automatic weapons, including hand grenades and anti-tank rockets (Organized Crime Consulting Committee, 1986). The explosives and weapons were reportedly to be used in their war with the Outlaws. A two-year undercover investigation by an FBI agent begun in 1982, known as "Operation ROUGHRIDER," involved 11 HAMC chapters in seven states and led to the arrests of 125 members and associates (Operation ROUGHRIDER, 1985). Several of the Hells Angels informed on their

Angels brothers for lighter sentences (Reynolds, 2000). Drugs confiscated during this operation included: methamphetamine, cocaine, marijuana, hashish, PCP, and LSD. Also beginning in 1982 a member of the HAMC Alaska chapter, Anthony Tait, became a FBI informant and remained one for three years. The resulting arrests of 35 Hells Angels included the National President, Sonny Barger (Reynolds, 2000). Tait was paid $250,000 and now reportedly lives in Europe under an assumed name.

The FBI also moved against the Outlaws Motorcycle Club. A 1982 RICO prosecution against Outlaws MC members from Florida, Georgia, North Carolina, and Tennessee involved white slavery and transporting women across state lines for immoral purposes (Smith, 2002). The National President of the Pagans MC, Antonio "Tiny" Martinez, was killed in a shootout with the FBI on Interstate 80 near Hubbard, Ohio, in 1984 (Organized Crime Consulting Committee, 1986). He had $69,820, a 9mm pistol, and a machine gun in his possession when stopped. The Pagans leader was "on the run" for failure to appear in a federal court in Delaware on the RICO charges of drug trafficking and operating a continuing criminal enterprise. The 1986 President's Commission on Organized Crime listed outlaw motorcycle gangs as being active in the United States during the 1980s. By the beginning of the 1990s, OMGs were recognized as an emerging new type of organized crime by law enforcement officials and others, and they appeared in the Congressional Record as such in 1991 (Brenner, 2002:4).

OUTLAW MOTORCYCLE CLUBS AS GANGS

The popular literature, including the autobiographies, and law enforcement activities support the official designation of outlaw motorcycle clubs as gangs—organizations whose members use their motorcycle club affiliations to engage in crime activity. We should also examine the behavior of one-percent biker members and clubs, using a generally accepted definition of gangs used by criminologists and other scholars. According to the National Gang Crime Research Center (NGCRC), a gang is defined as "a group of three or more persons, whether it is formal or informal in terms of its organizational sophistication, where the members engage in acts of crime over a continuous period of time, and this crime by members is either known to the group or is generally approved of, if not (more common to most gangs) actually sponsored or organized by the group itself" (NGCRC, 2004: 357). The most common types of criminal groups that fit this definition of gangs are: street gangs, prison gangs, and outlaw motorcycle gangs. Most legal statutes also add "having a common name or common sign or symbol." Under California law, in order to be classified a gang, "three or more people share the same group name and symbol and have an established history of criminal activity perceived as benefiting the group" (California Department of Justice, 2004:13). Do one-percent biker clubs fit the definition and label of gangs? We already know that they are composed of three or more persons sharing the same name and symbol (colors), but do they have an established history of criminal activity perceived as benefiting the group? The search for an answer begins with an examination of one-percent biker clubs and the criminal history of club members, especially the leaders.

Members' Criminal History

The one-percent bikers with celebrity status today—Hells Angels' Sonny Barger, former chapter and national president, and best-selling author; Chuck Zito, former chapter president, best-selling author and bodyguard to the stars; and former Devils Disciple MC member Duane "Dog" Chapman, bounty-hunter extraordinaire and star of his own TV dramatic series—all are convicted felons who have served lengthy prison sentences. Barger readily admits that he sold drugs (Barger, 2000:252). All three of these biker celebrities have their own web sites. Barger, who markets himself as an "American legend," sells Hells Angels support merchandise, ranging from calendars, souvenirs, and beer to barbecue sauce (www.sonnybarger.net/main.html). Zito's web site and the dust cover of his book have a picture of him and former President Bill Clinton. The smiling former president has his arm around Zito's shoulder (www.chuckzito.com/default2.htm).

Media celebrities such as Barger, Zito, and Chapman are not the only biker club members with criminal histories. The established leaders of many clubs are, or have been, involved in criminal activities. The current National Hells Angel President George Christie Jr. and his son, George Christie III, the Vice President of the Ventura chapter of the Hells Angels, were recently sentenced to three years probation for conspiracy to sell drugs (www.gligic.org/00000007.htm). The elder Christie's ex-wife was also convicted. Father-son involvement in biker clubs and criminal activity are not uncommon. The son of the president of the Vancouver Canada East End chapter of the Hells Angels was recently sentenced to six years in prison for cocaine trafficking and extortion (Hall, 2007). The son was also a patched member of the chapter.

The Outlaws' International President, Harry "Taco" Bowman, was convicted (along with several other charges) of conspiracy to murder Barger and Christie (*United States v. Harry Bowman*, 2002). Testimony at the trial of "Taco" Bowman's successor, Outlaws International President James Wheeler, revealed that members of the Indiana and Florida Outlaws chapters who were not convicted felons were required to obtain gun permits to carry concealed weapons (www.bikernews.net/getnews.cfm?article, February 8, 2004). They acted as bodyguards at meetings and other gatherings when convicted felons could not. One Outlaws MC spokesman recently told the author that their days of "mugging and thugging" were over. The recent convictions of Outlaws international leaders calls this statement into question.

Other biker gang leaders have fared no better. The founding president of the Bandidos, Donald Eugene Chambers, an ex-Marine and Vietnam veteran, was sentenced to prison for a narcotics-related double murder. His successor, Ronnie Hodges, was imprisoned in 1988 for bombing the home of a member of a rival gang. The current Bandidos international and national president, George Wegers, pleaded guilty to RICO violations for his role in witness tampering and trafficking in stolen motorcycles and stolen vehicles. Three Bandidos chapter presidents also pleaded guilty to RICO charges ranging from threatening a federal informant to distributing methamphetamine at the same time as Wegers. The guilty pleas resulted from a two-year federal investigation into Bandidos activities in Washington, Montana, and South Dakota (Millage, 2006). In 2005, the president of the San Diego Hells Angels pleaded guilty to charges that he had conspired to distribute methamphetamines and kill members of the Mongols MC. Finally, in 2006, the former president of the Chicago Hells Angels pleaded guilty to federal drug and racketeering charges (Sher, 2006).

It is not only the Big Five outlaw motorcycle gang leaders who have been involved in criminal activities. Seven chapter presidents, one vice president, one treasurer, and seven sergeants-at-arms of the Vagos MC in Southern California were arrested in 2006 by a task force of ATF, local police, and sheriffs departments members (Risling, 2006). The crimes alleged ranged from illegal firearms to drug distribution. Vago leaders in the past have declared that it is a social club and not a criminal enterprise and have complained of law enforcement witch hunts. The arrest and convictions of established leaders of outlaw motorcycle clubs support the law enforcement argument that they are more gangs than clubs.

Many clubs/chapters are also composed of a majority of members with criminal records. The 1999 Criminal Intelligence Service Canada Annual Report stated that of the 249 Hells Angels in Canada—patched members (214) and prospects (35), 205 had criminal records, of which 105 were for drug-related crimes (www.cisc.gc.ca/AnnualReport 1999/Cisc99en/omg.htm). Denmark has the highest concentration of

European, Australian, and U.S. members of the Bandidos MC ride to the funeral of Uffe Larsen in Denmark. Larsen died in a shootout between the Bandidos and the Hells Angels at Copenhagen's international airport. *Photo courtesy of AP Photo/Joergen Jessen.*

outlaw bikers in the world. A 2004 survey by the Danish police reveled that all but one member of the Hells Angels and Bandidos had criminal records (Sher and Marsden, 2006:255). Eleven of the 18 Hells Angels MC members identified in the 2003 search warrant affidavit in Arizona had felony convictions (Search Warrant affidavit, BATF Agent Joseph Slatalla, July 2, 2003).

Criminal behavior, including murder, has been and is a prerequisite for some biker gang chapters. Prospects for Hells Angels Canadian chapters must commit crimes witnessed by other members to prove they are not cops (Lavigne, 1987). The founder of the Cleveland Hells Angels chapter says that prospects had to commit murder to become a member:

They have to kill someone . . . He has to roll his bones within six months . . . . The person he kills is someone that the intelligence will set up with security . . . If they renege on that, then they are killed . . . . He knows too much (quoted in Lavigne, 1987:72).

Law enforcement authorities say that HA members who kill for the club become members of a select group called the "Filthy Few," and wear that tattoo and a patch on their jacket (Southeast Connecticut Gang Activities Group[SE-GAG], 2002). This has been disputed as a myth by Hells Angels such as Sonny Barger and Chuck Zito (Barger, 2000; Zito, 2002). However, when Barger was called before a federal grand jury in the Southern District of New York that was investigating the criminal activity of the HAMC, he refused to answer "What is the Filthy Few?" (*Appellant v. United States*, No. 85-6528, 1985). Testimony by an FBI expert on outlaw motorcycle gangs at a 1999 evidentiary hearing revealed that the FBI in their seminars and training of law enforcement officers teaches as an accepted fact that the "Filthy Few" patch and the accompanying lightening bolts signifies that the wearer has killed for the Hells Angels (*United States v. John David*

Ward, 1999). The same expert testified that although more than 100 HA members wear the patch, none of them has ever been charged and convicted of murdering for the club. Nevertheless, law enforcement sources report that the Long Island, New York, Vice-President of the Hells Angels received the "Filthy Few" patch for shooting a Pagans member during the 2002 brawl between the two groups in Plainville, New York. Law enforcement officials allege that other biker gangs have designated enforcers who can and do kill for the club—Hells Angels' Filthy Few, Outlaws' SS squad, Pagans' Black T-shirt squad, and the Bandidos' Nomads Chapter (SE-GAG, 2002). Testimony in the Harry "Taco" Bowman case confirms this, at least for the Outlaws MC. In one federal case—*United States v. Carl Warneke et al.* (2002)—testimony revealed that one of the Outlaws defendants was awarded a patch bearing a skull with crossed pistons and an "SS" insignia for a club murder.

Some Canadian one-percent biker clubs are more into crime than biking. David "Wolf" Carroll (Quebec Nomads Hells Angels) lamented to another member, "The Nomads judge you by the size of your portfolio. If you don't have money, you're no good. Our club is no longer really a real biker gang. There are some members who have told me that they don't even like biking" (quoted in Sher and Marsden, 2003: 217). Peter Paradis, former president of the Canadian Rock Machine MC, in his autobiography states that members did not have to own or ride a motorcycle, but they had to be good drug pushers (Paradis, 2002).

There are other biker clubs reported to be more gangsters than bikers. For example, testimony in the Bowman trial mentioned earlier revealed that an "Outlaw who commits murder, attempts murder, or explodes a bomb on behalf of the Outlaws is entitled to wear 'Lightning bolts,' a Nazi-style 'SS' tattoo. An Outlaw who has spent time in jail [prison] may receive an 'LL' tattoo, which stands for 'Lounge Lizard'" (*United States v. Bowman.* 2002: 2). Lavigne (1987) states that the sentimental notion of "brotherhood" that supposedly binds the Hells Angels together has been replaced by the drug business that is now the backbone of the club. When Barger began contemplating a move from Oakland, California, to Arizona in 1994, there were no Hells Angels chapters in Arizona. He set up a fast track to patch-over the "baddest" biker gang in the state, the Dirty Dozen. Eighty-five percent of the Dirty Dozen members selected to become Angels had felony arrest records (Sher and Marsden, 2006). Barger officially changed chapters in 1998. National and international law enforcement authorities say that other biker clubs, such as the Pagans, Outlaws, and Bandidos, compete nationally and internationally for control of drug trafficking.

There are also numerous allegations that biker gangs are involved with other organized crime groups. Lavigne (1987) states that HA chapters in California, Canada, Connecticut, Missouri, Ohio, and New York have collaborated with traditional organized crime families in criminal activities, even acting as hitmen for these groups. He also states that members of the Pagans MC act as couriers, enforcers, bodyguards, and hitmen for traditional organized crime groups in Pennsylvania, New Jersey, and New York (Lavigne, 1989). The New Jersey report mentioned earlier states that both the Pagans MC and the Warlocks MC (headquartered in Philadelphia) have ties to LCN (La Cosa Nostra) groups. Lavgne (1987) says that the Florida Outlaws get their cocaine from Colombian and Cuban crime groups. Outlaws MC members have also formed alliances with traditional organized crime groups in Chicago, Tampa, and New Orleans. Crazy Joe Spaziano, an Outlaws member on Florida's death row for more than 20 years for a rape and murder he supposedly did not commit (Mello, 2001), acted as one of two bodyguards in a meeting with the Outlaws' national enforcer and Chicago's Outfit (Lavigne, 1987:212). The Criminal Intelligence Service Canada (2004) reports that the Hells Angels in Canada, particularly those in British Columbia, Ontario, and Quebec, have links to traditional (Italian-based) organized crime. Lyman and Potter (2007) also state that there have been cooperative relationships between OMGs and traditional organized crime groups since the early 1980s. The NGIA reports that Russian organized crime groups have been associated with outlaw motorcycle gangs (NAGIA, 2005: 3). In addition, the same association reports that northern California Hispanic gangs have ties to OMGs (NAGIA, 2005:8).

SUMMARY

The involvement of one-percent biker clubs/chapter in criminal activities leads law enforcement authorities and others to argue that "[t]oday's biker organizations are sophisticated, calculating, extremely violent—nothing less than the insidious new face of global organized crime" (Queen, 2005: 22). These same law enforcement authorities see biker gangs as organized and as dangerous as traditional organized crime groups such as La Cosa Nostra—and even more violent. The National Alliance of Gang Investigators Association (NAGIA) reports that the National Drug Intelligence Center views gangs—street gangs, OMGs, and prison gangs—as the primary distributors of drugs throughout the United States (NAGIA, 2005: 1). Furthermore, law enforcement officials throughout the world, including Interpol and Europol, refer to one-percent biker clubs as outlaw motorcycle gangs (OMGs) involved in international organized crime. These officials say that one-percent criminal organizations (i.e., gangs) whose members use their membership in a motorcycle club as a basis for criminal activities are literally gangsters on wheels. The available evidence supports the designation of outlaw motorcycle clubs as outlaw motorcycle *gangs* and criminal organizations.

Recall the four principles of the network approach to organized crime presented in Chapter 1:

First Principle:
All group crime begins with a dyadic network between individuals with criminally exploitable ties.

This is the basic unit in any form of criminal cooperation. As we have seen thus far, the members of one-percent biker clubs are very homogeneous in race, sex, social class, and behavior patterns, including latent and manifest dispositions for criminal behavior by many members.

Second Principle:
Networks between criminal actors will depend on a common basis of trust.

The biker subculture's key value is brotherhood—trust between bikers as a group and club members as groups of righteous bikers. One-percent bikers pledge fidelity to each other and their club forever. This may be more rhetoric than reality in many cases, but there is no denying that during their membership process these clubs seek to ensure its existence and continuation. Therefore, criminal actors in one-percent biker clubs come together in criminal networks feeling that they can trust their partners and other members (even those not involved in criminal activities) not to rat them out. In addition, the long prospecting periods of most biker clubs/gangs serves to eliminate the most unstable and untrustworthy potential members: the hard-core alcoholics, drug addicts, and the most violent.

Third Principle:
A criminal organization consists of a combination of individuals linked through criminally exploitable ties.

Some crimes require more than two actors. When the dyadic relationship requires a third person, the nucleus for organized crime appears. This occurred early on in the history of the HAMC. Criminal organizations evolve into group criminal networks—a set of three or more people linked by criminally exploitable ties. There are two criminal organizations that apply to the study of biker clubs/gangs: *economic criminal organizations,* those set up for the sole purpose of achieving material gain, and *social criminal organizations,* those that support the criminal activities of its members indirectly. It appears that some one-percent biker clubs/gangs, such as the Mongols MC and the Philadelphia Warlocks MC, were originally set up as economic criminal organizations, while others, such as the Pagans MC and the Hells Angels MC or chapters of these clubs, evolved into economic criminal organizations. Some may be more akin to social criminal organizations in which the club or chapters of the club have a substantial or majority of its members involved in criminal activity. This is an empirical question addressed in the next chapter.

REFERENCES

Auger, M. (2001). *The Biker Who Shot Me: Recollections of a Crime Reporter.* Toronto: McClelland & Stewart.

Barger, R., with K. Zimmerman and K. Zimmerman (2000). *Hell's Angel: The Life and Times of Sonny Barger and the Hell's Angels Motorcycle Club.* New York: William Morrow.

Barker, T. (2006). *Busting Biker Gangs.* Paper presented at the Academy of Criminal Justice Annual Meeting. Baltimore, Maryland, February 2006.

Bowe, B. (1994). *Born to Be Wild.* New York: Warner Books.

Brenner, S.W. (2002). "Organized Cybercrime? How Cyberspace May Affect the Structure of Criminal Relationships." *North Carolina Journal of Law and Technology* 4(1):1-50.

B.W. (1980). "Feds Step Up Biker Gang Probe." *American Bar Association Journal* 66(12):1508.

California Department of Justice (2004). *Organized Crime in California: Annual Report to the California Legislature 2004.*

Charles, G. (2002). *Bikers: Legend, Legacy, and Life.* London: Independent Music Press.

Cohen, S. (1980). *Folk Devils and Moral Panics: The Creation of the Mods and Rockers.* Oxford, UK: Martin Robertson.

Davis, R.H. (1982). "Outlaw Motorcyclists: A Problem for Law Enforcement." *FBI Law Enforcement Bulletin* 13-22.

Detroit, M. (1994). *Chain of Evidence: A True Story of Law Enforcement and One Women's Bravery.* New York: Penguin Books.

Fuglsang, R.S. (1997). *Motorcycle Menace: Media Genres and the Construction of a Deviant Culture.* Unpublished Ph.D. Dissertation, The University of Iowa.

Hall, N. (2007). "Low-ranking Hells Angel Gets Six Years." *Vancouver Sun*, April 11, 2007. Found at: http://www.canada.com

Harris, M. (1985). *Bikers: Birth of a Modern Day Outlaw.* London: Faber & Faber.

Haut, F. (1999). "Organized Crime on Two Wheels: Motorcycle Gangs." *ICPR* 474-475.

ICPO-Interpol (1984). "Motorcycle Gangs." Report by Division II of the Interpol General Secretariat, May 10-11, 1984.

Johnson, W.C. (1981). "Motorcycle Gangs and Organized Crime." *The Police Chief* 32-33 & 78.

Kaye, H.R. (1970). *A Place in Hell: The Inside Story of 'Hell's Angels'—The World's Wildest Outsiders.* London: New English Library [First published in 1968 by Holloway Publishing, USA].

Kingsbury, K. (1995). *The Snake and the Spider.* New York: Dell.

Lavigne, Y. (1987a). *Hell's Angels: Taking Care of Business.* Toronto: Ballantine Books.

Lavigne, Y. (1987b). *Hell's Angels: Three Can Keep a Secret if Two Are Dead.* New York: Kensington.

Lavigne, Y. (1996). *Hells Angels: Into the Abyss.* Toronto: HarperCollins.

Lavigne, Y. (1999). *Hells Angels at War.* Toronto: HarperCollins.

Lyman, M.D., and G.W. Potter (2007). *Organized Crime,* 4th ed. Upper Saddle River, NJ: Pearson/Prentice Hall.

Lyon, D. (2003). *The Bikeriders.* San Francisco: Chronicle Books.

Lowe, M. (1988). *Conspiracy of Brothers.* Toronto: Seal Books.

Mandelkau, J. (1971). *Buttons: The Making of a President.* London: Sphere Books.

Martineau, P. (2003). *I Was a Killer for the Hell's Angels: the True Story of Serge Quesnel.* Toronto: McClelland & Stewart.

Mayson, B., with T. Marco (1982). *Fallen Angel: Hell's Angel to Heaven's Saint.* Garden City, NY: Doubleday & Co.

Mello, M. (2001). *The Wrong Man: A True Story of Innocence on Death Row.* Minneapolis: University of Minnesota Press.

Millage, K. (2006). "Major Bandidos Members Plead Guilty to Racketeering." *The Bellingham Herald*, May 9, 2006.

NGCRC (2004). "A Special Report of the NGCRC: White Racist Extremists Gang Members-A Behavioral Profile." In G.W. Knox and C. Robinson, eds., *Gang Profiles: An Anthology.* Peotone, IL: New Chicago School Press.

NAGIA (2005). *2005 National Gang Threat Assessment.* National Alliance of Gang Investigators Association: Bureau of Justice Assistance.

Operation ROUGHRIDER (1985). "After Three Years on the Road, FBI Arrests "Angels" in Nationwide Raid." *Narcotics Control Digest* 4-5, May 15, 1985.

Organized Crime Consulting Committee (1986). *1986 Report of the Organized Crime Consulting Committee.* Ohio Attorney General.

Paradis, P. (2002). *Nasty Business: One Biker's Gang's War Against the Hell's Angels*. Toronto: HarperCollins.

Pratt, A. (2002). "Modern America and its Discontents: The Ride-Hard, Die-Free Fantasy of Bike Week." *Americana: The Journal of Popular Culture* 1(1):1-16.

Queen, W. (2005). *Under and Alone*. New York: Random House.

Reid, K.E. (1981). "Expansionism—Hell's Angels Style." *Police Chief* 48(5):38-40.

Reynolds, F., as told to Michael McClure (1967). *Freewheeling Frank: Secretary of the Angels*. New York: Grove Press.

Reynolds, T. (2000). *Wild Ride: How Outlaw Motorcycle Myth Conquered America*. New York: Grove Press.

Risling, G. (2006). "Vagos Motorcycle Club Targeted in Southern California Crime Sweep." Associated Press, March 10, 2006.

Sanger, D. (2005). *Hell's Witness*. Toronto: Penguin Group.

Shellow, R., and D.V. Roemer (1966). "The Riot That Didn't Happen." *Social Problems* 14:221-233.

Sher, J. (2006). "Hell's Angels' Road Gets Rougher: The Outlaw Gang is Leaving a Trail of Death and Busts." *San Francisco Chronicle*, May 7, 2006.

Sher, J., and W. Marsden (2003). *The Road to Hell: How Bikers Are Conquering Canada*. Toronto: Alfred Knopf.

Sher, J,. and W. Marsden (2006). *Angels of Death: Inside the Biker Gang's Crime Empire*. New York: Carroll & Graf.

Simpson, L., and S. Harvey (2001). *Brothers in Arms: the Inside Story of Two Bikie Gangs*. Crows Nest, NSW, Australia: Allen & Unwin.

Smith, R. (2002). "Dangerous Motorcycle Gangs: A Facet of Organized Crime in the Mid Atlantic Region." *Journal of Gang Research* 9(4):33-44.

Southeastern Connecticut Gang Activities Group (SE-GAG). (2002). *Motorcycle Gangs*. Found at: http://www.segag.org/frmcgang.html/

Thompson, H.S. (1996). *Hell's Angels: A Strange and Terrible Saga*. New York: Ballantine Books.

United States v. Bowman (8/20/2002), No. 01-14305). Found at: http:///law.emory.edu/11 circuit/aug2002/01-14305.opm.html

United States v. John David Ward (July 1, 1999). Nos.SA 99-01M and SA 99-0200M-002. Found at: http://80-web.lexis-nexis.com

Veno, A. (2003). *The Brotherhoods: Inside the Outlaw Motorcycle Clubs*. Crows Nest, NSW, Australia: Allen & Unwin.

Wolf, D.R. (1999). *The Rebels: A Brotherhood of Outlaw Bikers*. Toronto: University of Toronto Press.

Wethern, G., and V. Colnett (1978). *A Wayward Angel*. New York: Richard Marek.

Wood, J. (2003). "Hell's Angels and the Illusion of the Counterculture." *The Journal of Popular Culture* 37(2): 336-351.

Zito, Z., with J. Layden (2002). *Street Justice*. New York: St. Martin's Press.

7

Biker Gangs as Organized Crime

INTRODUCTION

In the late 1980s, the academic community began to view organized motorcycle gangs as organized crime groups. For example, in 1990, Boston University Professor Edwin J. Delattre stated that four American "white-supremacist" outlaw motorcycle gangs (the Hells Angels, the Outlaws, the Pagans, and the Bandidos) were—along with indigenous black street gangs and Hispanic gangs—becoming the new faces of United States organized crime (Delattre, 1990). Quinn and Koch recently opined that "most law enforcers and academic experts agree that the largest one-percent motorcycle clubs are a form of organized crime despite their origins as barroom brawlers" (Quinn and Koch, 2003:281). Law enforcement authorities are in agreement that one-percent bikers clubs are engaged in organized crime. Furthermore, based on the number of criminal prosecutions of one-percent clubs and the convictions of their leaders/officers, it appears that some one-percent biker clubs or chapters of these clubs, particularly the Big Five (the Hells Angels, the Outlaws, the Bandidos, the Pagans, and the Sons of Silence) are more like criminal gangs (organized for profit through crime) than like clubs (voluntary associations based on an interest in motorcycles). Even if not criminal organizations, many clubs are social organizations that have a large number of members who are involved in criminal activity. Nevertheless, there are some who caution against labeling all one- percent motorcycle clubs as organized crime groups (Albanese, 2004; Veno, 2003). Albanese and Veno among others point to the clubs and members of these clubs who are not involved in serious criminal activities or organized crime. There is support for both positions. In fact, one's view often depends on the focus of analysis—the clubs themselves or members of clubs.

Using clubs as the focus of analysis, there is no doubt that the Big Five clubs or chapters of these clubs, along with a number of other one-percent biker clubs, have and are engaged in organized crime, particularly drug trafficking. However, the few research studies of outlaw bikers from the seminal work of Wolf (1991) and forward have found members who have broken the law but not for profit and who have not organized their activities when engaged in criminal activities. Albanese (2004) has observed that OMGs vary widely in the extent to which they engage in criminal activity, and some law enforcement sources support this thesis. Law enforcement organizations provide evidence that all the members of some biker clubs (or gangs) are not engaged in organized crime or any serious crime, for that matter. For example, the MAGLO-CLEN Assessment on Outlaw Motorcycle Gangs, using clubs as the focus of analysis, states that "[o]utlaw motorcycle gangs are sophisticated, organized, criminal organizations that have extended their sphere of influence around the globe in a relatively short period of time" (2003:1). However, this same law enforcement source recognizes that in some instances ". . . [club] criminal acts are endorsed by the leadership of the club, and at other times these criminal enterprises are the work of a handful of individual members" (MAGLOCLEN Assessment, 2003:4).

GANG AND MEMBER CRIMINAL ACTIVITY

Focus: Gang/Club Criminal Activity

There has been very little data gathered on the criminal activities of one-percent biker gangs/clubs using gangs/clubs as the focus of analysis. However, the National Alliance of Gang Investigators' Associations (NAGIA) in their *2005 National Gang Threat Assessment* reports that a compilation of information from the FBI, the National Drug Intelligence Center (NDIC), and the International Outlaw Motorcycle Gang Investigators Association (IOMGIA) reveals that four of the major outlaw motorcycle gangs—Hells Angels, Bandidos, Outlaws, and Pagans—have been involved in a variety of criminal activities (see Table 7.1).

Table 7.1: Criminal Activities of Outlaw Motorcycle Gangs

Criminal Activities	Hells Angels	Bandidos	Outlaws	Pagans
Drugs				
Production	X	X	X	
Smuggling	X	X	X	
Transportation	X	X	X	
Distribution	X	X	X	X
Weapons Trafficking	X	X	X	X
Murder	X	X	X	X
Prostitution	X	X	X	
Money Laundering	X	X	X	
Explosives Violations	X	X	X	X
Bombings	X	X	X	X
Motorcycle and Motorcycle-Parts Thefts	X	X	X	X
Intimidation	X	X	X	
Extortion	X	X	X	X
Arson	X	X	X	X
Assault	X	X	X	X
Insurance Fraud	X	X	X	
Kidnapping	X	X	X	
Robbery	X	X	X	
Theft	X	X	X	
Stolen Property	X	X	X	
Counterfeiting	X	X	X	

Source: Modified from National Alliance of Gang Investigators, *2005 National Gang Threat Assessment,* page 14. The number of times each gang was involved in the criminal activities is not shown. The time period for gathering the information is also not shown.

Drug trafficking is generally considered to be the number-one crime activity engaged in by organized crime groups. According to the NAGIA report, all the OMGs examined were involved in some form of drug trafficking. The Pagans MC was reported to be engaged in the distribution of drugs but not the production, smuggling, and transportation of drugs. All the gangs were involved in the organized crime activities of weapons trafficking, motorcycle and motorcycle parts thefts, extortion, counterfeiting, and insurance fraud. The four gangs were also involved in the violent activities of murder, explosive violations, bombings, and arson, all crimes that typically accompany or facilitate organized crime activities. Surprisingly, according to the NAGIA report, the Pagans were not involved in money laundering, a criminal activity made necessary by organized crime involvement, or prostitution, another typical organized crime activity.

Also using gangs/clubs as the unit of analysis, Table 7.2 is a compilation of organized crime activities by biker gangs/clubs, large and small, taken from a variety of sources in the 10 years between 1995 and 2005—newspapers, court cases, and so on. It is meant to be illustrative, not exhaustive.

Figure 7.1: Organized Crime Activities by Selected One-Percent Biker Gangs

Avengers MC

Now, here's the deal, gentleman. I'm gonna tell you guys flat out: Anybody in this room that doesn't want to be involved in criminal activity, you can be excused.

I'm serious. You're excused because our backs are against the . . . wall, man. If we have to start doing felonious . . . stealing motorcycles, dealing dope or whatever the . . . that we got to do (Elyria, Ohio, Chapter President, Avengers Motorcycle Club, 1999-Caniglia, 1999).

In 1999, Tom Hakaim, a prominent South Lorain, Ohio, businessman and treasurer and road captain of the Avengers MC, pleaded guilty to charges of racketeering and attempting to commit a violent crime on behalf of an enterprise. Hakaim testified against fellow members to have several charges dropped (Anon. 1, 1999).

In 2001, a member of the Avengers MC was convicted of interstate commerce facilitation in the commission of murder for hire, interstate travel in aid of a crime of violence, and conspiracy to distribute cocaine. The cocaine supplier was the Medellin Cartel in Colombia (*Wright v. U.S.*, Civil Case No. 05-71569, Crim. Case No. 96-80876).

Bandidos MC

George Wegers, the international president and chapter president of the Bellingham Chapter of the Bandidos MC, pleaded guilty to federal racketeering and conspiracy charges (Millage, 2006).

Breed & Pennsylvania Warlocks MC

The Breed and the Pennsylvania-based Warlocks MC were once bitter enemies, but in 2006 members and leaders in both biker gangs were arrested and charged with cooperative crimes of meth and crystal meth (ice) distribution. Arrested were the presidents of the Pennsylvania chapter of the Warlocks and the Breed's New Jersey Mother Club. Also arrested were five of the seven-member Pennsylvania Breed's executive board and two executive members of the New Jersey Breed. Seized were 22 pounds of crystal meth; $500,000; 44 firearms, including a submachine gun; 10 explosive devices; numerous vehicles; and 24 motorcycles (Anon. 2, 2006).

Diablos MC

In 1998, the president of the Connecticut Chapter of the Diablos MC and 12 other members of the Connecticut and Massachusetts chapters were charged with RICO and racketeering charges. The president of the Connecticut chapter was

Figure 7.1—continued

convicted of 26 charges, including RICO, murder for hire, narcotics, and auto theft violations. (*U.S. District Court for the District of Massachusetts*, 145 F. Supp. 2d 111; 2001 U.S. Dist. Lexis 5362).

Freelancers MC

Following the 2004 arrest and seizure of "substantial quantities of methamphetamine and cocaine," the founding member and former vice president of the New Hampshire Freelancers MC was found guilty of possession with intent to distribute dangerous drugs (*U.S. v. Belton*, No. 04-cr-192-01-JD).

Hells Angels MC

On August 12, 1986, members of the Outlaws motorcycle club shot and killed John Cleve Webb, a member of the Anchorage, Alaska, chapter of the Hells Angels in Louisville, Kentucky. Shortly thereafter, Barger, a member of the Oakland chapter of the Hells Angels, said that it was time to start killing Outlaws again. [Barger was later convicted of conspiracy charges related to attempts at revenge.] (*U.S. v. Barger,* Nos. 89-5606, 89-5607 1990).

A defense attorney and three Hells Angels members of the Troy, New York, chapter pleaded guilty to being a part of a drug ring that distributed methamphetamines in central New York (*New York Lawyer,* April 29, 2004).

The president of the San Diego chapter of the Hells Angels pleaded guilty to racketeering charges—distributing methamphetamine and conspiracy to kill members of the Mongols MC. Nine other members also pleaded guilty to racketeering charges (Soto, 2005).

The former president of the Chicago Chapter of the Hells Angels pleaded guilty to federal racketeering charges related to the sale of cocaine and methamphetamine (Anon. 2, 2006).

Two officers (president and former president) of the Spring Valley, Illinois, chapter of the Hells Angels pleaded guilty to selling drugs, to intimidation, and to robbery charges (Kravetz, 2006).

Iron Horsemen MC

In 2002, two members of the Maine Iron Horsemen MC were charged and subsequently found guilty of possession with intent to distribute a controlled substance (oxycodone and methamphetamine) (*U.S. v. Fournier*, Crim. No. 02-57-B-S, U.S. District Court for the District Court of Maine 2002 US. Dist. Lexis 20732).

Loners MC

A 1999 arrest led to the conviction of two Loners MC officers (former president of the Quapaw, Oklahoma, chapter and the president of the Kentucky chapter) for the production and distribution of methamphetamine (*U.S. v. Cervine*, No. 00-40024-21-SAC).

Outlaws MC

[Harry "Taco" Bowman] served as international president for 13 years, until 1997. As international president, Bowman handled matters large and small, from setting the Outlaws' policies regarding other gangs to monitoring the activities of members.

In the early 1990s. the Warlocks, another Florida club, allied with the Hells Angels, began selling drugs on their behalf. This ignited a war between the Out-

Figure 7.1—continued

laws and the Warlocks. When the Outlaws learned that Raymond "Bear" Chafin, a former member [of the Outlaws], was the leader of a Warlocks chapter in Edgewater, Bowman told Hicks to find Chafin and kill him. [Chafin was later killed by an Outlaws prospect who received his patch and lightening bolts].

On New Year's Eve 1993, Bowman announced a meeting of all Outlaws at a party in Fort Lauderdale. During the meeting, Bowman announced that the Outlaws would escalate their hostilities in 1994, showing no tolerance for Hells Angels or their sympathizers. [The Outlaws' national president has final authority over all club activities.]

. . . At a 1994 meeting in Chicago, Bowman told Hicks [Wayne "Joe Black" Hicks. Bowman's "right-hand man"] and others that an Outlaw had become a snitch. Bowman said that the snitch would be killed and explained that the killing would be made to look like an enemy had done it. He also said that the murdered snitch would be given an Outlaw funeral. [The Outlaw snitch was later killed and received an Outlaw funeral.]

. . . At a meeting near the end of 1994, Bowman, . . . announced that the Outlaws would take the war against the Hells Angels to California. Bowman planned to send a group of trustworthy Outlaws to California to conduct surveillance on, and possibly assassinate, either Sonny Barger, the international president of the Hells Angels, or George Christie, a national officer [Outlaws went to California but no one was assassinated]. (*U.S. v. Bowman*, No. 01-14305).

Pagans MC

The 1998 arrests and subsequent convictions of 27 Pagans for conspiracy to commit murder, extortion, arson, weapons violations and assault eliminated four Pagans chapters on Long Island, New York (MAGLOCLEN Assessment, 2003:17).

Renegades MC

In November 1999, 28 members of the Virginia Chapter of the Renegades MC were convicted of distributing methamphetamines in the Tidewater area. The drug trafficking had gone on for several years (MAGLOCLEN Assessment, 2003:43).

Road Saints MC

In 1996, the President of the Columbus, Ohio, chapter of the Road Saints MC was charged and convicted of possession of a firearm by a person convicted of a crime punishable for a term exceeding one year (*U.S. v. Scarberry*, No. CR2-98-00008).

Sons of Silence MC

In 1995, 13 Sons of Silence MC members were charged and subsequently found guilty of conspiracy to commit racketeering; conspiracy to distribute and possession to distribute methamphetamine; obstruction of justice; possessing with intent to sell a motor vehicle part knowing that the vehicle identification number of the part had been removed, obliterated, tampered with, and altered; money laundering; the commission of violent crimes in aid of racketeering activity; and engaging in a continuing enterprise (*U.S. v. Gruber et al.*, No. CR(4-MJM. 1998).

Sundowners MC

In 1998, several members of the Sundowners MC were tried and convicted of conspiracy to sell narcotics, conspiracy to distribute methamphetamine, and use

Figure 7.1—continued

---

of the telephone in the commission of a drug offense (*U.S. v. Johnson* No. 99-CR-23B).

Warlocks MC

In 2005, the "enforcer" for the Shenandoah County, Virginia, chapter of the Warlocks MC [Florida-based Warlocks] pleaded guilty to numerous charges related to the distribution of drugs (*U.S. v. Dezzutti*, No. 5-05CR00005-1).

Related to the case above, the acting enforcer of the Brevard County, Florida, chapter of the Warlocks MC pleaded guilty to numerous charges related to the distribution of drugs (*U.S. v. Framelli*, No. 5-05CR00005-2).

Focus: Member Criminal Activity

As stated, there is very little data on outlaw motorcycle gangs. However, there has been one attempt by law enforcement officials to measure OMG club and member criminal activity through survey research. The Bureau of Justice funds the MAGLOCLEN (Middle Atlantic-Great Lakes Organized Crime Law Enforcement Network) Regional Information Sharing System (RISS) as part of the government's efforts to address gang violence (www.ojp.usdoj.gov/BJA/topics/law_enforce.html). In 2003, MAGLOCLEN surveyed 1,061 member agencies on criminal activities of OMGs in the region, with 819 responding. Thirty percent of the agencies reported OMG activity in their areas within the years between 2000 and 2003). Sixty-two percent of the agencies had arrested OMG members during the last four years. There were 201 agencies that reported that investigations (undercover, task force, and informant) and intelligence were the leading causes of OMG arrests, but the single leading cause was routine traffic arrests in 74 agencies (see Table 7.2.).

Table 7.2: Causes of Arrest by MAGLOCLEN Agencies

Cause	Number of Agencies
Customs Interdiction	3
Undercover Investigations	36
Task Force Investigations	42
Citizen complaints	58
Informants Investigations	61
Intelligence	62
Routine Traffic Stops	74
Other	21

Source: Modified from MAGLOCLEN Assessment, 2003:15.

Findings related to the association between OMGs and other organized crime groups in the regions reporting (with the club as focus of analysis) are shown in Table 7.3. The OMGs were most likely to be associated with traditional organized crime groups such as the Mafia/Cosa Nostra (41 agencies). A disturbing finding is the number of agencies responding that the OMGs in their areas had associations with white supremacist groups (22) and street gangs (23). The report also stated that OMGs use street gangs in their narcotics distribution activities to isolate club members from law enforcement (MAGLO-CLEN, 2003:18). In these cases, one or two club members controlled the activities of the street gang, further isolating the club and making the prosecution of OMG leaders and members more difficult.

Table 7.3: Organized Crime Groups Associated with Outlaw Motorcycle Gangs

OC Groups	Number of Agencies
Russian Organized Crime	1
Colombian Organized Crime	6
Asian Organized Crime	6
White Supremacists Groups	22
Street Gangs	23
Traditional Organized Crime [Mafia, La Cosa Nostra]	41
Other	6

Source: Modified from MAGLOCLEN Assessment, 2003:19.

Survey respondents reported that the primary source of income for OMGs in their areas is the manufacture and distribution of illegal narcotics. Again, this finding is more related to the gang/club and not to its members. When asked about the occurrence of various types of crimes committed by OMG members in their jurisdiction, some interesting results were obtained (see Table 7.4).

Table 7.4: Crimes Committed by Outlaw Motorcycle Gang Members

(Agencies asked whether they experienced members committing these crimes frequently, occasionally, or never)			
Crime	Frequently	Occasionally	Never
Narcotics Distribution	49%	41%	10%
Narcotics Manufacturing	29%	47%	24%
Assault	24%	64%	12%
Motorcycle Theft	21%	51%	28%
Money Laundering	17%	36%	47%

Table 7.4—continued

Witness Intimidation	16%	57%	27%
Fencing Stolen Property	15%	54%	31%
Prostitution	14%	39%	47%
Firearms Trafficking	12%	55%	33%
DL/Registration/Title			
Fraud	11%	38%	51%
Extortion	9%	48%	43%
Automobile Theft	8%	49%	43%
Gambling	7%	34%	59%
Rape	4%	34%	61%
Attempted Homicide	3%	53%	44%
Robbery	3%	45%	52%
Arson	3%	38%	59%
Home Invasions	2%	25%	73%
Homicide	2%	50%	48%
Counterfeit	1%	19%	80%
Bombings	1%	25%	74%
Other	2%	11%	47%

Source: Modified from MAGLOCLEN Assessment, 2003:20.

Even though the agencies reported that 90 percent of the OMG members in their area had engaged in narcotics distribution frequently or occasionally, respondents reported that 10 percent of the *members* had never done so. Seventy-six percent of the OMG members were involved in narcotic manufacturing, but 24 percent had never committed this organized crime activity. Moreover, large numbers of OMG members never engaged in the organized crime activities of money laundering (47%), fencing stolen property (31%), and firearms trafficking (33%). The law enforcement agencies also reported that 28 percent of the OMG members had never engaged in motorcycle thefts and 43 percent had not engaged in automobile thefts, a crime typically associated with outlaw motorcycle gangs. Furthermore, although gang rapes created the original moral panic associated with biker gangs, respondents reported that 61 percent of the OMG members never committed rapes. However, only 12 percent of the members had never committed an assault, which serves as evidence of the violent nature of these gangs/clubs.

These results indicate that although the law enforcement respondents believe a majority of the members of these clubs/gangs are involved in serious and organized criminal activities, they also believe that some members are not. Therefore, the group dynamics and social structure within these clubs/gangs are important for an understanding of biker gangs.

There is also limited data on OMG-member criminal activity outside the United States. In Sweden, there are 300 motorcycle clubs, 20 of them classified as "motorcycle gangs" (National Council for Crime Prevention, 1996). Reports in Sweden focused on the behavior of members and concluded that "motorcycle gangs are seen as confederations that entertain certain subcultural values, and in which certain forms of organized crime are present, although the groups are not per se criminal organizations" (National Council for Crime Prevention, 1996:51). The report states that 75 of the 100 Hells Angels and Bandidos members have been formally charged with crimes. They have been brought to trial 756 times. However, 20 members have been responsible for 505 of the 756 trials. The report concludes that "Swedish motorcycle gangs' crimes are mainly committed by certain groups of members, and not necessarily in an organized form" (National Council for Crime Prevention, 1996:51).

GROUP CRIMINAL ACTIVITY AND EVOLUTION INTO CRIMINAL ORGANIZATIONS

In investigating member criminal activity Quinn and Koch (2003) point out that the informal groupings within clubs is a topic often neglected in the discussions of biker clubs. These informal groupings encourage or discourage certain forms of criminality. At the group level in biker clubs/gangs, it is common for cliques of like-minded members (sharing criminally exploitable ties) to commit criminal acts together, sometimes without the knowledge of their fellow brothers (Quinn and Koch, 2003:291). Quinn and Koch (2003:299) also say:

> None of the available evidence contradicts the thesis that these criminal conspiracies are the creation of cliques, factions, or chapters that are merely facilitated by the club as a trustworthy network rather than directly created by it [Lampe's social criminal organization].

> This statement fails to recognize the existence of biker economic criminal organizations. However, it makes clear that the extent of member and group criminal involvement is crucial to defining the club as a club or a gang.

As stated earlier, those one-percent biker gangs that fit the definition of criminal organizations at their origin or at a later stage of their development are considered *economic* criminal organizations—set up to engage in crime for profit. Those one-percent clubs or chapters of these clubs that evolved into criminal organizations are or were *social* criminal organizations that facilitated the criminal activities of their members only indirectly. Economic criminal organizations such as the Mongols MC and the Pennsylvania-based Warlocks MC came into being for the purpose of committing organized crime activities. It is an empirical question as to whether all the chapters of these two clubs are economic criminal organizations, but the available evidence and law enforcement sources tend to support the argument that the members of the Pennsylvania-based Warlocks MC are literally "gangsters on two wheels."

Social criminal organizations such as many biker clubs and chapters of clubs evolve or have evolved into club/chapter-sponsored organized crime. At some point in the evolution of a one-percent biker club or chapters of these clubs, this evolution happened relatively early in their history. According to Barger (2000), Thompson (1967), and Wethern (1991), this happened to the Hells Angels in the mid- to late 1960s as they moved into organized drug trafficking. Prior to this time, individual or small groups of HA members had engaged in drug dealing, but it was not the main focus of the clubs. The expanding drug trade caused other biker clubs, such as the Outlaws MC

A Hells Angels MC member stands defiantly outside the group's clubhouse in Sparks, Nevada, on December 3, 2003, vowing to fight for the return of items seized during a federal raid. Federal agents raided Hells Angels motorcycle gang hangouts across the West, making 55 arrests after a two-year undercover investigation into drugs and guns. *Photo courtesy of AP Photo/Debra Reid.*

and the other California clubs, to evolve into criminal organizations and resulted in an increase in violence as the clubs (now gangs) competed with each other for territorial control.

CRIMINAL ORGANIZATION CONTINUUM

Whether any particular one-percent biker club or chapter of a club is an organized crime entity lies along a criminal organization continuum depending on the members' involvement in organized crime activities or whether the officers and leadership are involved. On the left side of the continuum are the one-percent clubs or chapters of clubs that live the deviant life style of the one-percent biker but no members engage in organized criminal activities. Members who do engage in serious criminal activity risk losing their patch. These clubs are true motorcycle clubs. The categories of clubs and gangs are ideal types that exist along a continuum of biker clubs so that gradations of one-percent clubs will fit in between. Law enforcement authorities have a tendency to place all one-percent clubs on the extreme (gang) end of the continuum, while club and biker spokesmen would place the clubs on the other end as clubs. Complicating the placement of any one club or chapter along the continuum is the tacit support of fellow members for their criminal brothers because of the Biker's Code of Brotherhood.

Those clubs in which individual members or small groups of members engage in organized criminal activities, sometimes without the knowledge of the members or leaders or with their tacit support, are *social criminal organizations*. Social criminal organizations provide the basis for evolution into criminal gangs.

Those clubs or chapters of clubs in which all the members are involved in organized criminal activities at the direction of the leadership coalition are examples of *economic criminal organizations* and criminal gangs organized for profit through crime. Many one-percent biker gangs of all sizes, such as the Mongols, the Pennsylvania-based Warlocks, the Renegades, and the Dirty Dozen, appear to fit this category. Numerous chapters of all the one-percent biker clubs, particularly the Big Five (Hells Angels, Bandidos, Outlaws, Pagans, and the Sons of Silence), can be placed in this category also. Once the leadership and the majority of the members of any one chapter decide to engage in organized criminal activities, they can ensure the safe operation of their activities through the membership process by selecting only those prospects who have engaged or will engage in crime. Those members who do not engage in criminal activities will provide tacit support to their fellow brothers because of the Biker's Code of Brotherhood.

Figure 7.2: Continuum of One-Percent Motorcycle Clubs as Criminal Organizations

Clubs	Social Criminal Organizations	Gangs

CONCLUSION

All one-percent biker clubs are deviant clubs, but they are all not criminal gangs organized for profit through crime. All the clubs are not criminal organizations engaged in organized crime activities. Some clubs or chapters of clubs operating as gangs have members who follow the deviant lifestyle of the only biker, but they do not engage in serious criminal activity. Whether the club or chapter is a gang or criminal organization depends on the extent of the involvement of its members and the leaders in criminal activities. In other words, there is a continuum of one-percent motorcycle clubs as criminal organizations. Gangs are on one end of the continuum, and pure clubs are on the other, with numerous clubs or chapters of clubs that are social criminal organizations in between.

REFERENCES

Albanese, J.S. (2007). *Organized Crime in Our Times,* 5th ed. Newark, NJ: LexisNexis Matthew Bender.

Anon. 1 (1999). *Organized Crime Digest*, October 6, 1999.

Anon. 2 (2006). "Meth Arrests Hurt 2 Motorcycle Clubs: Breed and Warlock Ties." *The Philadelphia Daily News*, July 7, 2006.

Barger, R., with K. Zimmerman and K. Zimmerman (2000). *Hell's Angels: The Life and Times of Sonny Barger and the Hell's Angels Motorcycle Club.* New York: HarperCollins.

Delattre, E.J. (1990). "New Faces of Organized Crime." *American Enterprise* (May/June):38-45.

Kravetz, A. (2006). "Two Hells Angels Members Plead Guilty." *Journal Star*, February 9, 2006.

MAGLOCLEN Assessment (2003). *Outlaw Motorcycle Gangs.* Publisher not listed.

National Council for Crime Prevention (BRA) (1996). *Crime among Motorcycle Gangs.* BRA-report 1996:6.

Quinn, J., and D.S. Koch (2003). "The Nature of Criminality Within One-percent Motorcycle Clubs." *Deviant Behavior* 24:281-305.

Soto, O.R. (2005). "Local Hells Angels Boss Gets Prison as Racketeer." *Union Tribune,* September 23, 2005.

Thompson, H.S. (1967). *Hell's Angels: The Strange and Terrible Saga of the Outlaw Motorcycle Gangs.* New York: Ballantine Books.

Veno, A. (2003). *The Brotherhoods: Inside the Outlaw Motorcycle Clubs.* Crows Nest, NSW, Australia: Allen & Unwin.

Wolf, D.J. (1991). *The Rebels: A Brotherhood of Outlaw Bikers.* Toronto: University of Toronto Press.

8

Criminals Without Borders: Exporting American Organized Crime

INTRODUCTION

The social-outcast image of American outlaw bikers popular in the 1950s and 1960s transformed outlaw bikers into media celebrities and fostered the image of a biker subculture (Reynolds, 2000). The image was carried overseas by the entertainment media, creating a desire to become a member of the American biker subculture and leading to a number of Hells Angels imitators and indigenous outlaw clubs, who accepted the one-percent biker lifestyle (Barker, 2004; Harris; 1985; Mandelkau, 1971). At one time, the American bikers who described themselves as one-percenters and their international imitators and fellow club members lived the life of drinking binges, brawls, and rowdiness with a true sense of alliance and fellowship. However, as described in Chapter 7, there is a darker side to these clubs. Today, many chapters of these clubs here and abroad resemble gangs organized more around criminal activities and the profit motive than motorcycle clubs organized around partying and brotherhood. Many experts, particularly law enforcement authorities, such as the Los Angeles Police Department, say that outlaw motorcycle gangs are criminal organizations whose members use their membership in a motorcycle club as a basis for criminal activities (Haut, 1999).

Outlaw motorcycle gangs have been called the "only organized crime group developed in the United States (without ethnic ties) that is being exported around the world" (Smith, 1998: 54). One law enforcement expert on OMGs says that "[b]iker gangs are the only sophisticated organized crime groups that we export from the United States" (Trethaway and Katz, 1998). To further strengthen this argument, many biker gangs have established ties and working relationships with international organized crime groups such as La Cosa Nostra, Colombian cartels, and even the Chinese Triads (Barker, 2004; Haut, 1999; Trethaway and Katz, 1998). OMG members have acted as contract killers for traditional OC groups (Smith, 2002). Furthermore, international organizations such as Interpol, Europol, and the United Nations recognize the criminal potential of American-based outlaw motorcycle gangs. Interpol categorizes OMGs with Mafia-type organized crime organizations: highly structured hierarchies, internal rules of discipline, codes of ethics [sic], and diversity of illegal and legitimate affairs (Kendall, 1998).

INTERNATIONAL EXPANSION

Interlocking networks with indigenous OMGs in other countries allowed American-based OMGs to link common criminal enterprises and the benefits derived from these. This marked the entrance of these clubs, now gangs, into the global marketplace of crime. The international implications of American-based OMGs were recognized by the law enforcement community in the early 1980s (Doughtie, 1986). In a 1984 report from the General Secretariat of Interpol, the Hells Angels MC and the Outlaws MC were reported to have chapters in Canada that were involved in organized crime activities (Interpol, 1984). The report stated that the Hells Angels were the only motorcycle gang with chapters in 12 countries (seven Western European countries— Great Britain, West Germany, Netherlands, Denmark, Switzerland, France, Austria, Australia, New Zealand, Canada, and the United States). Since that time, the Angels have expanded internationally and other U.S. OMGs have established chapters in countries outside the United States.

In 1991, Interpol created Operation Rocker to deal with the rapid expansion of American-based OMGs throughout the world (Smith, 1998). Named after the banners on the top and bottom of the clubs' colors, Project Rocker (no longer in existence) had the following objectives:

- to identify motorcycle gangs that are engaged in continuous criminal activity
- to identify each gang's membership, hierarchy, modus operandi, and specific criminal activity

- to correlate the information for analysis and dissemination

- to assist member countries in the exchange of criminal intelligence information, and;

- to identify specific contact officers within the NCBs [Interpol's National Central Bureau in member countries] and law enforcement agencies having expertise with outlaw motorcycle gangs.

In 2000, in addition to the United States, there were 28 countries cooperating in Operation Rocker. These countries included all those with chapters of the Hells Angels. A Project Rocker Newsletter was initiated in 1998 (McClure, 2000). The newsletter contained international OMG activities from NCB reports and other intelligence sources. There was also a yearly meeting of those involved in Operation Rocker. Operation Rocker had some success in dealing with OMGs, but it did not stop their expansion.

The International Outlaw Motorcycle Gang Investigators Association (IOMGIA) was "organized to promote training and development of law enforcement professionals involved in the investigations of non-traditional organized crime groups, primarily outlaw motorcycle gangs . . ."(www.iomgia.com).

Figure 8.1: Interpol

Interpol is the world's largest international police organization, with 184 member countries. Created in 1923, it facilitates cross-border police co-operation, and supports and assists all organizations, authorities and services whose mission is to prevent or combat international crime.

Interpol's Three Core Functions

Secure global police communications services

Interpol runs a global police communications system called I-24/7, which provides police around the world with a common platform through which they can share crucial information about criminals and criminality.

Operational data services and databases for police

Interpol's databases and services ensure that police worldwide have access to the information and services they need to prevent and investigate crime. Databases include data on criminals such as names, fingerprints, and DNA profiles, and stolen property such as passports, vehicles, and works of art.

Operational police support services

Interpol supports law enforcement officials in the field with emergency support and operational activities, especially in its priority crime areas of fugitives, public safety and terrorism, drugs, and organized crime, trafficking in human beings and financial and high-tech crime. A Command and Co-ordination Centre operates 24 hours. 11a day, seven days a week

Source: http://www.interpol.int/Public/icpo/about.asp

Europol, the European Union's law enforcement organization that handles criminal intelligence, in its 2005 *EU Organized Crime Report* says that the three main outlaw motorcycle gangs throughout Europe are the Hells Angels, the Bandidos, and the Outlaws (Europol, 2005). The report says that members of these gangs are involved in drugs (cocaine, synthetic drugs, and cannabis), stolen-vehicles trafficking, and exploitation of prostitutes. Finland and Sweden also reported that OMGs were involved in firearms trafficking. Europol says that these gangs use extreme violence, including inter-group violence, as the gangs battle each other for territory, and intra-group violence used to maintain discipline and compliance from club members and associates. The use of violence also extends outside the gangs in their extortion operations. Europol reports that the use of violence and intimidation against law enforcement agents by OMGs is a serious problem in Sweden.

As in the United States, the European gangs use legitimate means to mask the criminal nature of their groups. They register their clubs as legal associations or even foundations; they protect their "colours" as registered trademarks, and sue companies that misuse them. The gangs sell support merchandise and engage in legitimate businesses. The Europol report concludes with the statement:

Outlaw motorcycle gangs are present in force in the Nordic countries, Germany, and Belgium, but they are expanding their activities to the new Member States with the support of existing gangs in Russia and Eastern Europe. They are involved in a variety of crimes such as drug trafficking, smuggling of commodities and illegal prostitution. They have no scruples about using violence (Europol, 2005:31).

Figure 8.2: Europol

Mission

Europol is the European Union law enforcement organization that handles criminal intelligence. Its aim is to improve the effectiveness and cooperation between the competent authorities of the Member States in preventing and combating serious international organized crime and terrorism. The mission of Europol is to make a significant contribution to the European Union's law enforcement action against organized crime and terrorism, with an emphasis on targeting criminal organizations.

Mandate

Europol supports the law enforcement activities of the Member States mainly against:

- illicit drug trafficking;
- illicit immigration networks;
- forgery of money (counterfeiting of the euro) and other means of payment;
- trafficking in human beings (including child pornography)
- illicit vehicle trafficking
- money laundering

Source: http://www.europa.eu.

The United Nations in their 2002 *Bulletin on Narcotics* reports that 30 different outlaw motorcycle gangs (this includes chapters of the Hells Angels, Bandidos, and Outlaws) operate mainly on the East Coast of Australia (United Nations, 2002). OMG groups are primarily involved in drug production and distribution (mainly amphetamines and cannabis), prostitution, and the trafficking of stolen vehicles. However, the report states that OMG groups have also been involved in a wide variety of crimes: trafficking in counterfeit goods, serious fraud, insurance scams, money laundering, armed robbery, illegal immigration, extortion, manufacturing of firearms/ammunition, trafficking in explosives, trafficking in endangered species, murder, assault, arson, tax evasion, social security and licensing fraud, and illegal fishing. The gangs have no overriding ethnic identity, but they are predominately drawn from white, male, and working-class communities. The Australian OMGs do exclude Asians from membership. Australian OMGs are particularly violent; there were 10 murders of OMG members by rival gangs between 1997 and 2001. The United Nations also reports that most of the cannabis operations in Canada are operated by OMGs such as the Hells Angels (United Nations, 2006).

OMG CRIMINAL ACTIVITIES IN SELECTED COUNTRIES

In addition to the global efforts by Interpol, Europol, and the United Nations against outlaw motorcycle gangs, there are several countries that consider these gangs, particularly the United States-based gangs, to be national problems.

Australia

Australia is a commonwealth federation consisting of six states (Queensland, New South Wales (NSW), Victoria, Tasmania, South Australia, and Western Australia) and two territories (Australian Capital Territory and Northern Territory). The country has two levels of law enforcement agencies: state police and the Australian Federal Police (AFP). Each state and the Northern Territory have their own police force; the Australian Capital Territory is under the jurisdiction of the AFP. Since 1992, these forces have come together in five national task forces coordinated as national responses to particular complex organized crime activities (National Crime Authority: www.nca.gov.au). The Panzer Task Force formed in 1995 targets the criminal activities of outlaw motorcycle gangs.

Figure 8.3: Panzer Task Force

Mission

Targets the organized criminal activities of outlaw motorcycle gangs, especially those related to the cultivation and supply of cannabis, the manufacture and supply of amphetamines, and organized violence.

Agencies

New South Wales Police New South Wales Crime Commission
Victoria Police Queensland Crime Commission
Queensland Police Tasmania Police
South Australia Police Northern Territory Police
Western Australia Police Australia Federal Police—ACT Region
Australian Federal Police Australian Bureau of Criminal Investigation
Australian Customs Service Australian Securities & Investment Com.
AUSTRAC [Australian Transaction Reports & Analysis Centre—Money Laundering]
Department of Immigration & Multicultural Affairs
Australian Taxation Office National Crime Authority

Activities

More than 1,800 task force members have participated in the investigation of OMG criminal activities. Each agency has a representative on the Panzer Co-ordination Committee, and this Committee meets three times a year to coordinate and monitor the progress of the Panzer Task Force. In addition to drug activities, Panzer investigations have revealed that OMG members have been involved in the organized theft of motor vehicles and motorcycles, currency counterfeiting, and fraud.

Source: Modified from National Crime Authority, http://www.nca.gov.au/html/pg_TskFce.htm

The United Nations reports that there are approximately 30 different OMGs in Australia. This includes indigenous gangs, such as the Coffin Cheaters, the Commancheros, the Gypsy Jokers, the Finks, and the Rebels (Australia's largest one-percent club, with 63 chapters), and the American-based OMGs (the Hells Angels, the Bandidos, and the Outlaws). The Rebels, founded in the late 1960s, originally called themselves the Confederates after the South in the American Civil War. They still fly the Confederate battle flag.

Police authorities report that the Bandidos and the Outlaws often use street gang members for low-level drug distribution, car thefts, and break-ins (Miranda, 2003). At times, the gangs have worked together in criminal activities. A 2004 operation by NSW, South Australia, and Queensland authorities arrested members of the Rebels, Nomads, Gypsy Jokers, Hells Angels, and Finks who had formed a network to produce cannabis and methamphetamines (Anon. 2, 2004). In spite of cooperative networks for criminal profit, the gangs often engage in battles over turf and "showing class." In 2006, the Finks and the Hells Angels fought at a surfer's convention, resulting in five persons—one a bystander—being shot and stabbed (Anon. 3, 2006). The Rebels and the Hells Angels are involved in turf battles in South Australia. Law enforcement authorities claim the battles are over the drug trade (Anon. 4, 2006).

Table 8.1: OMG Violence in Australia

> **Motorcycle Gang Violence in Australia**
>
> **September 2, 1984: Milperra Massacre:** Seven people killed in battle between Commancheros and Bandidos.
>
> **August 31, 1997:** Six people wounded when 85 warring Outlaws and Odin's Warriors MC fought in the Queensland city of Mackay.
>
> **November 9, 1997:** Bandidos president and two other gang members shot dead at Sydney's Blackmarket nightclub.
>
> **October 14, 1998:** Coffin Cheater member shot to death at the wheel of his car in Perth.
>
> **May 1, 1999:** Arson attack on the Bandidos clubhouse in Adelaide's north-west.
>
> **May, 1999:** Violent clashes between Rebels & Black Uhlans MC in Gladstone, Queensland.
>
> **July 13, 1999:** Police use a bulldozer to raid the Melbourne headquarters of the Hells Angels as part of a murder investigation.
>
> **July 15, 1999:** A bomb blast demolishes a building in Adelaide that was to be the Rebel's new clubhouse, causing damage to nearby homes and businesses.
>
> **August 1, 1999:** Three biker club members charged after a shootout in Adelaide's northern suburbs , shots also fired the next day when the men due to appear in court.
>
> **August 3, 1999:** Federal and state police meet in Adelaide, form special operation codenamed AVATAR to crack down on bikie violence.
>
> **August 4, 1999:** Commanchero beaten to death and his body dumped outside his ex-wife's western Sydney home.
>
> **August 5, 1999:** Disused [abandoned} house firebombed on the Rebels' Bringley-based western Sydney chapter property.
>
> **August 6, 1999:** One-time Rebels president disappears from outside a hotel in Quueanbeyan, NSW.
>
> **August 8, 1999:** Bomb attack on Bandidos clubhouse in Geelong, Victoria.
>
> **September 20, 1999:** Homemade bomb attack on Bandidos clubhouse in Gosford, NSW.
>
> **September 22, 1999:** Rebels member shot dead in drive-by attack on the gang's central NSW coast chapters headquarters at west Gosford.
>
> **September 28, 1999:** Finks member shot in the head and arm by unidentified sniper in Coffs Harbour on NSW mid-north coast.
>
> **October 7, 1999:** Police detonate a device outside the Bandidos Ballarat, Victoria, clubhouse.
>
> **October 8, 1999:** Three Rebels gunned down outside the club's Adelaide headquarters.
>
> **September 2, 2001:** Former Western Australian detective Don Hancock and his friend killed in car-bomb by Gypsy Jokers.

Source: Modified from "Fed: Car-bomb Factbox." *AAP General News* (Australia), HighBeam Research, 11/4/2004. This list is illustrative, not exhaustive.

As shown in Table 8.1, the Australian OMGs have a history of violence. In 1984 in what is known as the Milperra Massacre, seven people (six bikers—two Bandidos and four Commancheros—and a 14-year-old girl) were killed in a shootout between the Commancheros and the Bandidos over a drug-selling disagreement (Stephenson, 2004). The Australian Bandidos were originally Commancheros who left the club because they were not allowed to sell drugs. Eight Commancheros received life sentences, and 16 Bandidos received 14 years for manslaughter. As reflected in Table 8.1, 1999 was an especially violent year for Australia's bikie [Australian term] gangs. In 1999, a Victoria Commanchero was tortured and beaten to death and the clubhouses of the Bandidos, Commancheros, and Rebels were bombed. The two bombs that exploded outside the Brompton Rebel clubhouse did $500,000 in damage. Three members of the Rebels MC were murdered in South Australia in 2001. In 2002, a NSW Commanchero sergeant-at-arms received 10 years for manslaughter after the beating death of another Commanchero, while administering discipline for violating club rules (Anon. 1, 2002). The Bandidos have also engaged in intra-gang violence. The Australian Bandidos' national sergeant-at-arms, on parole for a 1998 manslaughter of two men, killed the Australian Bandidos national president following an argument at dinner. He later committed suicide (Braithwaite, 2006).

Frequently OMG violence is directed at nonmembers for revenge. In 2004, the ex-wife of a Hells Angel member was murdered because she testified against him and other HA members, connecting them to a gun used in a 1996 South Australian double murder (McAloon, 2004).

The most notorious biker gang murder since the Milperra Massacre occurred when members of the indigenous outlaw motorcycle gang, the Gypsy Jokers, set off a car bomb killing Don Hancock, the retired chief of Western Australia's criminal investigations branch (CIB) and his best friend Lou Lewis, a former bookmaker. The bombing, called the worst criminal assassination in West Australia's history, was in revenge for the sniper killing of a Gypsy Joker member near Kalgoolie, West Australia, a year earlier. After his retirement, Don Hancock moved to a small mining community, Ora Banda, near Kalgoolie, where he owned a pub. Several Gypsy Joker members on a run stopped at the pub and insulted the barmaid—Hancock's daughter. Hancock threw the bikers out of the pub. An hour later when the bikers were sitting around a campfire, a sniper, generally believed to be Hancock, shot and killed one of them with a high-powered rifle. Two weeks later Joker members bombed Hancock's hotel, blaming him for the murder. They later bombed a general store adjoining the hotel and burned Hancock's house down. Hancock moved to Perth, refused to cooperate with the investigation, and turned down police protection. A year after the Joker was killed near Kalgoolie, a bomb planted in Lewis's car went off, killing both Lewis and Hancock.

The reaction to the assassination was immediate and vociferous. Public outcry led to the appointment of a task force—Operation Zircon—to find the killers and a clamor for new laws against "bikie" gangs. A Gypsy Joker who was present at the campfire and planted the bomb in Lewis's car confessed and turned against his fellow members. He was convicted of murder and sentenced to life in prison. The alleged mastermind of the attack was acquitted, and four other members were found not guilty for the destruction of Hancock's property. Operation Zircon received an international award from the International Motorcycle Gang Investigators Association in 2004 (Media Release—Western Australia Police Service, 16/09/2004).

OMGs operate throughout Australia; however, gang activity is a particular problem in the eastern state of Queensland. Queensland is considered Australia's Gold Coast and is the center of large casino operations and an international tourist market with an increasing methamphetamine market (Maxwell and Davey, 1997). The Queensland Crime and Misconduct Commission in its 2004 report on organized crime states that: "Members of outlaw motorcycle gangs (OMGs) have a significant involvement in organized crime in Queensland" (Queensland Crime and Misconduct Commission, 2004:4). They are primarily involved in the manufacturing and distribution of amphetamines. OMG members are to a lesser extent involved in the distribution of MDMA (ecstasy), cannabis, and occasionally heroin. Gang members have also been involved in fraud, identity crimes, motor vehicle thefts, firearms trafficking, extortion, loan sharking, and prostitution. A key finding was that criminal activity was characterized more by members acting as a part of a criminal network with non-OMG criminals and members from other OMGs, often competing with each other, rather than activity as a club/gang (Queensland Crime and Misconduct Commission, 2004:36). This finding would put the OMGs found in the Australian State of Queensland in the category of social criminal organizations on the continuum of one-percent motorcycle club as criminal organizations outlined in the previous chapter (refer to Figure 7.2).

Outlaw motorcycle gangs are expanding in Australia. The Australian Crime Commission reported in January 2007 that 10 of the nation's bikie gangs had added 26 new chapters (www.news.com.au/adelaidenow/story). Three new chapters were added in the state of South Australia, which has eight bikie gangs: Bandidos, Descendants, Finks, Gypsy Jokers, Hells Angels, MobShitters, Rebels, and Red Devils. This expansion has increased tension between the gangs and led to territorial disputes and violence.

Canada

Outlaw motorcycle gangs, particularly American-based gangs, are a significant organized crime problem in Canada. An entire chapter will be devoted to them.

Denmark

The Danish National Police in their report *Organized Crime in Denmark in 2004* (2004:8) states: "members of biker groups [are involved] in forms of organized crime such as robbery and narcotics smuggling." They are also involved in homicides, violence, intimidation, smuggling of goods subject to high levels of tax, and various forms of financial crime. The National Police also report that Serbian criminal networks have links with biker groups. According to the National Police, Danish biker groups have "special connections" with North American biker groups. Biker groups dominate the amphetamine market in Denmark. They are also involved in the distribution of MDMA (ecstasy). Biker groups operate legitimate businesses as "fronts" for their illegal activities and the laundering of money. In 2003, a Copenhagen Angels member was arrested in a bankruptcy fraud case involving 57 companies who had been cheated out of millions (Anon. 5, 2003).

There have been several biker wars in Denmark. The first occurred in the early 1980s as two indigenous Denmark motorcycle gangs, the Galloping Ghosts and Bullshit, fought over who would become the Danish Hells Angels chapter. Eight bikers were killed during the war. Bullshit lost the war after its leader was machine-gunned (Neely, 1996). The leader of the Angels, Jorn "Jonke" Nielsen, who killed the Bullshit leader, became a national celebrity, publishing two books and appearing on television. Former Bullshit members patched-over to the Bandidos in 1993.

In 1994, what was known as "The Great Nordic War" between the Hells Angels and Bandidos erupted in the Nordic countries of Denmark, Finland, Norway, and Sweden. Law enforcement authorities say the gangs were fighting over the lucrative drug markets. During the period 1994-1997, 11 bikers were murdered, and there were 74 attempted murders (see Table 8.2). Five of the murders and 40 of the attempted murders occurred in Denmark (National Commissioner of Police, 2002). In 1996, Bandidos members broke into the minimum-security prison where Hells Angel Jorn Nielsen was being held (Neely, 1996). They blew open his cell with a grenade and shot him four times. Nielsen survived, but the attack created a national outcry. Following this attack, Denmark passed a temporary "Biker Law" (now permanent) that allowed the police to prohibit certain people from gathering in residential areas if it presents a danger to the residents. Six hundred and fifty bans were issued against 200 bikers (Anon. 6, 1998).

The two gangs committed to a 1997 "peace agreement" that is still, more or less, in effect in the Nordic countries. The National Police claim that after the "peace agreement" the two gangs divided the country into regions of organized crime autonomy, with several towns declared "open" where both gangs can operate (Anon. 8, 2003). This would place the Danish Bandidos and Hells Angels MCs on the "gang" side of the Continuum of One-Percent Motorcycle Clubs as Criminal Organizations.

Table 8.2: Great Nordic War Casualties

Casualties of the Great Nordic War
13/02/1994: During a shootout at the Roof Top Club in Helsingborg, Sweden, a 23-year-old Hells Angel supporter was shot and killed.
22/06/1994: The president of Klan C—a biker club that supports Bandidos, was murdered by a Hells Angel.
17/07/1995: The president of the Swedish chapter of Bandidos was shot on his way home from a meeting in Finland.
01/03/1996: Two Finnish Bandidos were shot outside their clubhouse in Helsinki. One died on the spot; the other died later in hospital.
10/03/1996: A young Bandidos member was killed during a shootout at Copenhagen's Kaastrup.
15/07/1996: A Danish member of the Swedish chapter of Bandidos was shot in Norway.
05/10/1996: Two people died and 18 were seriously injured when a missile was fired at the Hells Angels clubhouse in Titangade, Copenhagen.
10/01/1997: A 26-year-old Hells Angel was shot dead in his car in Aalborg, Denmark.
04/06/1997: A car bomb exploded outside the Bandidos clubhouse in Drammen, Norway. A female passer-by became the first civilian causality when she was killed as she drove by in her car.
07/06/1997: A young Bandidos "trainee" was shot dead as he left a café in Liseleje in Northern Zealand, Denmark.

Source: Anon. 7 (1998).

The Netherlands

In 2004, the Dutch Hells Angels were involved in a bizarre multiple intra-club/gang murder with international connections. According to newspaper accounts and the recently published book *Angels of Death* (Sher and Marsden, 2006: 260-278), the vicious leader of the Amsterdam Nomads chapter of the Hells Angels, Paul "The Butcher" de Vries, decided to "rip off" a Colombian drug cartel. The drug deal had been arranged by the Hells Angels Curacao chapter. Drug-deal "rip offs" are forbidden by Hells Angels' rules. When other members of the Nomads chapter learned of the "rip-off," they decided to take retribution. Paul de Vries was hated by the other members and was called by one". . . the most evil man on the planet (Amoruso, no date)." He was alleged to have committed 11 to 15 murders. His "brothers" tortured and killed de Vries and two other HA members and dumped their bodies in a nearby stream. Two members of the Curacao-based Hells Angels were sent to Amsterdam as part of the international Angels internal investigation and were rescued by the police just before their murders. Twelve Nomads were sentenced to six years in prison for the manslaughter of de Vries. The court said that there was no premeditated decision to kill the three HAs. Based on this event and other drug deals by Dutch Hells Angels, it appears that they are more gangs than clubs. In spite of this it has been reported that several dozen soldiers in the Dutch army are also members of the Hells Angels (www.dutchnews.nl/news/archives).

New Zealand

The Criminal Investigative Branch of the New Zealand police reports that:

> There are many motorcycle gangs in New Zealand and they are frequently involved in the illegal manufacture and sale of drugs, violent crime and vice. Membership of these gangs can be of mixed race (www.police.govt.nz).

New Zealand OMGs with criminal networks from overseas established the domestic manufacture of methamphetamines (Wilkins et al., 2004). Although crime rates are high in New Zealand, it was generally free of OMG organized crime until the 1970s (Newbold, 1997). The first Hells Angels chapter was formed in Auckland in 1961, but it was not until the 1970s that the Angels became involved in organized crime (Newbold, 1997). According to Newbold, the Auckland Angels did not become involved n the manufacture and distribution of amphetamines and LSD, until the California Hells Angels became their main supply source. Drug dealing allowed the New Zealand Angels to become prosperous, leading to them purchasing real estate and a home in an Auckland suburb for a club house. In the 1990s, the Hells Angels were the best organized gang in New Zealand and the supplier of methamphetamines and LSD to the other gangs (Newbold, 1997). At one time, Andrew Sisson, a member of the a New Zealand Angels, was the

Hells Angels world secretary. He often made trips to the United States, Canada, Europe, South Africa, and Australia, conducting Hells Angels business (Anon. 9, 2005). Sisson and his wife were convicted in 1999 of conspiring to manufacture methamphetamine and money laundering.

Indigenous OMGs also became involved in organized criminal activities. New Zealand police say there are four indigenous outlaw motorcycle gangs in Christchurch, the Devil's Henchmen, Highway 61, Epitaph Riders, and the Road Knights (Anon. 8, 2004). The authorities say that a prospect must commit a criminal act to become a member of these gangs. In 1999, the Hells Angels and the indigenous Headhunters MC were reportedly making millions working together in criminal activities (Manning, 1999). There were wars between the OMGs earlier, but now it appears that they cooperate with one another in criminal activities.

Based on the available information above and the New Zealand law enforcement reports, it appears that the New Zealand Hells Angels and the indigenous OMGs are gangs and not motorcycle clubs. The New Zealand HAs became involved in organized drug activities with the help of the California Hells Angels.

Other Countries

As stated, American-based OMGs with chapters in other countries, such as Norway and Sweden, have been involved in organized crime activities. In addition, in 2004, 11 members of the Mainz, Germany Hells Angels chapter were sentenced to prison for extortion as well as drugs and weapons offenses, leading to their being banned (www.dw-world.de) The Hamburg and Duesseldorf chapters were banned in 2001 and 2002 after some of their members were convicted of crimes. A coordinated 2005 raid on Bandidos chapters in Germany, Luxembourg, Norway, and Sweden yielded weapons, drugs, and computers (www.aftenposten.no). The raids were conducted at the request of Italy after a Bandidos leader was killed in Bolzano, Italy. France has a special law enforcement unit, CRACO, that deals with OMGs.

SUMMARY

The one-percent biker subculture was transported outside the United States by the media and the entertainment industry, leading to the formation of one-percent outlaw motorcycle clubs in other countries. The American-based one-percent clubs—the Hells Angels, the Bandidos, and the Outlaws—through interlocking relationships with these indigenous clubs began forming international chapters. The American-based OMGs also transported organized criminal activities and began fighting with each other and the indigenous clubs/gangs over territory and criminal markets. Two common characteristics of OMGs—American-based and indigenous—in countries outside the United States are violence and organized criminal activities, particularly the manufacture and distribution of drugs. According to law enforcement authorities in these countries, including Interpol, Europol, and the United Nations, the one-percent motorcycle clubs in their jurisdictions are more gangs than clubs.

REFERENCES

Amoruso, D. (no date). "The Nomads From Limburg." *Gangsters Incorporated.* Found at: http://gangstersinc.tripod.com/HellsAngels/Nomads.html

Anon. 1 (2002). "Bikie Jailed 10 Years for Deadly Gang 'Discipline.'" *Sydney Morning Star*, May 17, 2002.

Anon. 2 (2004). "Raids Expose Alleged Drug Ring." *The Age*, May 26, 2004. Found at: http://www.theage.com.au/articles/2004

Anon. 3 (2006). "Man in Fort Case at Brawl." *The Advertiser.* Found at: http://www.theadvertiser. news.com.au

Anon. 4 (2006). "Time for These Men to Explain Themselves." *The Sydney Morning Advertiser*, May 20, 2006.

Anon. 5 (2003). "Chicago in the 30s or Denmark Right Now—Tax Authorities Implement a New Strategy to Fight Organized Crime." *The Copenhagen Post Online*, December 5, 2003. Found at: http://www.cphpost.dk

Anon. 6 (1998). "Biker Law Permanent." *The Copenhagen Post Online*, May 7, 1998.

Anon. 7. (1998). "Biker Gangs Here to Stay?" *The Copenhagen Post Online*, May 28, 1998.

Anon. 8. (2004). "From Overt to Covert." *The Press (Canterbury, New Zealand)*, October 29, 2004.

Barker, T. (2004). "Exporting American Organized Crime—Outlaw Motorcycle Gangs." *Journal of Gang Research* 11(2):37-50.

Braithwaite, D. (2006). "Fugitive Bandidos Shoots Himself." *The Sydney Morning Herald,* May 12, 2006

Crime and Misconduct Commission (2004). *Organized Crime Markets in Queensland: A Strategic Assessment.* Queensland: Crime and Misconduct Commission. Number 6.

Doughtie, J.A. (1986). "Motorcycle Gang Investigations: A Team Effort." *FBI Law Enforcement Bulletin* 19-22.

Europol (2005). *2005 EU Organized Crime Report: Public Version.* The Hague, October 25, 2005.

Harris, M. (1985). *Bikers: Birth of a Modern Day Outlaw.* London: Faber & Faber.

Haut, F. (1999). "Organized Crime on Two Wheels: Motorcycle Gangs." *International Criminal Police Review:* 474-475.

Interpol (1984). "Motorcycle Gangs." *ICPO- Interpol General Secretariat.*

Kendall, R.E. (1998). "The International Problem of Criminal Gangs." *International Criminal Police Review:* 469-471.

Mandelkau, J. (1971). *Buttons: The Making of a President.* London: Sphere Books.

Manning, S. (1999). "Major Organized Crime Network Reported." *Scoop Auckland.*

McAloon, C. (2004). "Vic: Slain Mum Feared Ex-hubby and Hells Angels Would Kill Her." *AAP General News,* January 29, 2004.

Miranda, C. (2003). "Bikie Pursuit as Police Target the 'X-Men Inside." *The Daily Telegraph.*

Maxwell, J.C., and J. Davey (1997). *Comparison of Patterns of Illicit Drug Use in Australia and the United States.* Austin: Texas Commission on Alcohol and Drug Abuse.

McClure, G. (2000). "The Role of Interpol in Fighting Organized Crime." *International Criminal Police Review-No 481.*

National Commissioner of Police (2002). *Plan of 25 September 2002 for Intensified Efforts to Combat Crime and Problems of Law and Order, Etc. Originating in the Biker Community.* Copenhagen: National Commissioner of Police.

Neely, T. (1996). "Hell's Angels-type Bikers Create Havoc in Denmark, Too." *Knight-Ridder/Tribune News Service* (HighBeam Research), August 28, 1996.

Newbold, G. (1997). "The Emergence of Organized Crime in New Zealand." *Transnational Organized Crime* 3(3):73-94.

Reynolds, T. (2000). *Wild Ride: How Outlaw Motorcycle Myth Conquered the World.* New York: TV books.

Sher, J., and W. Marsden (2006). *Angels of Death: Inside the Biker Gangs' Crime Empire.* New York: Carroll & Graf.

Smith, B.W. (1998). "Interpol 's "Project Rocker" Helps Disrupt Outlaw Motorcycle Gangs." *The Police Chief* 65(9):54-56.

Smith, R. (2002). "Dangerous Motorcycle Gangs: A Facet of Organized Crime in the Mid Atlantic Region." *Journal of Gang Research* 9(4):33-44.

Stephenson, R. (2004). *Milperra: The Road to Justice*. Sydney: New Holland.

Tretheway, S., and T. Katz (1998). "Motorcycle Gangs or Motorcycle Mafia?" *The Police Chief* 66(4):53-60.

United Nations (2002). *Bulletin on Narcotics: The Science of Drug Abuse Epidemiology*. LIV (1 & 2).

United Nations (2006). *2006 World Drug Analysis: Volume 1: Analysis*.

Wilkins, C., J. Reilly, E. Rose, D. Roy, M. Pledger, and A. Lee (2004). *The Socio-Economic Impact of Amphetamine Type Stimulants in New Zealand: Final Report*. Auckland: Massey University.

9

The Hells Are No Angels: Organized Crime, Death, and Mayhem in Canada

INTRODUCTION

Since 2002, there have been at least eight books on motorcycle clubs/gangs in Canada (Auger, 2002; Cherry, 2005; Langton, 2006; Martineau, 2002; Paradis; 2002; Sanger, 2005; Sher and Marsden, 2003; Sher and Marsden, 2006). The thesis of all these works is that Canadian one- percent motorcycle clubs, particularly the Hells Angels, are criminal gangs (outlaw motorcycle gangs) engaged in organized crime. The Canadian motorcycle gangs—both indigenous and American-based—are extremely violent, engaging in inter-gang, intra-gang, and gratuitous violence on nongang members, including criminal justice officials, reporters, and, on occasion, innocent civilians. Admittedly, all the authors, except Paradis—a former gang president—are journalists and sometimes engage in sensationalism. However, their view is shared by Canadian law enforcement authorities and confirmed by the available evidence. For the most part, Canadian one-percent motorcycle clubs are criminal gangs and not clubs. This is especially true for the American-based clubs—the Hells Angels, the Bandidos, and the Outlaws—that have established chapters in Canada.

CANADIAN LAW ENFORCEMENT ACTIVITIES

Criminal Intelligence Service Canada (CISC)

The Criminal Intelligence Service Canada (CISC) unites "the criminal intelligence units of Canadian law enforcement agencies in the fight against organized crime and other serious crime in Canada" (www.cisc.gc.ca). The CISC is composed of a Central Bureau, located in the capital of Ottawa and a system of nine Provincial Bureaus located in each of the Canadian provinces of Alberta, British Columbia, Manitoba, New Brunswick, Newfoundland, and Labrador, Nova Scotia, Ontario, Quebec, and Saskatchewan. The Province of Prince Edward Island is served by the Criminal Intelligence Service Nova Scotia; the territories of Yukon, Northwest, and Nunavut are served by Criminal Intelligence Service Alberta and Criminal Intelligence Service Ontario (CISC, 2005:i).

There are two levels of membership in the CISC. Level I members are federal, provincial, regional, or municipal police services and agencies that are responsible for the enforcement of federal and provincial statutes and have a permanent criminal intelligence unit. Level II members are agencies who are responsible for the enforcement of federal or provincial statues but cannot meet other qualifications—for example, they may not have a permanent intelligence unit. The intelligence units "supply their Provincial Bureaus with criminal intelligence and raw data related to organized and serious crime . . . for further analysis and dissemination" (www.cisc.gc.ca).

Every year the CISC issues an Annual Report on Organized Crime in order to inform and educate the public. The CISC seeks to elicit the public's help in partnership with law enforcement agencies. According to the CISC, "One of the keys to success in the fight against organized crime is partnership between law enforcement agencies as well as with policy makers and the public" (CISC, 2005:iii). The reports provide information on a number of organized crime groups in Canada (aboriginal-based, Asian-based, Eastern European, outlaw motorcycle gangs, and Italian-based). It is possible to trace the recent growth and criminal activities of Canadian OMGs through these annual reports.

CISC Annual Report—1997

In 1996, there were 38 OMGs in Canada, with the Hells Angels being the largest and best organized. The Hells Angels were in every province except Ontario (which was surprising because Ontario had the largest number of OMGs—13—and a lucrative drug trade). Law enforcement authorities said that the Angels were too busy fighting with the Rock Machine, an indigenous motorcycle gang, in Quebec to set up a chapter in Ontario. This "Biker War" with the Rock Machine had started over drug trafficking markets in Montreal and other parts of the Province of Quebec. The war, which started in 1994, had so far claimed 50 victims. There were 57 attempts or conspiracies to commit murder and 40 bombings and/or cases of arson.

Figure 9.1: 1997 CISC Highlights

> **Highlights**
> - The Hells Angels remain one of the most powerful and organized criminal groups in Canada.
> - Drug trafficking is the most lucrative activity of outlaw motorcycle gangs. This is especially true of the Hells Angels who, with the support of their affiliated clubs [puppet clubs] have taken over the distribution and sale of drugs such as cocaine, cannabis, LSD and PCP. Furthermore, the Hells Angels are involved in the hydroponic cultivation of marihuana.
> - The armed conflict between the Hells Angels and the Rock Machine still rages in the Province of Quebec.
> - The Hells Angels have moved into Alberta and forged ahead with their plans for expansion into the provinces of Saskatchewan, Manitoba and Ontario.

Source: CISC Annual Report on Organized Crime in Canada—1997

CISC Annual Report—1998

In 1998, there were still 38 known OMGs in Canada, with the Hells Angels still the most powerful and well-organized. The Biker War was still going on in Quebec, with 68 dead thus far. In a move to find allies in their battle with the Angels, members of the Rock Machine had contacted both the Bandidos and the Outlaws about possible membership, and it was believed that the Bandidos had granted hang-around status to the Rock Machine. The OMGs were still heavily involved in drug trafficking. In the spring of 1997, the Sûreté du Quebec [Quebec Provincial Police] disrupted three marijuana hydroponic operations in Montreal. One was run by the Hells Angels, and the other two were run by an Angels puppet club, the Death Riders.

The Quebec Hells Angels began a campaign of intimidation against the provincial criminal justice system, resulting in the destruction of 13 police vehicles and the murder of two correctional officers. The president of the Nomads chapter of the Quebec Hells Angels, Maurice "Mom" Boucher, was arrested and charged with the murder of the two correctional officers.

Law enforcement authorities moved against the indigenous Satan's Choice MC, arresting 135 members and associates on more than 1,085 charges. Authorities also investigated the St. Catherine's chapter of the Outlaws, arresting the chapter president and former national president, charging them with drug trafficking and weapons charges. Several indigenous OMGs—the Winnipeg-based Los Bravos, the Saskatoon-based Alberta Rebels, and the Alberta Grim Reapers—patched over to the Hells Angels.

The five British Columbia (BC) Hells Angels chapters, the wealthiest Angels' chapters in the world, controlled the drug trade in the province, particularly the hydroponic cultivation of marijuana. This marijuana, which was known as "BC Bud," was exported to the United States. The BC Angels were also in the production of live sex shows [pornography] over the Internet.

Figure 9.2—1998 CISC Highlights

Highlights

- The Hells Angels are still one of the most powerful and well-structured criminal organizations in Canada. In 1997, they continued to grow and added three new chapters to the 11 that already existed across the country.
- Drug trafficking remains their primary and most lucrative criminal activity.
- The armed conflict between the Hells Angels and the Rock Machine still rages in the Province of Quebec.

Source: CISC Annual Report on Organized Crime—1998.

CISC Annual Report—1999

As a result of patching over indigenous motorcycle gangs by American-based OMGs—the Hells Angels, the Bandidos, and the Outlaws—in 1999 there were 30 known OMGs in Canada. CISC reported that the Hells Angels had 214 patched members and 35 prospects. Two-hundred and five (205) of these members had criminal records; 105 of the members' records were for drug-related offenses. The BC Angels created a new chapter and increased their hydroponic marijuana trade. The Alberta HAs disbanded the indigenous King's Crew [only two members were allowed to patch-over to the Angels] and took over all biker-related criminal activities in Alberta. Forty-five of the 46 members of the Alberta Hells Angels had criminal records, with 25 of them having been convicted of serious crimes.

The Manitoba Los Bravos MC had been in existence for 30 years by this time and were expected to become Hells Angels during the year. Ontario still had the most OMGs, nine (down from 13 in 1997). The Angels still had the goal of establishing a chapter in the province once the Biker War was over. In Ontario, the indigenous Para-Dice Riders were the most prosperous and the Satan's Choice the most involved in criminal activities—fencing stolen goods, auto theft, insurance and credit card fraud, tractor trailer thefts, and smuggling. CISC also reported that Satan's Choice members worked with traditional organized crime (Italian-based) members in extortion and debt collection as well as firearms and narcotics distribution. In London, Ontario, two prominent members of the Outlaws were killed by indigenous OMG members in turf wars.

In the Province of Quebec, the Hells Angels now had six chapters and a vicious Nomads' chapter and seven puppet clubs. The Biker War between the Angels and the Rock Machine was still continuing. There were now 103 homicides, 124 murder attempts, nine missing persons, 84 bombings, and 130 incidents of arson, for a total of 450 violent incidents since 1994.

Figure 9.3: 1999 CISC Highlights

Highlights

- The Hells Angels are one of the most powerful and well-structured criminal organizations in Canada. In 1998, they formed two new chapters: one in British Columbia and one in Saskatchewan, for a national total of 16 chapters.
- The armed conflict between the Hells Angels and the Rock Machine is still raging in Quebec. In 1998, there were 27 related homicides and 27 murder attempts.

Source: 1999 Annual Report on Organized Crime—1999.

CISC Annual Report—2000

In 2000, OMGs, especially the Hells Angels, were a national priority for Canadian law enforcement during the year. OMGs were reported to be involved in a long list of crimes: importation and distribution of cocaine, the production and distribution of methamphetamines, the cultivation and exportation of high-grade marijuana, illegal trafficking of firearms and explosives, the collection of protection money from both legitimate and illegitimate business operations, fraud, money laundering, and prostitution.

There were a number of significant law enforcement actions against OMGs during the year. In British Columbia there were two trials going on against HA members. One involved Haney chapter members charged with three counts of cocaine trafficking. The other trial involved East End HA chapter members charged with trafficking cocaine, conspiracy to traffic cocaine, and laundering proceeds of crime. Members and associates of the Edmonton Rebels pleaded guilty to drug-trafficking offenses. In Quebec, the police dismantled a Hells

Angels drug ring with the arrest of 34 members and associates. Quebec police arrested 10 of the 11 members of a Hells Angels puppet club, Blatnois Mauricie, and they were going to use this arrest to test the new Bill C-95 anti-gang legislation (see below). A Calgary Hells Angels member was charged with a plot to cause serious harm to a Calgary alderman, a city hall staff member, and a member of a community association. The latter charges arose out of the destruction of the HA Calgary clubhouse for noncompliance with local building codes.

Figure 9.4: Bill C-95—Anti-Gang Legislation

Canadian police agencies, pointing to the United States RICO (Racketeer Influenced and Corrupt Organizations) law pressured Parliament for a similar law. In April 1997, "Parliament amended the Criminal Code to prevent and deter the commission of criminal activity by criminal organizations and their members, such as outlaw motorcycle gangs.

The Act defines a "criminal organization" as any group, association, or other body consisting of five or more persons whether formally or informally organized [later changed to three or more members].

(a) having as one of its primary activities the commission of an indictable offense under this or any other Acts of Parliament for which the punishment for five years or more and

(b) any or all members of which engage in or have within the preceding five years engaged in the commission of a serious offences

The Act does not make membership in a criminal organization a criminal offense in Canadian law, but rather, the commission of crimes within a criminal organization framework

The new amendments include:

- A new offense—participation in a criminal organization with a penalty of up to 14 years in jail
- Greater police discretion in using electronic surveillance against gangs for up to a year compared with the previous 60 days
- Expanded proceeds of crime laws to allow seizure of all proceeds from gang-related offenses
- Additions to the Criminal Code concerning the use of explosives in criminal gang activity
- A new peace bond, designed to target gang leadership, would allow a judge to prohibit associating or communicating with other gang members
- A change in bail provisions. Anyone charged with a gang-related offense would be held without bail until trial, unless he/she could show why detention was not justified
- Tougher sentencing
- New sentencing provisions in the Criminal Code aimed at delaying parole eligibility\ for certain organized gang offenses.

Source: RCMP, 1999.

Although the Angels still did not have a chapter in Ontario, the CISC reported that the majority of the OMGs in the province did business with the Angels (although the Rock Machine, of course, did not do business with the Hells Angels). Ontario now had 11 OMGs—up two from the year before—including the Para-Dice Riders, Outlaws, Satan's Choice, Vagabonds, and the Rock Machine. It appeared that the Hells Angels were trying to patch-over the Para-Dice Riders to form the first HA chapter in Ontario.

Figure 9.5: 2000 CISC Highlights

Highlights

- The Hells Angels remain one of the most powerful and well-structured criminal organizations in Canada. In 1999, they formed two new chapters, bringing the total to 18 chapters nationally.
- The armed conflict, which started in 1994 between the Hells Angels and the Rock Machine in Quebec, continues.

Source: CISC Annual Report on Organized Crime—2000

CISC Annual Report—2001

In 2001, the Hells Angels retained their status as the largest and most criminally active OMG in Canada. The Angels finally established a chapter in the Province of Ontario by patching over the Satan's Choice and the Last Chance. The Angels also patched over the Edmonton Rebels and the Winnipeg-based Los Bravos. The Bandidos countered the expansion of the Hells Angels in Ontario by making the Rock Machine probationary Bandidos on December 1, 2000, and patching over the Loners. They also established two probationary Bandidos chapters in Montreal and Quebec City. The Outlaws retained their seven chapters in Ontario.

Also in this year, members of the British Columbia Hells Angels were convicted for the first time for a serious crime: trafficking in cocaine. Two members of the Vancouver Hells Angels chapter were convicted of trafficking in cocaine, conspiring with four other men to traffic in cocaine, and possession of the proceeds of crime. In a test of the Bill C-95 anti-Gang Law, four members of the Rock Machine were found guilty of gangsterism.

The Hells Angels continued their intimidation of non-gang members and threats of violence. A prosecutor in the BC Angels case was approached by two men and had his life threatened. The ex-president of the Calgary Hells Angels was found guilty of two counts of counseling mischief and two counts of common assault in the 1999 plot to bomb the homes of the alderman and community activist mentioned earlier. A crime reporter for the *Journal de Montreal* was shot five times but survived. He had just completed a series of stories on the deaths and disappearances of Hells Angels and Mafia members as a result of drug-trafficking conflicts. The Edmonton police discovered that the Hells Angels were conducting counter-surveillance and intelligence on them.

It appeared that the Biker War had ended in Quebec when the leaders of the Hells Angels and the Rock Machine and their lawyers met at the Quebec City courthouse and declared a public truce in October 2001. The truce lasted two months, until the Rock Machine became probationary Bandidos, bitter enemies of the Angels, at which time sporadic violence broke out again.

Figure 9.6: 2001 CISC Highlights

Highlights

- The year 2000 saw dramatic growth for the Hells Angels as chapters were formed in Manitoba and Ontario. The Bandidos patched-over the Rock Machine as probationary Members (one step below full membership) in December 2000.
- OMGs in Canada continue to use violence, ranging from intimidation and assault to attempted murder and murder.
- OMGs continue to associate with street gangs and other organized groups at the regional, national and international levels.

Source: CISC Annual Report on Organized Crime—2001.

CISC Annual Report—2002

In 2002, the CISC reported that OMGs, particularly the Hells Angels, were engaged in a wide variety of criminal activities: money laundering, intimidation, assaults, attempted murder, murder, fraud, theft, counterfeiting, extortion, prostitution, escort agencies/strip clubs, after-hours clubs (selling alcohol illegally), telemarketing, and the possessing and trafficking of illegal weapons, stolen goods, and contraband.

The Hells Angels remained the largest and most criminally active OMG in Canada. Through the patching-over of indigenous biker gangs and active expansion, the Angels had 35 chapters, up from 14 in 1998. CISC reported that the gang continued to be involved in the importation and trafficking in cocaine, the cultivation and exportation of high-grade marijuana, and—to a lesser extent—the production and trafficking of methamphetamine and the trafficking of ecstasy and other illicit synthetic drugs. The BC Angels were criminally active in the province's marine ports and smuggling contraband, including drugs, into and out of Canada through the ports. The BC Angels had developed criminal alliances with Italian crime families and were forming alliances with Asian-based crime groups as well.

In Quebec, the Hells Angels continued their intimidation of witnesses and criminal justice officials. One witness' home was firebombed, and other witnesses had their homes fired on by a shotgun. A former gang-unit police officer had her vehicle torched and her residence firebombed twice. Members and associates appeared in court in "colors" in an attempt to intimidate witnesses, police officers, and members of the justice system.

The American-based motorcycle gangs took over the province of Ontario by patching-over the indigenous OMGs, violently disbanding other clubs, and establishing new chapters. The Hells Angels had 14 chapters and one prospect chapter in Ontario, up from zero in 1996. The Outlaws had 10 chapters, and the Bandidos had formed two chapters in Ontario. There were several incidents of violence between the Angels and the other two gangs. The CISC also reported that the three gangs had formed alliances with street gangs to perform lower-level criminal activities and security duties.

The Biker War continued between the Hells Angels and the Bandidos (Rock Machine patched over in 2001), with two civilian deaths in addition to the seven biker murders. A teenager was killed when he was

The Ontario Provincial Police Commissioner and an Ontario Provincial Police Biker Enforcement Unit Inspector examine Hells Angels vests in Toronto. Outlaw motorcycle gangs in Canada are among the most criminal and violent in the world. *Photo courtesy of AP PHOTO/CP, Aaron Harris.*

caught in the crossfire outside a bar. An innocent man was killed when his car was confused with that of a Bandidos member. There were also 26 arsons in bars and clubs associated with the Angels.

Mom Boucher, the infamous leader of the Quebec Hells Angels Nomads, was retried on charges of ordering the murders of two prison guards and the attempted murder of another in 1997. In his first trial, Boucher was acquitted, but the prosecution appealed and was allowed to retry him—a move allowed in Canada but not the United States. Boucher was found guilty on all three counts and sentenced to serve

25 years before being eligible for parole. He is currently appealing this conviction.

There were several important law enforcement actions against OMGs throughout the provinces. Operation SHADOW shut down seven methamphetamine labs in Calgary, Alberta, and Kelowna, Vancouver, and the Fraser Valley in British Columbia. In Ontario, Operation WOLF, against the Bandidos, resulted in 149 charges against 27 members and associates for hijacking and stealing cargo truckloads of merchandise. Drugs, weapons, and $3 million in stolen property were recovered. Project AMIGO targeted the Bandidos in Ontario and Quebec. Sixty-two arrest warrants were issued for offenses ranging from conspiracy to commit murder and trafficking in drugs (cocaine, heroin, ecstasy, and marijuana). CISC reported that the entire Bandidos Montreal chapter and half of the Bandidos Quebec City chapter were arrested. The Bandidos' National President was also arrested. Operation 4-H resulted in the arrests of 55 members and associates of the Quebec City Hells Angels and the New Brunswick Dammers (a puppet club). The charges were conspiracy to traffic in cocaine, ecstasy, and marijuana and conspiracy to launder the proceeds of crime. The operation identified a national drug network with drugs imported from British Columbia and Quebec into Atlantic Canada. Operation HAMMER led to the arrests of 20 individuals with ties to the Halifax Hells Angels.

Figure 9.7: 2002 CISC Highlights

Highlights
- Across the country, there have been a number of incidents of intimidation by OMGs and their affiliates against victims, witnesses, and law enforcement.
- Violence continues in Quebec between the Hells Angels and Bandidos over the protection and expansion of drug trafficking networks. There have also been a number of violent incidents between the Outlaws and the Hells Angels in Ontario.
- OMGs, particularly the Hells Angels, continue to form and maintain associations with street gangs.

Source: CISC Annual Report on Organized Crime—2002.

CISC Annual Report—2003

In 2003, the CISC reported that the American-based OMGs—the Hells Angels, the Outlaws, and the Bandidos—were the most influential OMGs in Canada. The Angels were noted as the most powerful of all, with 34 chapters. The Outlaws were concentrated in Ontario, with nine chapters. The Bandidos did not have any Canadian clubhouses but they had a small number of members and probationary members in Ontario. Law enforcement authorities continued to "hammer" the OMGs, particularly the Outlaws and the Bandidos.

In Ontario, Project RETIRE, a three-year operation against the Outlaws, resulted in the arrests of 60 members and associates, including two United States-based members, the Outlaws United States national vice-president, and the international president. Five Outlaws clubhouses in Ontario were seized and, according to authorities, the club chapters were in disarray and their criminal influence diminished. Project AMIGO, which targeted the Bandidos in Ontario and Quebec, ended in June 2002. Authorities said that the operation ended the criminal influence in both provinces. Megatrials against the Hells Angels as a result of the 2001 Operation SPRINGTIME were going on in this year as well.

Figure 9.8: 2003 CISC Highlights

Highlights

- Outlaw motorcycle gangs (OMGs) remain a serious criminal threat in Canada. They are involved in an array of criminal activities such as murder, drug trafficking, prostitution, illegal gambling, extortion, intimidation, fraud and theft.
- Successful law enforcement action within the last two years has had an impact on the degree of criminal influence of OMGs in Central and Atlantic Canada.

Source: CISC Annual Report on Organized Crime—2003.

CISC Annual Report—2004

In 2004 the Hells Angels remained the largest and most powerful Canadian OMG, with 34 chapters and 500 members. However, they were facing pressure from law enforcement authorities and other OMGs. CISC reported that the Outlaws and the Bandidos were maintaining a low profile following the 2002 law enforcement actions. The Outlaws had seven chapters in Ontario, but CISC reported that only three operated with any degree of stability. The Bandidos had a chapter in Ontario and established a probationary chapter in Alberta. CISC reported that the Alberta chapter may pose a challenge to the drug activities of the Hells Angels in western Canada.

The Canadian Hells Angels were reported to have significant links to other organized crime groups, particularly the BC Angels and Italian-based groups. These criminal networks were used to facilitate the importation and exportation of illicit commodities, especially drugs.

Figure 9.9: 2004 CISC Highlights

> **Highlights**
> - The Hells Angels remain the largest OMG in Canada; however, this group is experiencing varying degrees of weakness in Alberta, Manitoba, Quebec and Atlantic Canada due to law enforcement operations, internal conflict and increased competition from other criminal organizations.
> - Drug trafficking remains the primary source of illicit income of the Hells Angels in Canada though the group is also involved in a variety of other criminal activities.

Source: CISC Annual Report on Organized Crime—2004.

CISC Annual Report—2005

The format for the CISC reports was changed with the 2005 annual report. In this year, there was no longer a separate section on each of the organized crime groups in Canada, and highlights were no longer listed. Nevertheless, the report said that OMGs were still involved in marijuana growth operations (Hells Angels), cocaine trafficking, and methamphetamine production and distribution. OMGs were also reported to be involved in motor vehicle thefts.

The End of the Canadian Biker War

The Biker War in Canada between the Hells Angels and the Rock Machine (later the Bandidos) was the worst organized crime war in history in terms of numbers of dead and injured. The war raged on for eight years (1994 to 2001), resulting in 160 murders, including an innocent-11 year-old boy; 175 attempted murders; 200 people wounded; and the disappearances of 15 bikers (Roslin, 2002). The war began in 1994 when the Quebec Hells Angels, led by Maurice "Mom" Boucher, attempted to take over control of the province's cocaine, hashish, and marijuana markets from a coalition of the rival Rock Machine club, independent dealers, and some Mafia elements.

The Biker War ended with the implementation of law enforcement's Operation SPRINGTIME mentioned above. On March 28, 2001, 2,000 police officers spread out throughout Quebec and executed more than 130 arrest warrants and seizures of gang assets, including 20 buildings, 70 firearms, and $8.6 million Canadian and $2.7 million U.S. (Cherry, 2005). The operation may have ended the Quebec Biker War, but it did not end the violence associated with Canadian OMGs. The largest mass murder in Ontario's history would involve the Bandidos in 2006.

The Bandidos Massacre

On Sunday, April 8, 2006, the police were called to a rural farmhouse in Shedden, Ontario. The farm owners had discovered a minivan and a tow truck with a car hooked to the back. A fourth car was found about 100 meters down a dirt road. The police found eight bodies inside the two vehicles and began an investigation into the worst mass murder in Ontario's history. Within days, the eight men—all from the Toronto area—were connected to the Bandidos Motorcycle Club. One victim, John "Boxer" Muscedere, was the national president of the Bandidos Canada. He had eight criminal convictions since 1996, including assault with a weapon, breaking and entering, resisting arrest, and escaping custody. The Loners, the Bandidos, and the Hells Angels were all reported to be, or have been, active in the area. By the following Monday, the police had arrested and charged five people with first-degree murder. One of the five was a 46-year-old woman charged with helping in the killings. The first-degree murder charges against the woman and her common-law husband, who was also originally charged, were later reduced to eight counts of accessory after the fact.

Among those charged was Wayne Kellestine, a patched Bandidos member who was the former leader of the St. Thomas Annihilators and the St. Thomas Loners. The police contend that the mass murder was a case of "internal cleansing" and that no other criminal organization was involved. They reported that six of the dead were full-patched Bandidos members, one was a prospect member, and the other was an associate. However, Julian Sher, journalist, biker expert, and co-author of two books on Canadian biker gangs, holds that the slayings were the result of a turf war between the Hells Angels and the Bandidos (Anon., 2006). Another observer, Ed Winterholder, former president of the Oklahoma Bandidos and author of the only book on the Bandidos, said that the murders had to be fueled by methamphetamine (Boland, 2006). He went on to say that when the St. Thomas Loners disbanded, half the members became Hells Angels and the other half (including Kellestine and most of those who were murdered) became Bandidos. Finally, yet another theory says that Kellestine had become a problem for the Bandidos because he was a known white supremacist and a "loose cannon" who had a swastika cut into his lawn. According to this theory, 10 bikers were on their way to pull Kellestine's "patch" when they stopped for coffee and two of the bikers called Kellestine and alerted him. Allegedly, the two that ratted out their brothers are among the five arrested for the murders (Robertson, 2006). There is also speculation that the victims had announced plans to patch-over to the Hells Angels.

The investigation of the mass murder is still ongoing and has spread to other parts of Canada and the United States. In June 2006, three Winnipeg Bandidos—two full-patched members and a prospect— were charged with the eight murders (Lambert, 2006). One of those arrested was the Winnipeg Bandidos chapter president; the other full-patched Bandidos member was a former police officer.

According to a senior Texas Department of Public Safety investigator, in a surprising development, the Bandidos International President revoked the Canadian Bandidos' membership and barred them from wearing Bandidos colors (Appleby, 2006). Evidently, the "last straw" was when the American Bandidos learned that their Canadian brothers had let a former police officer become a member. An August 2006 check of the Bandidos web site lists no Canadian chapters (www.bandidosmc.com/). The ultimate outcome of the mass murder case and the status of the Bandidos in Canada will be decided in the future.

SUMMARY

The OMGs—both indigenous and American-based—in Canada are the most criminal and violent motorcycle gangs in the world. They are truly criminal organizations engaged in a variety of organized criminal activities. An indication of the criminal activity of the Canadian Hells Angels and other Canadian motorcycle clubs/gangs is the fact that the Sûreté du Quebec has determined that the Quebec Hells Angels had $18 million in drug sales from November 10 to December 19, 2000 (Cherry, 2005:168). That included 1,916 kilograms of cocaine, for a profit of more than $8 million. They also reportedly moved 838 kilograms of hashish during that period, for a profit of $680,000.

The Canadian OMGs are also extremely violent, especially with each other, having little regard for any sense of biker brotherhood. As the widow of a Bandidos member murdered in 2004 remarked upon learning of the 2006 Ontario mass murder, "How can one of their own allegedly take them? What happened to the whole (biker) brotherhood?" (Bhardwaj, 2006). The answers to her questions may lie in the words of an Ontario Provincial Police official: "It should be remembered that these individuals are criminals. They're not the motorcycle enthusiasts they try to portray themselves to be" (Diebel, 2006).

REFERENCES

Anon. (2006). "Mass Killings Mean Angels Win Biker Turf War: Expert." *CBC News*, April 11, 2006. Found at: http://www.cbc.ca

Appleby, T. (2006). "'It's the End of the Bandidos in Canada': Murder Charges Leave Biker Gang's Membership Depleted, Police Say." *Globe and Mail*, June 22, 2006. Found at: http://www.theglobeandmail.com

Auger, M. (2002). *The Biker Who Shot Me*. Toronto: McClelland & Stewart.

Bhardwaj, A. (2006). "Family's Flashback: Widow of Bandido Slain Two Years Ago Knew Some of Latest Victims." *Edmonton Sun*, April 15, 2006.

Boland, J. (2006). "Ex-biker Thinks Meth Fuelled Killings." *Toronto Sun*, April 11, 2006.

Cherry, P. (2005). *The Biker Trials: Bringing Down the Hells Angels*. Toronto: ECW Press.

CISC (2005). *2005 Annual Report: Organized Crime in Canada*. Ottawa: Criminal Intelligence Service Canada.

Diebel, L. (2006). "Long on Ideas, Short on Time: Seeking Ways to Fight Biker Crime." *Toronto Star*, April 16, 2006.

Lambert, S. (2006). "Police Charge 3 Winnipeg Men in Slayings of 8 Bikers in Ontario." *National Archive*, June 16, 2006. Found at: http://www.680news.com/news/national

Langton, J. (2006). *Fallen Angel: The Unlikely Rise of Walter Stadnick in the Canadian Hells Angels*. Mississauga, Ontario: John Wiley & Sons, Canada.

Martineau, P. (2003). *I Was a Killer For the Hells Angels*. Toronto: McClelland & Stewart.

Paradis, P. *Nasty Business: One Biker Gang's Bloody War Against the Hells Angels*. Toronto: HarperCollins, Canada.

RCMP (1999). Anti-Gang Legislation: Bill C-95, *Gazette* 61 (Nos. 7-12).

Robertson, I. (2006). "Bandidos Betrayal? Bloodbath Tip-off: A Source." *Sun Media*, April 13, 2006.

Roslin, A. (2002). "Quebec Biker War: A Hells Angel Chieftain Named "Mom" Stands Accused of Running a $1 Billion Drug Empire." *High Times Magazine*. Found at: http://hightimes.com/new/content

Sanger, D. (2005). *Hell's Angels*. Toronto: Viking Canada.

Sher, J., and W. Marsden (2003). *The Road to Hell: How the Biker Gangs Are Conquering Canada*. Toronto: Alfred A. Knopf, Canada.

Sher, J., and W. Marsden (2006). *Angels of Death: Inside the Biker Gangs' Crime Empire*. New York: Carroll & Graf.

10

Biker Gangs Now and in the Future

The club in and of itself is not a criminal organization. It's never been proven to be a criminal organization.

George Christie Jr.—2006 (Heinz, 2006)

INTRODUCTION

It has been more than 50 years since the one-percent biker clubs were established and, as reflected in the statement of George Christie Jr., chapter and national Hells Angels president, club/gang spokesmen are still asserting that the clubs are not criminal organizations. Christie, a convicted felon (on conspiracy to sell drugs) and reportedly the number-two man in the Hells Angels, is considered to be successor to Sonny Barger. His statement of impression management flies in the face of the available evidence. The nature of the membership and criminal activities attributed to one-percent clubs, chapters of one-percent biker clubs, and members of one-percent biker clubs continues today and shows no signs of changing in the future.

CLUBS-TO-GANGS EVOLUTION

One-percent biker clubs as subcultures share a specific set of deviant values and adhere to a certain code of conduct that instills in each member a common basis of trust known as "brotherhood." The nature, structure, and culture of the one-percent biker subculture attracts bikers with criminal or potentially criminal dispositions—i.e., criminally exploitable ties—and facilitates and supports the criminal networks that arise in these clubs. The selection process ensures the perpetuation of the deviant culture. Patchholders in many clubs and chapters invite for membership only those prospects who share their same criminal propensities, even making the commission of crimes a prerequisite for membership. Given their selection and socialization practices, many of these clubs have evolved into social criminal organizations, that is, organizations that indirectly support the criminal activity of their members. Over time this indirect support facilitates the individual and group criminal behavior of a club's members and leads to the formation of gangs organized for profit through criminal activities, including organized crime.

The American-based biker gangs such as the Hells Angels, the Bandidos, and the Outlaws are involved in organized criminal activities on a national and international scale. Two common characteristics of these American-based gangs are violence and organized criminal activities, particularly the manufacture and distribution of drugs. According to law enforcement authorities in these countries, including Interpol, Europol, and the United Nations, the one-percent motorcycle clubs in their jurisdictions are more gangs than clubs.

NOW AND IN THE FUTURE

George Christie Jr. shares the common characteristic of many leaders/officers in the notorious Hells Angels motorcycle "club"/gang; that is, he is a convicted felon, particularly of a drug offense. This trend continues today. On June 11, 2007, the Spokane, Washington, Hells Angels chapter president was convicted of racketeering acts, including mail fraud and extortion. Two other current and former Angels were convicted along with him. The federal prosecutor was quoted as saying the case "blows up the myth that [the Hells Angels] create—that they just get together to sell T-shirts and ride motorcycles" (Johnson, 2007). In July 2006, the former sergeant-at-arms of the San Diego Hells Angels chapter pleaded guilty to conspiracy to commit racketeering and conspiracy to commit and distribute methamphetamine and received a 14-year sentence (Anon. 2, 2006). Another Shasta County, California, Hells Angels sergeant-at-arms, a registered sex offender, was arrested for the murders of two young girls—ages 12 and 15—more than 20 years ago (Herendeen, 2006). After finishing a 13-month sentence for drug and weapons possession, his DNA was run against DNA found at the girls' murders and was found to match. A former member of the Arizona Hells Angels alleges that Sonny Barger, the iconic HA leader, ordered him to murder a person that was passing himself off as a Hells Angel (Wagner, 2006). Members of the Washington Nomads Hells Angels, including the president and also the former West Coast president, went on trial February 28, 2007, faced with RICO charges (Bowermaster, 2007). The government alleges that the Nomads are a highly organized criminal organization.

The federal government has also prosecuted the Washington Bandidos MC. In October 2006, the national and international Bandidos president, George Wagers, was sentenced to a 20-month prison term after he pleaded guilty to conspiracy to commit racketeering (McDonald, 2007). As part of the plea agreement, Wagers is not allowed to live or work in Whatcom County, Washington, which is the location of the Bandidos national headquarters and where Wagers owns a Harley-Davidson shop. The 65-year-old president of the Bellingham, Washington, Bandidos chapter was sentenced to four years in prison by the same federal judge after he pleaded guilty to racketeering.

In 2006, Delaware indicted 32 Pagans members and associates for drug trafficking, racketeering, and gang activity (Parra and Williams, 2007). During the investigation, law enforcement authorities recovered cocaine, hallucinogenic mushrooms, Percocet, marijuana, firearms, and bullet-proof vests. During the execution of the search warrants, a 25-year-old Marine combat veteran and Pagans member was killed. His widow and parents have filed a federal civil rights lawsuit over the killing. In the Midwest, a police undercover operation in Louisville, Kentucky, led to the arrest and convictions of two Outlaws members—one of them the regional enforcer—for being felons in possession of a firearm.

THE CRIMINAL ACTIVITY OF OTHER AMERICAN ONE-PERCENT CLUBS

The Angels and other Big Five clubs are not the only one-percent biker "clubs"/gangs engaged in criminal activities today. In the Northeast, 16 members of the Diablos MC were arrested on federal and state narcotics and firearms charges (Anon. 1, 2005). The arrests were the result of an undercover operation by a Massachusetts state trooper. Also in the Northeast, 15 members of the Breed MC were arrested for running an $11 million methamphetamine ring in Pennsylvania and New Jersey (Naedale, 2006). Law enforcement authorities report that the Avengers MC has established a chapter in Huron County, Ohio, after a six-year absence. On the west coast, 25 members and associates of the Vagos MC were arrested for charges ranging from murder, attempted murder, and weapons and drug violations (Risling, 2006).

THE CRIMINAL ACTIVITY OF OTHER ONE-PERCENT CLUBS OUTSIDE THE UNITED STATES

In addition to the arrests in Canada for the massacre of eight Bandidos mentioned in Chapter 9, three members of the Denmark Bandidos were charged with extortion, money laundering, and six counts of illegal sale of public land in Thailand. An "Outlaw Motor Cycle Gang Squad" was recently formed in Queensland, Australia, "to fight against bikie [Australian term for biker] gangs who are involved in drug dealing, extortion and violence" (Wilson, 2006). The impetus for this bikie squad was a shoot-out between the Hells Angels and the Finks MCs. In that shootout, which took place at a kickboxing tournament, three people were shot and two people stabbed.

The Netherlands public prosecutor's office attempted to have the Hells Angels banned nationwide as a criminal organization. The prosecutors filed seven cases against all seven HA chapters (Amsterdam, Haarlem, Alkmaar, IJmuiden, Rotterdam, Kampen, and Harlingen), declaring that they were criminal organizations united in crime efforts. Dutch judges in the first case agreed that Hells Angels were involved in crime, but said there was insufficient evidence to suggest that the biker gang "threatens public order to the extent it should be banned" (Associated Press/AP Online, 2007). The judges in the case involving the Haringen chapter said that they could not be held responsible for criminal acts by members of other chapters. They also said that the criminal records of some members did not prove that the chapter was a criminal organization. The prosecutor's office said it would appeal; therefore, their efforts to ban the gang are not over.

Outlaw motorcycle gangs are expanding in Australia. The Australian Crime Commission reported in January 2007 that 10 of the nation's bikie gangs had added 26 new chapters (www.news.com.au/adelaidenow/story). Three new chapters were added in the state of South Australia, which now has eight bikie gangs: Bandidos, Descendants, Finks, Gypsy Jokers, Hells Angels, MobShitters, Rebels, and Red

Devils. As gang violence escalates between biker gangs over control of the drug markets, there is growing concern in New Zealand (Anon. 5, 2007).

Canadian authorities also continue to apply pressure on the biker gangs. A raid in April 2007 in the greater Toronto area by the Provincial Biker Enforcement Unit, a task force composed of Toronto police, provincial police, and the RCMP, served warrants on 12 locations, including the Hells Angels clubhouse, and led to the arrest of 30 bikers (Nguyen, 2007). Using a full-patched Angels member as a mole to infiltrate the gang, the police seized weapons and drugs as well as the largest HA clubhouse in Canada. The authorities also arrested a police officer for leaking police information to gang members. The existence of the mole leads to the conclusion that the Code of Brotherhood among biker gang members is eroding under intense police pressure. This was the third time in two years that Canadian police had been able to use full-patch members as police informants. The oft-repeated saying that "Three can keep a secret if two of them are dead" may be a truism, even for Angels brothers.

The head of the OPP (Ontario Provincial Police) Biker Enforcement Unit said that the raid proved that the gangs claim that they were a group of motorcycle enthusiasts is "misleading propaganda" (Vallis, 2007). He further sated that:

> The goals of outlaw motorcycle gangs are to create criminal enterprises in Ontario and Canada for financial gain through violence, threats and attempts to control various criminal activity focusing on drug trafficking.

Nevertheless, all the Canadian courts do not view biker gang members as criminals. A Hells Angels member convicted of assaulting a Canadian police officer, leaving him with a split lip, was given a 30-day sentence even though the Crown asked for four months. The Justice commented that the Angel had been a contributing member of society for a decade and that his offense was spontaneous and out of character (www.theglobeandmail.com).

OMG VIOLENCE

Enmity between one-percent "brothers" here and overseas goes on unabated. The violence often results from longstanding feuds and hatred. In January 2007, the sergeant-at-arms for a New Hampshire Outlaws chapter shot and killed a man for refusing to take off or turn inside out a Hells Angels support shirt before entering a bar that was an Outlaws hangout (Anon. 3, 2007). Similarly, Washington Hells Angels Nomad members are also accused of murdering a biker who misrepresented himself as a "full-patched" Angel. Two Hells Angels, one a prospect of a Canadian chapter, were recently arraigned for shooting five members of the Outlaws at Custer State Park in South Dakota (Walker, 2006). Both gangs were in the area for the annual Sturgis Motorcycle Rally. It was the first violence between one-percent biker gangs at the rally since 1990 when a bar brawl between the Outlaws and the Sons of Silence left an Outlaw shot and two Sons of Silence members stabbed.

Violence between biker gangs is still related to control of illegal markets, particularly drugs. The Australian Hells Angels announced their move into Sydney, Australia, by the shooting of a local bouncer (Gibbs, 2006). The shooting was meant to be a signal to Sydney's other biker gangs—the Rebels, Bandidos, Nomads, Finks, Commancheros, and Gypsy Jokers—that the Angels wanted a part of the lucrative drug trade. The Rebels are currently moving into territories controlled by the Outlaws and the Bandidos, spurring turf wars with these gangs. Five Bandidos were charged with arson for setting fire to the Brisbane clubhouse of the Rebels (Sid, 2007). The clubhouse was demolished because of fire damage. In April 2007, the Hells Angels and the Finks brawled in the Adelaide, Australia, airport when they met by chance while waiting for members on different flights.

CLUBS-VS.-GANGS CONTROVERSY

Julian Sher, biker expert and co-author of the best-selling book *Angels of Death*, commenting on the latest actions against the Angels stated:
These kinds of raids do tremendous damage to the Hells Angels' PR campaign to try to present themselves as just good old boys on bikes (Nixon, April 5, 2007).

There is still controversy surrounding the distinction between biker clubs and gangs. All members of outlaw motorcycle clubs qua gangs may not be criminals. For example, the FBI reports that members of the Hells Angels, including an Army lieutenant colonel, has served in Iraq (Main, 2007). Some members of the Canadian and Dutch military are also reported to be HA members. One of the Hells Angels killed in the 2002 Laughlin shootout between the Angels and the Mongols was a member of the U.S. Coast Guard. In 2002, the president of the London chapter of the Hells Angels led a phalanx of motorcycles during Queen Elizabeth's Golden Jubilee parade. However, the notoriety of the club/gang labels members as criminals. For example, the state of Washington is moving to revoke the state gambling license of a Hells Angels member who was the security supervisor of a state-licensed casino (Anon. 4, 2007). Video tapes show the security supervisor wearing his colors while working. The state considers the Hells Angels to be a "criminal offender cartel"; therefore, members are not eligible for licensure in the tightly regulated gambling industry. The security supervisor was, at the time, vice-president and acting president of the Washington Nomads chapter of the Hells Angels, based in Spokane. Members of the Nomads chapter, including the president— and former west coast HA president—and four members, are on trial for trafficking in stolen motorcycle parts, robbery, racketeering, and murder. The security supervisor was not charged.

Membership in OMGs also taints "good deeds." The clubs/gangs routinely participate in charitable events, such as Christmas toy events, but law enforcement groups say they do this to mask their true nature or rehabilitate their criminal reputation. The Queensland, Australia, Police Minister says that because some members of the Australian OMGs— Rebels, Bandidos, Finks, Outlaws and Hells Angels— are murderers, rapists, robbers, and drug traffickers, charities should stop accepting their donations (Viellaris, 2007), contending that the donations give the gangs an undeserved "veneer of respectability."

Approximately 5,000 bikers from around the New England area gather for a Harley rally that raises donations for the Ronald McDonald House in Brookline, Massachusetts. Outlaw motorcycle gangs routinely take part in such charitable events. *Photo courtesy of AP Photo/Tory Wesnofske.*

In addition to causing conflict between rival clubs/gangs, the wearing of gang colors has an intimidating effect on nonmembers, leading to bans in many public places, such as bars and restaurants. The Hells Angels are banned from wearing their colors to the Ventura California County Fair. They have gone to court to have this ban lifted. Colors bans of this nature will likely expand in the future in the United States and abroad as more jurisdictions define the clubs as gangs or criminal organizations.

LAW ENFORCEMENT INTELLIGENCE

In the future we can expect law enforcement authorities in the United States and overseas to expand their intelligence activities on OMGs. This includes the expanded use of biker informers, undercover operations, and electronic surveillance. In 1994, Congress passed the Communications Assistance for Law Enforcement Act to foil the use of communications by organized crime networks (Nolin, 2006). This act authorizes and compels the telecommunication industry to cooperate with the law enforcement agencies in electronic surveillance while assuring the privacy rights of citizens. The police can intercept virtually any cellular or Internet communications as long as they follow accepted procedural law. Electronic surveillance has been and will continue to be an important tool in law enforcement actions against biker gangs engaged in criminal activities.

The OMGs are also involved in intelligence activities directed at law enforcement. A recent search of a high-ranking Canadian Hells Angels member's home found Corrections Department profiles of Angels and associates, internal police memos, and secret road block plans (Pritchard, 2007). Canadian police authorities were disturbed but not surprised by the finding. The Winnipeg police chief said, "it's no secret organized crime groups like the Hells Angels conduct intelligence-gathering and counter-surveillance on police and justice officials" (McIntyre, 2007). Among the items found were names and phone numbers of Angels and associates around the world, including in Canada, United States, Denmark, South Africa, Germany, England, England, Portugal, France, Brazil, Australia, Italy, and Holland. This was a coup for police intelligence efforts. Because of the fear of infiltration by OMG members, the OMG sessions at the Annual Meeting of the National Gang Research Center are restricted to badge-carrying police officers.

A curious development that could have implications for police intelligence-gathering and the use of undercover police officers against biker gangs has recently come to light. ATF Special Agent Jay Dobyns, who spent three years investigating the Arizona Hells Angels, sued the Department of Alcohol, Tobacco, Firearms, and Explosives, claiming that his agency has failed to provide protection to him and his family following his undercover work (Shannon, 2007). Dobyns claims that the agency said protection would be too expensive. He also claims that once he filed suit the ATF Bureau began spreading allegations that he is mentally unfit to serve as a Special Agent. Because undercover law enforcement officers are so important in the investigation of biker gangs, this suit and the publicity surrounding it could have a dampening effect on the willingness of ATF agents to volunteer for these assignments.

REFERENCES

Anon. 1 (2005). "Several Members of Diablos Motorcycle Gang Arrested." December 9, 2005. Found at: http://www.inqnews.com/Articlephp?id=657

Anon. 2 (2006). "Former Hells Angels Member Gets 14 Years." July 28, 2006. Found at: http://www.signonsandiego.com

Anon 3. (2007). "Biker Rivalry Murder Trial Starts, Outlaws, Hells Angels Feud Seen as Motive." Associated Press, February 3, 2007. Found at: http://www.concord monitor.com

Anon 4. (2007). "Hells Angel Got State Gambling License: 'Full-Patch' Member Hired for Security at Valley Casino." *The Spokesman-Review*. Found at: http://www.highbeam.com/DocPrint.aspx?DocId=1Y1:104515487

Anon 5. (2007). "Gang Violence Escalates in Wanganui." April 5, 2007. Found at: http://www.stuff.co.nz

Associated Press/AP Online (2007). "Dutch Judges Refuse to Ban Hells Angels." March 6, 2007. Found at: http://highbeam.com

Bowermaster, D. (2007). "Hell's Angels Case Going to Court. *Seattle Times,* February 28, 2007. Found at: http://seattletimes.nwsource.com

Gibbs, S. (2006). "Sydney's Big Bikie Gangs Are Armed and Dangerous. And Now the Hells Angels Are Rolling into Town." Found at: http://www.smh.com.au.au/news/national

Heinz, (2006). "Angels 'Share Cody Values' in Peaceful Rally." Found at: http://www.codyenterprise.com

Herendeen, S. (2006). "Murder Suspect Built Life on the Coast." Found at: http://www.modbee.com

Johnson, G. (2007). "Guilty Verdicts in Hells Angels Trial." *FoxNews.com*, June 11, 2007.

Main, F. (2007). "FBI Details Threat from Gangs in Military." *Sun Times*. Found at: http://www.knowgangs.com/news/jan07/0120.php

McDonald, C. (2007). "Hells Angels Leaders on Trial Today: Biker Gang Charged with Racketeering." *Seattle Post-Intelligencer,* March 12, 2007. Found at: http://seattle epi.nwsource.com

McIntyre, M. (2007). "Hell's Angels Trial: See the Evidence: Leaked Files No Surprise to Ewatski; Gangs Gather Counter-intelligence." *The Winnipeg Free Press*. Found at: http://www.winnipegfreepress.com

Naedale, W.F. (2006). "Motorcycle Gang's $1 Million Meth Ring Broken." *The Philadelphia Inquirer*.

Nguyen, L. (2007). "Thirty Arrested as Police Raid Biker Gangs." *Toronto Star,* April 4, 2007. Found at: http://www.thestar.com

Nixon, G. (2007). "Hells Angels 'Reeling' After Cross-country Raids, but War Not Over: Expert." *Canadian Press,* April 5, 2007. Found at: http://www.canada.com

Nolin, C.A. (2006). "Tellecommunications as a Weapon in the War of Modern Organized Crime." *Common Law Conspectus: Journal of Communications Law and Policy* 15(1):231-260.

Parra, E., and L. Williams (2007). "Pagan Attorneys Seek Investigation Details." March 29, 2007. Found at: http://www.delawareonline.com

Pritchard, D. (2007). "Cop Papers Found at Hells Angels Home, Court Found." *Sun Media*. Found at: http://winnipegsun.com/News/Winnepeg/2007/03/13/pf-3741887.html

Risling, G. (2006). "Sweep of Motorcycle Club Leads to 25 Arrests, Seizure of Firearms." *The San Diego Union-Tribune*, March 10, 2006. Found at: http://www.signonsandiego.com/uniontrib/20060310/news_1n10gang.html

Shannon, M. (2007). "Federal Agent: No Protection After Dangerous Undercover Work." All Headline News, February 5, 2007. Found at: http://www.allheadlinesnews.com

Sid (2007). "Bandidos to Face Court Over Fire, April 16, 2007. Found at: http://www.ozbiker.com

Viellaris, R. (2007). "Charities Told to Outlaw Bikie Gifts," April 1, 2007. Found at: http://www.news.com.au/perthnow/story

Wagner, D. (2006). "Informer Links Top Hells Angel to Murder Plot." *The Arizona Republic*.

Walker, C. (2006). "Hells Angels Bikers Indicted." *Rapid City Journal*.

Vallis, M. (2007). "Ontario Police Officials Praise Informant's Help in Hells' Raids." *National Post*, April 5, 2007. Found at: http://www.canada.com

Wilson, T. (2006). "New Cop Squad to Focus on Bad Bikies." *The Gold Coast Bulletin*.

Appendix A
By-Laws—Bandidos
Motorcycle Club, 1999

Note: These by-laws have been reproduced with the original capitalization, misspellings, and punctuation errors.

1: Requirements for a Chapter:
Five (5) member minimum — One (1) "Charter Member".
Charter Member = 10 years.
Keep pictures and information on all members.
Hold weekly meetings.
$25.00 per month, per member to National treasury (by the 1st of each month).
Probationary Chapters (new) will pay a one-time donation of $1000.00 to National Treasury.
Probationary Chapter members bikes and titles will be pledged to National Chapter for the first year.

2: Patches:
Only a Top and Bottom rocker, Fat Mexican, 1% diamond and MC patch should be on the back of your cut-off, It should be visible from 150 feet.
A 1%er diamond will be worn over the heart.
Anything else is up to the individual.

Year patches & buckles are not to be given early.

National can grant a "Lifer" patch or membership on a person to person basis.

One Property Patch per member. If she rides her own bike it is NOT to be worn while riding with or around Patcholders or Prospects. It should not be worn in public without her old man in view.

There is no limit on Property Belts.

3: Do's:

Labor Day and Memorial Day are MANDATORY RUNS. A Chapter may leave one (1) member behind from a mandatory run. A member on medical leave or a Life Member is that member. This is for security reasons, that person should have access to a phone as much as possible.

When you are traveling you should attend your host chapter's meetings. You must abide by those chapters [sic] By-Laws and policies.

4: Don'ts:

Things that will cost you your patch:
You don't lie.
You don't steal.
This includes OL' Ladies as well.

Needle use will not be tolerated.
Neither will smoking of any chemicals—coke, speed, mandrax...if it didn't grow, don't smoke it!

5: Motorcycles:

Each member will OWN at least one (1) Harley Davidson or facsimile of at least 750cc.
No more than 30 days a year down time.
After 30 days that members Chapter will pay National $500.00.
Have a good reason? Ask for more time.

Road Captains should inspect all bikes regularly.

6: Membership:

*Hangaround period to be determined by chapter President.

*Harley Davidson Motorcycle or facsimile capable of meeting the demands of Pledge period.

*Members must be at least 21 years of age

*Sponsor—May be individual (preferably charter member) or may be Sponsored by chapter as a hole. Sponsor,

> Do not turn your Pledge loose without help. If you think enough of him to sponsor him into this club, it's up to you to teach him the right way, the BANDIDO WAY. If you're not ready to sacrifice your time and share your knowledge. Don't do it. The simple things—Who's the neatest M.F. in the world? Or don't wear your Patch in a vehicle. Trivial things that will get a Prospective BROTHER run off.

> > *Pay $275.00 to National Treasury.
> > *Pledge bike and title.
> > *Be voted in as Pledge by Chapter (100% vote).
> > *Receive your Patch or Rocker.
> > *DO YOUR TIME.
> > Prospect 6 months MINMUM.
> > Probationary 1 year MINIMUM.

> This man is pledged to the whole BANDIDO NATION, not just one Chapter or area, City or State. He will attend every meeting, party, bike event or gathering of any kind in his area where Bandido Patcholders will be present.

> He will not miss any National or Regional runs, especially Funerals.

> This club is about sacrifice, get used to it! His motorcycle should be in up and running condition his whole Pledge period, ready to go anywhere. In other words, NO DOWN TIME.

> *Pledge is not eligible for vote if there are any outstanding debts, Chapter, National or Private, (inside club), he should start into this club on a level playing field.

*After the mandatory time period has passed, and the Sponsor feels the Pledge is ready, a meeting should be called. All surrounding Chapter Secretaries should also be notified, (in advance).

*The Pledge should be voted in by a 100% Chapter vote. Club members outside the chapter should have a chance to voice their opinions. The Pledges Sponsor should base his decision on these things, for he is the One whom will have to fade it if things go foul.
It is a lifelong commitment, DON'T RUSH IT.

*Charter Member is 10 years of unbroken service.

*National may grant Leave of absence—this is not automatic.

*Two (2) year members are eligible for transfer, only if both Presidents involved have agreed and a $50.00 fee is paid to National Treasury.

Other national Fees:

New Patch Fee	$ 275.00
Transfers	$ 50.00
New Charter	$1000.00
30 Day Downtime rule	$ 500.00

Index

Abbott, K., 82

Alain, M., 77

Albanese, J., 12–13, 16, 116

Alberta Grim Reapers MC, 148

Alberta Rebels MC, 148

Aliens MC, 9, 41

Altamont Speedway incident, 38–42

"American iron" motorcycles, 46, 56–57

American Motorcycle Association (AMA), 23, 25, 45

American popular culture, one-percent bikers and, 2

Anastasia, G.G., 81

Anderson, A.C., 17

Angels of Death (Sher and Marsden), 139–140, 166

Anti-gang legislation, Canadian, 150

Appellant v. United States, 91, 106

Appleby, T., 158

Aryan Brotherhood, 52, 53

Aryan Nation, 52

Asian organized crime, 122

Associates, 62–63

Auger, M., 3, 145

Australia
 Bandidos MC in, 77
 bikie gangs in, 7, 136
 HAMC chapters in, 77
 outlaw motorcycle gangs in, 133–137, 164
 Outlaw Motor Cycle Gang Squad, 164

Autobiographies
 biker club members, 5–6
 HAMC, 97–100

Avengers MC, 9, 118, 164

Baers, M.J., 38–40
Bandidos MC, 5, 50
    affiliation with Outlaws MC,
        79
    in Australia, 7, 77
    Bandidos Massacre, 157–158
    as Big Five club, 78–79
    biker wars and, 10
    black member in, 54
    in Canada, 153–154
    criminal activities of, 117
    in Europe, 132
    in Great Nordic Bike War, 10
    journalistic accounts of, 3
    membership outside U.S.,
        78–79
    Milperra Australia Massacre
        and, 6
    Nomads chapter, 78
    as one-percent biker club, 8
    organized crime activities,
        118
    recruitment process for, 62
    "Red and Gold World,"
        88–89
    relationship with Sons of
        Silence, 83
    turf battle between Hells
        Angels and, 7
    women and, 57
Barger, Ralph "Sonny," 71, 96,
    97
    on Altamont Speedway, 40
    assassination attempt, 10
    autobiography of, 99
    as convicted felon, 2, 104
    domestic violence complaints
        against, 51
    drug dealing by, 98

    on "elite men's clubs," 46
    grand jury testimony, 91
    at Hellraisers Ball, 10
    in Hell's Angels Forever, 2
    as media celebrity and best
        selling author, 2
    move to Arizona, 107
    on organized crime, 125
    personal attorney for, 76
    quotation, 95
    RICO action against, 102
    as signator on London char-
        ter, 5
    as technical advisor for Hell's
        Angels on Wheels, 2
    testimony by, 106
Barker, T., 9, 45, 46, 129, 130
Beare, M.E., 3
Becker, H.S., 46
Belli, Melvin, 41
Big Five clubs, 8–9, 76–83
    Bandidos MC, 78–79. See also
        Bandidos MC
    as criminal organizations, 126
    HAMC, 76–78. See also Hells
        Angels Motorcycle Club
    Outlaws MC, 79–80. See also
        Outlaws MC
    Pagans MC, 80–82. See also
        Pagans MC
    racist restrictions in, 54
    Sons of Silence MC as, 82–83.
        See also Sons of Silence MC
"Big Red Machine," 76
Bike Lust: Harleys, Women, and
    American Society (Joans),
    65–66
Biker, defined, 65, 66
Biker clubs
    ideals of, 7–8

in popular literature, 3–4
See also One-percent biker
clubs; Outlaw motorcycle
gangs (OMGs); *and entries
for specific clubs*
Biker-friendly bars, 63
Bike Riders, The (Lyon), 4
Biker justice, 100
Biker literature. *See* Literature
Biker movies
classics, 2
Easy Rider, 2, 33
Wild Angels, The, 38
Wild One, The, 33
Biker music, 2
*Bikers: Birth of a Modern Day
Outlaw*, (Harris), 6
Bikers Atlas, 64
Biker's Code of Brotherhood,
126
Biker subculture, 129
Biker wars, 9–12
Biker women
as necessary nuisances, 47
prostitution and, 48–49
sexual rituals and, 48
status roles for, 47–50
Bikie gangs, 8, 136
Black Pistons MC, 88, 89
Black Uhlans MC, 8
Black Urban Ryders Nation MC,
24
Blatnois Mauricie MC, 150
Blitzkrieg MC, 89
Boland, J., 157
Boozefighters MC, 27–28, 47
Born to Be Wild (Steppenwolfe),
2
Born Killers Motorcycle Gang,
41

Boucher, Maurice "Mom," 100,
147, 153, 156
Bowe, B., 3
Bowermaster, D., 163
Bowman, Harry "Taco", 5, 107
conviction of, 105
on FBI Most Wanted List, 10
as murderer of Warlocks
President, 86
trial of, 54
war against HAMC, 119–120
Bragg, M., 83
Braithwaite, D., 136
Brando, Marlon, 34
Breed MC
biker wars and, 9
organized crime activities,
118
as regional one-percent biker
group, 8
Brenner, S. W., 103
Brotherhood, 162
as biker club ideal, 7
criminal organization
continuum and, 126
as overriding value, 66
Brown wings, 98–99
Buell motorcycles, 56
Bullshit MC, 138
Bureau of Alcohol, Tobacco,
Firearms, and Explosives
(ATF), 19, 85
BURN MC, 24
*Buttons: The Making of a
President* (Mandelkau), 98

California, Southern, appearance of OMCs in, 25

California Highway Patrol (CHP), Hollister Motorcycle incident, 29

Canada
HAMC in, 77, 145–158
pressure on biker gangs in, 165
war between Rock Machine and HAMC in, 5, 147, 152, 156
Canadian law enforcement Bandidos Massacre and, 157–158
Criminal Intelligence Service Canada (CISC), 146–156

Canadian Rock Machine MC, 17

Canoga Park Alabama, 17

Caparella, K., 81

Carroll, David "Wolf," 107

Cavaliers MC, 24

Chafin, Raymond "Bear," 119–120

Chambers, Donald Eugene, 78, 105

Chapman, Duane "Dog," 104

Charles, G., 3

Cherry, P., 16, 145, 156

Chinese Triads, 130

Ching-a-lings MC, 52

Choir Boys MC, 11

Choppers (Discovery Channel), 2

Christie, George, III, 104

Christie, George, Jr., 104, 161, 162

Clauson, C. B., 27

Clothing
distinctive, 15
as symbolic representation, 17
See also Colors

Club bar, 61
recruitment process and, 63–65

Clubs-to-gangs evolution, 162–163

Clubs-vs.-gangs controversy, 166–167

Coffin Cheaters MC, 7, 134

Cohen, Stanley, 30–31, 96

Colnett, V., 5, 36–37, 97

Colombian Cartels, 130

Colombian organized crime, 122

Colors, 72
HAMC ban from wearing, 167
as message to others, 45
one-percenters', 2
as symbolic representation, 17

Colors parties, 71

Commancheros MC, 8, 134
biker wars and, 10
journalistic accounts of, 3
Milperra Australia Massacre and, 6

Commitment, as biker club ideal, 7

Connecticut Ed, 5. *See also* Winterhalder, E.

Conquistators MC, 50–51

Conventional motorcycle clubs, 23

Covarrubias, A., 17

Crash truck, 70

Crime, organized. *See* Organized crime

Criminal activities
one-percent biker clubs and, 3, 8–9, 12

by outlaw motorcycle gangs, 122–123
outside the U.S., 164–165
Criminal Intelligence Service Canada (CISC), 146–156
Criminally exploitable ties, 14
Criminal networks, 14
Criminal organization
    continuum of one-percent motorcycle clubs as, 126
    economic, 16
    quasi-governmental, 17
    social, 17–18
    structural complexity of, 18
Crips, 17
Curvin, Chris, 79
"Cyclist's Raid" article, 32–33

Danner, T.A., 53
Davey, J., 137
Davidson, Arthur and Walter, 23
Davis, John, 4
Davis, R.H., 101
Daytona, Florida, Bike Week and, 1
Daytona Bike Week, Pagan-Outlaw clash at 1976, 9
Death head, 35
Delattre, Edwin J., 115
Denmark
    Bandidos MC in, 164
    outlaw motorcycle gangs in, 138–140
Dequiallo, 91
Desroches, F.J., 15, 18, 63
Detroit, M., 3
Deviant clubs, 24. *See also* One-percent biker clubs; Outlaw motorcycle gangs

de Vries, Paul "The Butcher," 140
Diablos MC, 9
    criminal activity of, 163
    organized crime activities, 118–119
Dirty Dozen MC, 9, 126
Dobkins, Lou, 80
Dobyns, Jay "Jaybird," 63
Documentary films, 2
Donald E. Chambers v. State of Texas, 78
Doughtie, J. A., 130
Drug trafficking, 88, 117
Drug-trafficking organizations (DTOs), 13
Dykes on Bikes MC, 24

East Bay Dragons MC, 5, 52, 89
Easy Rider, 2, 33
Economic criminal organizations, 17, 124–126
Edmonton Rebels MC, 149
Eischeid, Paul, 55
England, Outlaw chapters in, 5
Ethnicity trap, 13
EU Organized Crime Report, 132
Europol, 132

Fallen Angel: Hell's Angel to Heaven's Saint (Mayson), 99
Fates Assembly MC, 9
Father-son involvement, 104
Federal Bureau of Investigation (FBI), 18–19
Federation of American Motorcyclists (FAM), 25
"Filthy Few," 106

Finks MC, 8, 134
Finland, OMGs in, 132
Florida-based Warlocks MC,
    85–86
Folk devils image, 11, 30–32, 99
*Folk Devils and Moral Panics:
    The Creation of the Mods and
    Rockers,* 30
Forkner, "Wino Willie," 26–29
Forsaken Few MC, 88
Foster, D., 82
Freelancers MC, organized
    crime activities, 119
"Freewheeling clubs," 35
Friedl, Otto, 34–38
"Friends of the club," 67–68
Fuglsang, R.S., 23, 25, 28, 96

Galloping Ghosts MC, 138
Galloping Gooses MC, 27, 37
Gang, defined, 103
Gangs
    evolution from clubs to,
        162–163
    outlaw motorcycle clubs as,
        103–108
Ghetto Riders MC, 89
Gibbs, S., 166
Gimme Shelter, 39, 41
Givvons, T.J., 81
Glendale Stokers MC, 28
Gotcha Sportswear, 76
Great Nordic Bike War, 10
Great Nordic War, 138–139
Guisto, Betsy, 47, 50–51, 54
Gypsy Jokers MC, 7, 37, 134,
    136–137
Gypsy tours, 28–30, 32

Hakaim, Tom, 118
HAMC. *See* Hells Angels
    Motorcycle Club
Hancock, Don, 136–137
Harley, William, 23
Harley-Davidson Company
launching of, 23
100th Anniversary, 1
Harley-Davidson motorcycle, as
    outlaw machine, 25, 56–57
Harper's Magazine, "Cyclist's
    Raid" article, 32–33
Harris, Maz, 6–7, 54, 71–72,
    96, 129
*Hartmann's Chicagoland Guide
    to Biker Bars,* 63–64
Harvey, S., 3
Haut, F., 77, 100, 129, 130
Hayes, Bill, 26, 32
Hell's Angels (Discovery
    Channel), 2
Hell's Angels (Marvel Comics),
    76
*Hell's Angels: The Life and
    Times of Sonny Barger,*
    (Barger), 2
Hell's Angels Forever, 2
Hell's Angels Motorcycle Club,
    (Barger), 2
Hell's Angels on Wheels, 2
Hell Bent for Glory Motorcycle
    Club, 35
Hell's Angel: Demon of Lust, 76
Hells Angels Motorcycle Club
    (HAMC)
    AFFA web site, 11
    Alberta chapter, 148
in American popular culture. 2
    in Australia, 7, 77
autobiographies, 97–100

Bandidos vs., 7

Barger, Ralph "Sonny," 35–36. *See also* Barger, Ralph "Sonny"

biker wars and, 9

British Columbia chapters, 148

in Canada, 77, 145–158

confrontation with anti-war demonstrators and, 7

criminal activities of, 117

as criminal offender cartel, 167

Danish chapter, 138

Death Riders puppet club, 147

in Europe, 132

"Filthy Few," 106

first chapter of, 76

formation of, 34–35

in Great Nordic Bike War, 10

history of, 34–38

journalistic accounts of, 3

as largest one-percent club in world, 46

literature on formative years, 5

members in Arizona club, 55

in mid-1960s, 37–38

Monterey "rape," 38

movies about, 3

New York puppet clubs, 63

Nomads chapter, 149

Oakland chapter, 36–37

as one-percent biker club, 8, 37

Ontario chapter, 151

organizational structure, 91–92

organized crime activities, 119

other names for, 76

outlaw subculture and, 6

Philadelphia chapter, 82

photodocumentaries on, 5

puppet clubs, 88

Quebec Nomads chapter, 16, 87–88, 147, 149

San Francisco chapter's restrictions, 53

as security for Altamont Speedway concert, 39

significance of lightening bolt patch, 107

undercover female officer riding with, 100–101

violence among chapters of, 11

war with Outlaws, 102

war with Rock Machine in Canada, 5, 147, 152, 156

See also One-percent biker clubs; Outlaw motorcycle gangs

Hells Lovers MC, 52, 89

Henderson, Wild Bill, 98

Herendeen, S., 163

Hessians MC, 71

Hicks, Wayne "Joe Black," 120

Highwaymen MC, 63

Hodges, Ronnie, 105

Hogan, Alan, 77

Hollister Independence Rally, July 2004, 1

Hollister Motorcycle Incident/Riot (1947), 28–31

Holthouse, D., 81

Hopper, C.B., 47–49, 52

Hunter, Meredith, 39–41

Independent one-percent clubs,
    83–87
    Iron Horsemen MC, 87
    Mongols MC, 86–87
    Warlocks MC, 84–86
Indian motorcycles, 56
Ingalls, Paul A. "German," 36
Initiation nights, 71
Initiation runs, 71
*In Search of History: Hell's
    Angels* (Arts and
    Entertainment Network), 2
International Outlaw
    Motorcycle Gang
    Investigators Association
    (IOMGIA), 131
Interpol, 101, 130–131
Iron Horsemen MC, 87, 119

Jackson, Peter, 5
Joans, Barbara, 65–66
Johnson, G., 162
Johnson, W.C., 102
Journalistic accounts of biker
    clubs, 3–4, 55
Justice, street or biker, 100

Katz, T., 55, 130
Kaye, H.R., 5, 97, 98
Kellestine, Wayne, 157
Kendall, R.E., 130
Kessler, R.E., 81
Kilzer, L., 82
Kingsbury, K., 3
Koch, D.S., 115, 124
Kravetz, A., 119
Ku Klux Klan, 17, 52, 53

Laconia, New Hampshire, Bike
    Week, 1
La Cosa Nostra, 17, 108, 122,
    130
La Eme, Mongol's relationship
    with, 86
Lambert, S., 158
Langton, J., 145
Larsen, Uffe, 106
Lasky, R., 41
Lavigne, Y, 3, 46, 52, 53, 54, 77,
    80, 107–108
Law enforcement
    Canadian activities, 146–156.
        See also Canadian law
        enforcement
    early efforts, 100–103
    at federal level, 101–102
    intelligence, 168
Leo, J., 63–65
"Letting off steam," 26, 27
Levingston, G., 5, 52
Lewis, J., 18
Lewis, Lou, 136–137
Lindberg, K., 62
Literature
    autobiographies, 5–6, 97–100
    journalistic accounts, 3–4, 55
    photodocumentaries, 5
    scholarly, 6–8
"Local 81," 76
Loners MC, organized crime
    activities, 119
Los Bravos MC, 148
Lowe, M., 3, 97
Lynn, Massachusetts, 64
Lyon, Danny, 4, 97

McAloon, C., 136

McCook Outlaws Motorcycle Club, 79

McDonald, C., 163

McIntyre, M., 168

McKee, M., 76

Mafia, 13, 122

MAGLOCLEN Assessment on Outlaw Motorcycle Gangs, 116, 121

Main, F., 166

Mamas, 47–48, 50

Mandelkau, J., 5, 97, 98, 129

Marijuana, hydroponic cultivation, 148

Market Street Commandoes MC, 27–28

Marron, John Vernon "Satan," 80

Marsden, W., 3, 54, 55, 88, 100, 106, 107, 139–140, 145

Martineau, P., 5, 145

Martinez, Antonio "Tiny," 103

Marvel Comics, 76

Maticka-Tyndale, E., 18

Maxwell, J. C., 137

Mayson, Barry, , 975, 99

Mello, M, 4, 108

Mexican Mafia, Mongol's relationship with, 86

Miles, James "Mother," 35

Miles, Pat, 35

Millage, K., 105, 118

Milperra Australia Massacre, 6, 136

Milwaukee, Wisconsin, Harley Davidson 100th Anniversary, 1

Miranda, C., 134

Mofos MC, 37

Money laundering, 63

Mongols MC, 63, 86–87, 126
  biker wars and, 10
  ferocity of, 83
  as lesser-known one-percent biker group, 8
  Queen as undercover ATF agent in, 68

Monterey, California, Labor Day Rally in (1964), 7

Moore, J., 47, 48–49, 52

Moral panic, 30–31

Morrison, Jim, 31

Morsani, A., 11

Motorcycles
"American iron," 46, 56–57

foreign, 4, 65

production of first, 23

Motorcycle culture, 6

Movies. See Biker movies

Murphy, Mark .G., 6

Muscedere, John "Boxer," 157

Music, biker, 2

National Alliance of Gang Investigators' Associations (NAGIA), 75, 78, 116

National Drug Intelligence Center (NDIC), 19

National Gang Crime Research Center (NGCRC), 52

National Gang Threat Assessment (2005), 116

Nazis, 53

Neo-Nazis, 52

Netherlands
  banning of HAMC in, 164
  outlaw motorcycle gangs in, 139–140

Newbold, G., 140

New Orleans Gay Motorcycle
  Club, 24
New Zealand
  gang violence in, 165
  outlaw motorcycle gangs in,
    140–141
Nguyen, L., 165
Nielsen, Jorn "Jonke," 138
Nixon, G., 166
Nolin, C.A., 168
Nomads MC, 78, 140

Oakland Panthers MC, 35
Odin's Warriors MC, 8
Ohio, motorcycle gangs in, 102
Old ladies, 48, 50
Olsen, Arvid, 34
One-percent biker club
  Outlaws as first, 79
  recruitment process, 61–73.
    See also Recruitment
    process
One-percent biker clubs
  at Altamont Speedway, 38–42
  "American iron" motorcycles
    and, 56–57
  in American popular culture,
    2
  Big Five. *See* Big Five
  biker wars and 9–12
  black or interracial, 52–54, 89
  club bars and, 64. *See also*
    Club bar
  as clubs vs. gangs, 96
  colors of, 45
  connection to traditional orga-
    nized crime, 6
  criminal activities of, 3, 8–9,
    97

as deviant clubs, 24
deviant life style of members,
  8
estimated number of, 75
folk devils image, 11, 30–32, 99
foreign motorcycles and, 4
  gender roles in, 47
  independent. *See* Independent
    one-percent clubs
lesser-known groups, 8
for lower/working class, 55–56
  major independents, 84–87.
    See also Independent one-
    percent clubs
  organizational structure, 90
  as outlaw motorcycle gangs
    (OMGs), 11
  as portrayed in movies, 2
  puppet clubs, 88–89
  regional 8
  relationships among, 83–84
  symbolic representation, 17
  violence of, 8–9
  white males and, 46–47
  as white supremacists or
    racists, 52
  women and, 46–52. *See also*
    Biker women
One Percent (Upright), 4–5
Operation Rocker, 130–131
Operation ROUGHRIDER,
  102–103
Operation SHADOW, 153
Operation SPRINGTIME, 156
Operation WOLF, 154
Operation Zircon, 137
Organized crime, 12–14
  biker gangs as, 115–127

criminal organization continuum, 125–127

enumeration method to define, 13–14

gang/club criminal activities, 116–121

from group activity to criminal organizations, 124–125

international, OMGs and, 11

Mafia as metaphor for, 14

member criminal activity, 121–124

network approach to, 14–18

traditional, relationship to one-percent biker gangs, 6

typology of activities, 13

Organized Crime in Denmark in 2004, 138–140

Orient-Aster motorcycle, 23

Osgerby, B., 38

Outlaw motorcycle gangs (OMGs), 11, 25–33

appearance of, 25

in Australia, 133–137

Boozefighters MC (1946), 27–28

cyclist's raid, 32–33

first biker movies about, 33

Forkner, "Wino Willie," 26–27

as gangs, 103–108

HAMC and the one-percenters, 34–38

list of crimes committed by, 122–123

members' criminal history, 104–108

moral panics, folk devils and, 30–31

organized crime groups associated with, 122

international expansion, 130–133

official information on, 18–19

Riverside motorcycle riot (1948), 32

violence and, 165–166

white-supremacist, 115

Outlaws MC

affiliation with Bandidos MC, 79

in Australia, 7

as Big Five club, 79–80

biker wars and, 9

in Canada, 153

criminal activities of, 117

in Europe, 132

journalistic accounts of, 3

member on death row for murder, 4

as one-percent biker club, 8

organized crime activities, 119

Pennsylvania chapters, 82

photodocumentary on, 4–5

Project RETIRE against, 154

puppet clubs, 88–89

rockers and colors, 5

at Sturgis Motorcycle Rally, 166

Upright's photos of, 53

war between HAMC and, 102

Outlaw subculture, development of, 6

Pagans MC, 47

as Big Five club, 80–82

biker wars and, 9

criminal activities of, 117
drug trafficking by, 117
  journalistic accounts of, 3
  as one-percent biker club, 8
  organized crime activities,
    120
  puppet clubs, 89
  ties to La Cosa Nostra, 108
  violence and, 82
Pagans Mother Club, 81
Pagans Mother Group, 90
Panzer Task Force, 133–134
Para-Dice Riders MC, 148–149
Paradis, P., 5, 145
Partying, as biker club ideal, 7
Passaro, Allen, 41
"Patched over," meaning of
  term, 7, 62
Patches, 72
  as Outlaw rocker, 5
  as symbolic representation, 17
Patchholder, stages in becoming,
  62, 65–72. *See also*
  Recruitment process
PEN1, 53
Pennsylvania-based Warlocks
  MC, 84–85, 118, 126
Peterson, Barney, 29
Photodocumentaries, biker clubs
  and 4–5
Piscottano, Gary, 53
Pissed Off Bastards of
  Bloomington MC (POBOB),
  27, 29, 34, 76
*Place in Hell: The Inside Story
  of 'Hell's Angels'—The
  World's Wildest Outsiders*
  (Kaye), 98
Porter, Walt, 27
Pratt, A., 96

Presidents MC, 37
Prison gang, 104
Pritchard, D., 168
Project AMIGO, 154
Project RETIRE, 154
Project Rocker, 130–131
Prospecting, purpose of, 69
Prostitution, biker women and,
  48–49
Puppet clubs, 88–89

Quasi-governmental criminal
  organization, 17
Quebec Nomads, 17
Queen, W., 68, 71–72, 86, 92,
  95, 96
Queensland Crime and
  Misconduct Commission, 137
Quesnel, Serge, 6, 100
Quinn, James, 18, 45–48, 55,
  62, 71, 79, 115, 124

*Rebels, The: A Brotherhood of
  Outlaw Bikers*, (Wolfe), 6–7
Rebels MC, 134
  in Australia, 7, 134
  Edmonton, Canada, 7
  women in, 49
Recruitment process, 61–63
  club bar and, 63–65
  friend of the club/hang-
    around stage, 67–68
  initiation-patchholder stage,
    71–72
  patch/colors and, 72
  righteous biker stage, 65–67
  stages of, 62
  striker/prospect/probate stage,
    68–71

Red Devils MC, 63, 89

"Red and White," 76

Reid, K.E., 100

Renegades MC, 120, 126

Research methodology, 18–19

Reshetylo, Daniel A., 7. *See also* Wolfe, Daniel A.

Reynolds, F., 3, 5, 97

Reynolds, T., 26, 27, 28, 31, 37, 41, 103, 129

Richards, Keith, 40

RICO (Racketeer Influenced and Corrupt Organizations)

application to motorcycle gangs, 9, 101–102

prosecutions, 90–91

Riding, as biker club ideal, 7

Righteous biker, 62, 65–67

Risling, G., 105

Riverside motorcycle riot (1948), 32

Road Hogs (MTV), 2

Road Rats MC, 37

Road Runners MC, 28

Road Saints MC, 120

Road Warriors, the Biker Brotherhood (Arts and Entertainment Network), 2

Robertson, I., 157

Rockers, 5, 72

Rockers MC, 3, 88

Rock Machine MC

biker wars and, 10

as economic criminal organization, 16

journalistic accounts of, 3

war between HAMC and

war with HAMC, 5, 147, 152, 156

Roemer, D.V., 96

Rolling Stones, Altamont Speedway concert, 38–42

Roslin, A., 156

Royal Canadian Mounted Police (RCMP), 6

Russian organized crime, 108, 122

Sadilek, Frank, 37

St. Thomas Annihilators, 157

St. Thomas Loners, 157

San Francisco Chronicle, photo of drunken motorcyclists in, 29

Sanger, D., 88, 100, 145

Satan's Choice MC

criminal activities of, 149

initiation by, 71

journalistic accounts of, 3

members in prison for murder, 4

Satan's Dead MC, 48

Satan's Sinners MC, 27

Satan's Slaves MC, 37

Scholarly literature on biker clubs, 6–8

Secret Life of Outlaw Bikers, 2

Sexual rituals, 48–49

Shannon, M., 168

Shaylor, Andrew, 5

Sheep, 48

Shellow, R., 96

Sher, J., 3, 54, 55, 88, 100, 105, 106, 107, 139–140, 145, 157

Side Winders MC, 28

Silverman, I.J., 53

Simpson, L., 3

Sisson, Andrew, 141

Skinheads, 52–53

Slatalla, Joseph, 91,106

Smith, B.W., 130

Smith, R., 103

Smurfs, 63

Social criminal organizations, 17–18, 125–126

Socializing process, striker period as, 68–71

Sons of Silence MC, 166
    as Big Five club, 82–83
    as one-percent biker club, 8
    organized crime activities, 120
    relationship with Bandidos MC, 83

Soto, O.R., 119

Spaziano, Crazy Joe, 4, 108

Sponsor, 67–68

Stephenson, R., 5–6, 136

Stidworthy, D., 33

Storm Troopers MC, biker wars and, 9

Street gangs, 15, 104, 122

Street justice, 100

Street Justice, (Zito), 2

Striker period, 68–71

Sturgis Motorcycle Rally, 1, 166

Sundowners MC, organized crime activities, 120

Sweden
    motorcycle gangs in, 124
    OMGs in, 132

Sweetbutts, 47–48

Syder, A., 33

Tattoos
    1%, 37
    as symbolic representation, 17

Terry the Tramp, 98

Thailand, Bandidos MC in, 164

13 Rebels MC, 26

Thompson, Hunter S. , 3, 37–38, 45, 53, 97, 125

Thunderguards MC, 89

Trelease, T.W., 17

Trethaway, S., 55, 130

Tribe MC, 89

Triumph motorcycle, 4

Trudeau, Yves "Apache," 100

Trust, in criminal milieu, 15

Ugly Motorcycle Club, 1

United Nations, 2002 Bulletin on Narcotics, 133

United States v. Barger, 119

United States v. Belton, 119

United States v. Bowman, 107

United States v. Carl Warneke et al., 107

United States v. Cernine, 119

United States v. Dezzutti, 121

United States v. Fournier, 119

United States v. Framelli, 121

United States v. Gruber et al., 120

United States v. Harry Bowman, 54, 105

United States v. John David Ward, 107

United States v. Moran et al., 63

United States v. Scarberry, 120

United States v. Starrett et al., 57

Upright, Michael, 5, 53

Vagos MC, as lesser-known one-percent biker group, 8

Van Duyne, P., 13
Veno, Arthur, 7–8, 33, 37, 57, 62, 66, 68, 70, 77, 96, 116
Ventura, Jesse (Gov.), 86
Violence
    one-percent biker clubs and, 8–9
    outlaw motorcycle gangs and, 165–166
Von Lampe, Klaus, 12, 14-15, 16, 78

Wagner, D., 163
Walker, C., 166
Walker, Robert, 101
Warlocks Counsel, 90
Warlocks MC, 82
    Florida-based, 85–86
    journalistic accounts of, 3
    as lesser-known one-percent biker group, 9
    organized crime activities, 121
    Pennsylvania-based, 84–85
    relationships with other clubs, 83–84
    ties to La Cosa Nostra, 108
Watson, J.M., 47
Wegers, George, 105, 118
Welsh, Peter "Buttons", 5, 98
Wethern, George "Baby Huey,", 5, 36–37, 97, 125
    in federal witness protection, 98
Wheeler, James, 105
Wheels of Soul MC, 52, 89
White supremacists groups, 122
White Trash Networks, 46
Wild Angels, The, 38

Wild One, The, 2, 32–33, 79
Wild Pigs MC, 11
Wilkins, C.J., 140
Wilson, T., 164
Winterhalder, E., 5, 7, 52, 88, 89, 157
Winton, R., 17
Wolf, Daniel, 7, 25, 46, 55–57, 64, 65, 67–68, 71, 72, 89, 96, 116
Women, one-percent biker clubs and, 46–52. *See also* Biker women
Women on Wheels Motorcycle Association, 24
Wood, J., 96
World War II veterans, 27
Wright v. U.S., 118

Yates, B., 25, 31, 56–57

Zito, Chuck, 2, 5, 45, 71, 96, 97
    autobiography of, 99–100
    on biker brotherhood, 66–67
    as Ching-a-Ling member, 52
    as convicted felon, 104
    domestic violence complaints against, 51
    at Hellraisers Ball, 10
    quotation, 95